" ...where do we start, on the threshold, before a door. Here it is - simplified so we can see its complexities. . . doors are very potent symbols."
Phi-Neter:
Power of the Egyptian Gods

By same author
Tankhem: Seth & Egyptian Magick
The Bull of Ombos (Seth & Egyptian Magick II)
Supernatural Assault in Ancient Egypt
Egyptian Magick: A Spirited Guide
Phi-Neter: Power of the Egyptian Gods
(with Soror Nephthys) *The Desert Fox Oracle*

Seth
& The Two Ways

Ways of seeing the "demon" god of Egypt

Mogg Morgan

Copyright © Mogg Morgan 2019
First paperback Edition

All rights reserved. No part of this work may be reproduced or utilized in any form by any means electronic or mechanical, including *xerography, photocopying, microfilm*, and *recording*, or by any information storage system without permission in writing from the publishers.

Published by
Mandrake of Oxford
PO Box 250
OXFORD
OX1 1AP (UK)

"I am the son, Seth, who causes the turbulence of the storm, circling within the horizon of the sky, like the crooked god" Book Of The Dead 39.8 (Trans. T G Allen)

"I am the son, Seth, who *clears* the turbulence of the storm, circling within the horizon of the sky, like the crooked god" Book Of The Dead 39.8 (Trans. Stephen Quirke)

One word changes the sense of our understanding of this ancient god, seen by some as the personification of bad things.

Contents

Introduction 9

Chapter One
  Historical views of Seth: Plutarch's Anti-God 22
Seth in Plutarch's Isis & Osiris 22
Sacrifice 30
Eating magic 33
Apep, Apophis 38
The Evil Eye 52
Plutarch's Seth 55
The Corn Mummy 61
Astronomical Associations 68
Spell to Cause Evil Sleep 78
Seven Spells or Utterances of Nekhbet 83

Chapter Two
  Modern views of Seth: The Nagada Hypothesis ... 116
Plutarch's influence on Modern Religion 116
The Revelation 124
The Nagada hypothesis 130
The Demonic Calendar 147
Birth Demons 148
Isolated Consciousness 152
Sexuality & Politics 155

Chapter Three
  The Outsider 164
Human Geography 164
The Common Demon 167

Chapter Four
Gods of Sex and Death 175
Sex & Death 182
Sacred Prostitution 184
Trance 188
Sex & Religion after the Pharaohs 192

Conclusions 196
The Two Ways 200

Liturgy, Ritual and Appendices 201
1.   Drawing down the Plough 201
An Ancient Sethian Rite 203
Appendix I Forms of the Decans 209
Appendix II Book(s) Of Overthrowing Apep 216
Overcoming Apep - A Personal View 269
Notes 274
Index 291

Introduction

Seth is an ancient Egyptian deity, much maligned in popular, academic and theological thought. Up until fairly recently the only thing one needed to know about Seth was that he was the personification of evil and the prototype of the devil, Satan and all bad things in the world. He is the god who in one of the world's most ubiquitous myths, kills another god, (his own brother Osiris no less), then usurps his role as king, and persecutes the orphaned Horus, who only survives to manhood, due to the cunning of his sorcerer-mother Isis. Horus then overpowers Seth and ensures he gets his just deserts.

However, over the last few decades this perception has changed; and the star of the ancient Egyptian god has risen. Once upon a time, knowledge of his mythos was confined to a handful of Egyptologists together with few scholars of the weirder byways of Egyptian religion. These days scholarly articles and books about the god proliferate, all steadily changing the way we look upon him. He has also become the focus of several modern reconstituted cults, all of whom attempt in their own way to revive his worship and to renovate his image. Even for those contemporary neo-Pagans who would not count themselves as devotees, there is a newfound respect for Seth. Hardly any text published by contemporary practitioners these days, can fail to express some sort of view on the ethical questions raised by this ancient myth, so relevant to the human condition, and the problems we still encounter in the modern world. Most notable the problem of good versus evil.

The roots of this modern turnabout in religious sensibility lie in the 1960s. More specifically in San Francisco, which for a short moment of time was the beating heart of the counter-culture. The unlikely herald of the new Sethian age couldn't have been further away from Egyptian mythology. The ground for his resurgence was made fertile, initially in 1966 by the appearance of a new form of counter-cultural Satanism.

The chosen vehicle was an organisation called the Church of Satan.[1] It would have to wait a further nine years, a significant number for many, for this organisation to give birth to a fully formed cult of Seth. Thus it was that in the summer of 1975 a new organisation emerged from or, depending on your point of view, transmogrified from the Church of Satan after a series of internal conflicts. This was the Temple of Set, which adopted as its patron, the ancient Egyptian god Set, or to use the standard Egyptological transcription "Seth".[2]

"Wait a minute", I hear you scream, "surely several other occultists had traversed this ground before!" The first that springs to mind would be the late, great Kenneth Grant, the widely respected interpreter of Aleister Crowley. Crowley is for many, Britain's most famous "satanist"; even styling himself after the Beast 666 from the New Testament Book of Revelation! Kenneth Grant was for many years the head of a magical order, which was viewed by some as the true successor to Crowley's Ordo Templi Orientis; however in recent, more litigious times, it has changed its outer name to, you guessed it; the Typhonian Order.

Kenneth Grant is famous for his "Typhonian" interpretation of Aleister Crowley's magical system of Thelema - "the way of one's own will". Typhon is one of several ancient Greek words used to designate the Egyptian god Seth. Analysis of ancient texts makes it clear that Typhon was no more than an outer name and was never meant to be used as a word of power. We know this because many spells in the ancient Magical papyri (including the Papyru Graecae Magicae or PGM) call upon the power of Seth. Scholarly consensus tells us that the ancient scribe who compiled the collection of Theban Magical Papyri was an Egyptian and that he used a special convention or code to indicate which are the most important words in any particular spell. In the illustration you

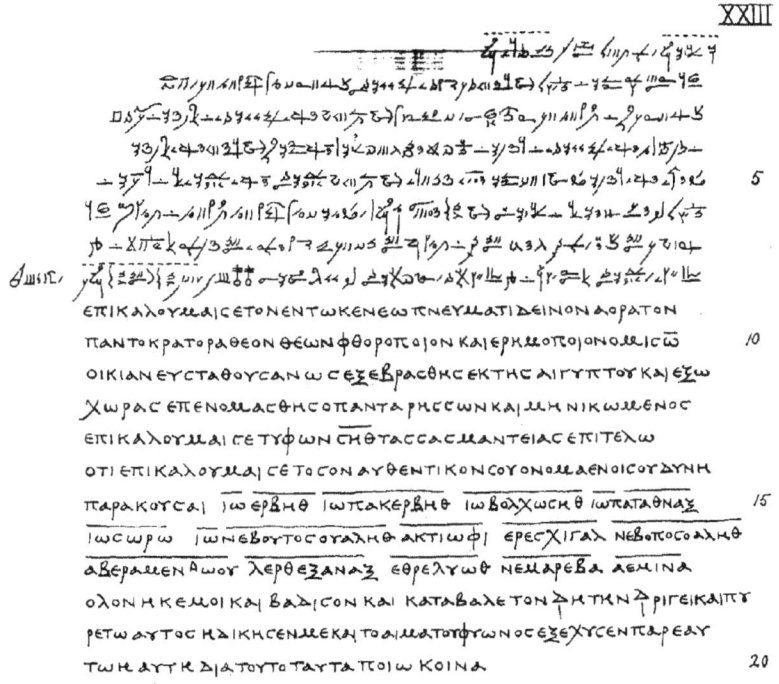

Text of spell from PGM - line 12 has line over name of Seth
PDM xiv 675-94 [PGM xivc 15-27]

might just make out that the name Seth, written in the uncial script, has a line over it, which indicates it is the power in the equation. This was never done for the word Typhon. The Typhon was simply the name of a Greek god.

Kenneth Grant published a series of monographs, which have become known as the Typhonian trilogies. The first of these, *The Magical Revival,* was published in 1972, and in it Grant equates Aiwass, the discarnate entity who supposedly dictated Liber Al vel Legis, with Shaitan and Seth. The history of Thelema (The "way of one's own will") in the modern world begins with a literary creation known as "Liber Al vel Legis". Everything Crowley subsequently wrote was a variation on this theme. Kenneth Grant is an early and important populariser of what we might call the Sethian mythos.

Commenting on an Ancient Egyptian stele which is famous to followers of the Thelemic way as the "Stele of Revealing" (actually a funeral stele of Theban priest Ankh-fn-Khonsu "Khonsu is his life" 25th Dynasty):

> "The [ie this] stele is a talisman of great power in Crowley's system. It shows the goddess Nuit arched over the solar-phallic Fire of (shin), Spirit, the letter of Abrasax or Abrahadabra, the Word of the Aeon of which Aiwass is the current expression. Sin also the letter of Shaitan or Set, the Fire of Desire (Hadit) at the Heart of Matter (Nuit)." [3]

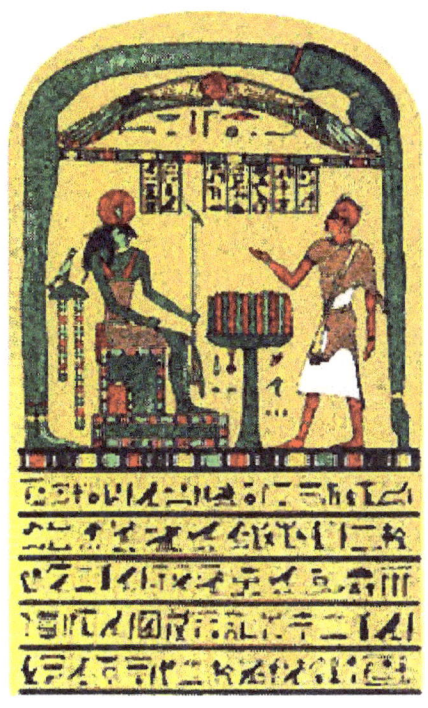

Stele of Revealing

For all things Egyptian, Kenneth Grant relied heavily on the works of Gerald Massey (1828-1907). Massey is an interesting figure, a Victorian Chartist, Theosophist, and amateur Egyptologist. Massey made good use of the leading academic authorities of his day, including Flinders Petrie, Wallace Budge, and Heinrich Brugsch. It is noteworthy that despite the many years separating Kenneth Grant from Massey's time, the former's theorising reads very like many passages from the latter's masterwork *Ancient Egypt: Light of the World*:

"The battles of Sut [Seth] and Horus are represented in both the apocryphal and canonical gospels. In the *Gospels of the Infancy* there are two boys—the bad boy and the good boy. In this form the two born antagonists continue their altercation with a root-relationship to the Osirian mythos. Sut is the representative of evil, of darkness, drought, sterility, negation, and non-existence. It is his devilry to undo the good work that Horus does, like Satan sowing tares [weeds] amongst the wheat. It was Sut who paralysed the left arm of Osiris and held it bound in Sekhem. It is the express delight of the bad boy, the child of Satan, to destroy the works of Jesus, the child of light. There is one particularly enlightening illustration of the mythos reproduced as *märchen* [folk tales]. The power of resurrection was imaged by the lifting of the arm from the mummy-bandages; Horus in Sekhem is the lifter of the arm. Whilst the arm is fettered in death, Sut is triumphant over Horus in the dark. When Horus frees his arm, he raises the hand that was motionless. He strikes down Sut, or stabs him to the heart. The power of darkness, one form of which was Sut, is designated the 'eater of the arm.'"[4]

Michael Aquino, the founding head of the modern day Temple of Set, is scornful of Kenneth Grant's attempts to connect "Set with Crowley's philosophy in general and Aiwass in particular."[5] Aquino cites Grant's introduction to *The Magical Record of the Beast 666*,[6] published in 1972 and his *Aleister Crowley and the Hidden God*, published in 1973.[7] Not that Aquino disliked the equation Shaitan/Satan equals Seth; merely that he is felt that most of the mythological basis of Crowley's *Liber AL vel Legis* is essentially dominated by the role of Osiris and Horus. Seth is of course part of the action, but the reader of the received text seems hardly aware of it.

Crowley rather famously was a devotee of the god Horus, who he believed was the dominant spiritual force of our modern age. Thus Michael Aquino thought that from Crowley's point of view, Seth was and continues to be an unwarranted intrusion.[8] Nowadays, more than 100 years after the creation of Crowley's spiritual manifesto, *Liber Al Vel Legis*, one cannot help but reflect that Crowley did actually miss something. The full significance of the god Seth in Egyptian religion is something that has only been fully explored and revealed by more recent scholarly research.

So Michael Aquino is mostly right when he says: "Crowley practically ignored Set, except for an occasional mention of the god in an Osirian mythic context. In his principal discussion of the Devil on page 296 of *Liber ABA: Magick*, for instance, he does not even include Set."

Nevertheless, Kenneth Grant's published theories concerning Seth and Shaitan, his *Typhonian* interpretation, that undoubtedly had a wide influence on the small but soon to be influential group of occult intellectuals. It could be argued that one of the first fruits of this, coming just as few years after publication of Grant's *The Magical Revival*, was the foundation of the Temple of Set in 1975. Kenneth Grant would be seen a their likely inspiration were it not for the publication of two other books, which are rarely mentioned in Kenneth Grant's Ordo Temple Orientis, but are very well known within the Temple of Set.

Whatever the source, the Temple of Set has since its foundation, played a major role in the subsequent popularisation of the god amongst neo-pagan groups. So ubiquitous is this influence, that one only need express an interest in the Egyptian god Seth in almost any pagan discussion group, to be met with the assumption that one must have a connection with the Temple of Set. In fact, since the 1970s there have been several other groups claiming an allegiance to Seth, although none as successful in terms of membership as the Temple of Set.[10]

Its founding leader Michael Aquino boasts that he had succeeded where Kenneth Grant had failed, Aquino had his own novel theory of how the name Satan is derived from an epithet of Seth; viz: the Middle Egyptian phrase "set heh" (Eternal Seth). This source of this insight is S G F Brandon, former priest and professor of comparative religion at Manchester University.[11]

It has already been pointed out that Seth did not play an obvious role in occult theory and praxis before 1972. One might also say that this date marks the beginning of modern academic studies of magick, which, like research into the god Seth, had been largely marginalized within the scholarly world as a "Cinderella subject".

In the case of Sethian studies, this neglect is also the result of the relative rarity of surviving artefacts and texts. Other than archaeological traces and fragments, there is no substantial, surviving, ancient shrine of the god like there is for deities such as Amun, Osiris, Isis, Horus, etc. The ancient Egyptians seem to have fallen out of love with their god, and with a few notable exceptions, tended to neglect or even destroy his monuments. This also explains the difficulty for the modern scholar, assuming one is interested. From the evidence Seth appears to be a minor god, although, as we shall see, this is far from the case.

Prior to the translation of the Egyptian Hieroglyphs by Champollion in 1822, the contents of the very many papyri and inscriptions were a closed book, the subject only of speculation. Egypt was known from classical Greek and Roman sources, as well as records of other Near Eastern cultures such as the Assyrian, and of course for most of us, from the Bible, the Talmud, and the Koran.

One extremely lively and informative late classical text was Plutarch's *Isis & Osiris*.[12] It is a rich source of information on Egyptian mythology; this book was probably the most widely read of all classical Greek texts, and still commonly consulted by Egyptologists. Enlightened Greek theologians practised "inter-translation", that is to say, they translated the names of non-Greek deities into more familiar gods from their own tradition. Contrast this with later Christian practice, which tends to recast pagan deities as demons.

So in the Greco-Egyptian Magical Papyri, the PGM:
Ra becomes Helios;
Shu, "sender of winds";
Tefnut is Aphrodite;
Geb is Chronus;
Nuit is "Mother of the Gods";

Seth becomes Typhon;

Isis, Osiris and Nephthys keep their Egyptian names but transcribed into Greek phonemes. [13]

Seth is in the above equated with the Greek anti-god Typhon, the personification of chaos.[14]

The template for this was set by the ancient Greek poet Hesiod, a near contemporary of Homer in the 7th century BCE. He wrote, (Theogony ll. 306-332) "Men say that Typhon the terrible, is outrageous [and] lawless." and more extensively in (ll. 820-868):

> "When Zeus had driven the Titans from heaven, huge Earth bore her youngest child Typhoeus of the love of Tartarus, by the aid of golden Aphrodite. Strength was with his hands in all that he did and the feet of the strong god were untiring. From his shoulders grew an hundred heads of a snake, a fearful dragon, with dark, flickering tongues, and from under the brows of his eyes in his marvellous heads flashed fire, and fire burned from his heads as he glared. And there were voices in all his dreadful heads which uttered every kind of sound unspeakable; for at one time they made sounds such that the gods understood, but at another, the noise of a bull bellowing aloud in proud ungovernable fury; and at another, the sound of a lion, relentless of heart; and at another, sounds like whelps, wonderful to hear; and again, at another, he would hiss, so that the high mountains re-echoed. And truly a thing past help would have happened on that day, and he would have come to reign over mortals and immortals, had not the

father of men and gods been quick to perceive it. But he thundered hard and mightily: and the earth around resounded terribly and the wide heaven above, and the sea and Ocean's streams and the nether parts of the earth. Great Olympus reeled beneath the divine feet of the king as he arose and earth groaned there at. And through the two of them heat took hold on the dark-blue sea, through the thunder and lightning, and through the fire from the monster, and the scorching winds and blazing thunderbolt. The whole earth seethed, and sky and sea: and the long waves raged along the beaches round and about, at the rush of the deathless gods: and there arose an endless shaking. Hades trembled where he rules over the dead below, and the Titans under Tartarus who live with Chronos, because of the unending clamour and the fearful strife. So when Zeus had raised up his might and seized his arms, thunder and lightning and lurid thunderbolt, he leaped form Olympus and struck him, and burned all the marvellous heads of the monster about him. But when Zeus had conquered him and lashed him with strokes, Typhoeus was hurled down, a maimed wreck, so that the huge earth groaned. And flame shot forth from the thunder-stricken lord in the dim rugged glens of the mount (26), when he was smitten. A great part of huge earth was scorched by the terrible vapour and melted as tin melts when heated by men's are in channelled (27) crucibles; or as iron, which is hardest of all things, is softened by glowing fire in mountain glens and melts in the divine earth through the strength of Hephaestus (28). Even so, then, the earth melted in the glow of the blazing fire. And in the bitterness of his anger Zeus cast him into wide Tartarus." [14]

Image of Typhon from Greek postage stamp

In the late Victorian era, Typhon was given a minor role in some of the rituals of the Order of the Golden Dawn. For example in the Lesser and Greater rituals of the Hexagram, the performer makes: "The sign of Typhon" several times, a yoga-like posture based on descriptions in the Egyptian magical papyri.

The Typhon posture

Sometimes it seems, and indeed I suspect, that the modern day Temple of Set initially modelled their re-creation of the cult on the way it was described in Plutarch's *Isis & Osiris*. Indeed some contemporary Sethians might still defend this point of view, arguing that all religious reconstruction is "post-modern", in the sense that one chooses, in rather an arbitrary manner, which period in a god's history to treat as typical. There is no inherent reason to suppose the final version of a long dead cult is somehow more valid as a religion than say the form it took at the beginning, its pre-historic, or in its so-called heyday. Egyptian religion is no static thing, all of its gods have a history; they wax and wane in importance, change form and character over the several thousand years of their time-line. Some argue that their current incarnation a no more or less valid a moment to take up the thread, and in the post-modern era there are no rules about how one should do this.

Chapter One
Historical views of Seth:
Plutarch's Anti-God

Plutarch of Chaeronea

SETH IN PLUTARCH'S ISIS & OSIRIS

I turn then to the presentation of Seth as he emerges in the pages of Plutarch, a reflection of post-pharaonic Egypt and the religious views of his time.

Plutarch uses the name of the Greek titan Typhon to refer to the Egyptian Seth. The first thing he tells us about Typhon is that he

" ... is hostile to the goddess [Isis] and demented by ignorance and deceit; he scatters and destroys the sacred Word [Osiris] which the goddess collects and puts together and delivers to those undergoing initiation. " [15]

Thus Typhon is presented as an anti-god, and one whose character is *totally* defined by the role ascribed to him in the cult of Isis and Osiris. This characterisation of Seth is repeated and amplified at several points in Plutarch's text. A little further on he writes how "They say that these and similar things are told of Typhon, how through envy and spite he wrought terrible deeds and produced confusion everywhere, filled the whole earth and seas with evils but then paid the penalty." [16]

For many this is all there is to know about Seth-Typhon. The translator of the standard English language edition of Plutarch's *De Iside et Osiride* is John Gwyn Griffiths, a task he undertook at the suggestion of Professor Battiscombe Gunn, as a sequel to (1960) *The Conflict of Horus & Seth: a study in an ancient mythology from Egyptian and Classical sources*, published in 1960. Thus Gwyn Griffiths already knew that Plutarch's understanding of the god Seth as "satanic" was really only a partial view. In many ways, as he makes clear in the accompanying commentary to *Isis & Osiris*, it was often a distortion or imposition on the native original. We are told that in Egyptian sources, Seth is never this kind of absolute devil; whereas in Greek mythology, Typhon is always "satanic".

Gwyn Griffiths' view had in the meantime been challenged by scholar Herman Te Velde in another classic book, *Seth, God of*

Confusion: A study of his role in Egyptian Mythology and Religion, Brill published in 1967. Unlike Gwyn Griffiths, Te Velde was happy to accept Plutarch's interpretations of native Egyptian myth. And this he does because, for Te Velde, Plutarch's *knew* Egypt, if not from direct contact, he was certainly closer in time to the historical events he describes. Te Velde takes Plutarch's point of view and runs with it, constructing an impressive thesis that Seth was always malign, even in native sources.

But for Gwyn Griffiths this was wrong, the idea of a "satanic" Seth is really a product of the Greek intellectual tradition, although he admits that, "This evolution of Seth into Satan requires some explanation." In another essay Gwyn Griffiths presents his discoveries from Greek sources of the first equation of Typhon with Seth, the earliest example of which appeared in the 6th century BCE works of Pherecydes of Syros. This is a century before the better known syncreticism of Egyptian Seth with Greek Typhon found in Herodotus. [17]

It reads:

> "[H]Oros the son of Osiris, whom the Hellenes call Apollo:
> he was king over Egypt last, having deposed Typhon." [18]

In Greek mythology, "Typhon was a revolutionary and a rebel" and nothing much else. Whereas in Egypt, Seth could be rebellious but he could also be a lot of other things, as we shall see. It was only after the rise of Greek power in Egypt that the two gods were fused, but the net result of this assimilation was the deepening of the conception of Seth as rebel and obliterations of his "redeeming features."[18] In other words the Greek views have been imposed on the Egyptian in such a way as the original nature of the God has been distorted and lost.

Plutarch, in a passage a little later on, obligingly defines for us the distinction between magick of the left and of the right hand path. This is one of the earliest instances of a way of looking at magic and religion that many in our own day still find important. One regularly sees discussions on the Internet and elsewhere about the supposed distinction between left and right hand magic. Depending on where one considers one's self to be on the scale you might feel inclined to criticise those in the other camp. Left-hand path practitioners regard themselves as serious magicians who in turn see those on the right hand as hide-bound by too many taboos and conventions. For example Stephen Flowers, an articulate contemporary ideologue of the Temple of Set, wrote a book entitled *Lords of the Left hand Path*. Those of the right naturally see themselves as taking a more adult approach, often criticising those of the left for their supposed lack of a moral compass.

Plutarch was not the only ancient philosopher to have used these categories. Some find it in the Hindu scriptures, especially the cult known in the west as Tantra. I think it is possible that it plays to an ancient taboo concerning left and right-handedness. One talks about the left-hand of darkness. Sinister, a Latin term, means to the left. Plutarch, whose world we are considering, tells us that "Plato in his long speculation on Law (Laws 717a-b) ascribes to the Olympian gods the right side and the odd numbers, and to the opposite of these he assigns the daemons." [19]

More orthodox gods, such as Helios, the sun, are associated with the right hand. If the sun is associated with the right hand then it comes naturally to view the left as the realm of darkness.

The Greeks divided creation into four distinct categories. Aside from (1) gods and (2) daemons, there are (3) heroes and (4) men. This distinction is traceable to the poet Hesiod, a huge influence on all later Greek thinkers. Thus Plato and the students of his philosophical school, of which Plutarch was a product, accepted his distinction.

For me this raises the question of whether each of the four would itself be divisible into two subcategories of good and bad? Plutarch says this is true of the demons, which are capable of being good and bad. Applying this the Egyptian myth, Plutarch says explicitly that the gods Osiris and Isis were originally good demons. Presumable, because of their trials and tribulations they became gods.[20]

From the Greek perspective all entities have a place in a larger hierarchy, from which they can ascend or descend. Other native traditions in Egypt say similar things. Manetho, a Greek-Egyptian priest of Ra, wrote a history of the kings of Egypt whose first chapter describes a mythical primeval time when Osiris and the other gods ruled as kings.

Abydos, the most famous of all ancient pilgrimage destinations in Egypt, is where a 1st dynasty tomb of king Hor'aha was venerated by later Egyptians as the actual tomb of Osiris. This tendency to turn real kings into gods is well attested. And not only kings. Imhotep, the architect of the first pyramid, that of Djoser at Saqqara; was a man of flesh and blood, but obviously very special, with his own religious cult dedicated to him centuries after his death.

Nowadays few scholars believe that Osiris was the deified ghost of king Menes, and may also recognise that the myth of Osiris and Isis is not as timeless as was claimed. Their cult comes into existence at about the same time as the building of the great pyramids (circa 2630-2100BCE) and therefore centuries after King Menes lived.

From a native Egyptian perspective Osiris and Isis were always gods; but were they? Plutarch seems to be saying that they were not always divine. One can certainly see how the status of Osiris and Isis had changed over the many millennia of Egyptian history. Rather surprisingly there is very little archaeological evidence of Isis as the great goddess we know and love, before the texts that appear inside the pyramids.

These texts mark the beginning of the Egyptian chronicle, so one might legitimately ask what other evidence could there be for their existence at an earlier time? In fact there are short or fragmentary inscriptions, proto-hieroglyphs that can be read, based on what came later. There is also a great number of non-textual relics, iconography, statues, and shrines. Put these all together and we have a multitude of evidence from a time before the Pyramids, right back to the foundation of Hierakonpolis (citadel of the Falcon) in 4000BCE!

The Narmer pallet, found in the main deposite at the,
Horus temple, Hierakonpolis (Nekhen)

There is, a wealth of material before this. With the caveat that none of it can be easily read, in the way that the long inscriptions of the pyramid texts can be read. This reservation in mind, one has to say that Isis and Osiris are significant by their *absence*!

The archaeological record shows that there were other supernatural entities in Egypt that would later be associated with Isis. One of the most important goddesses was a horned cow variously known as BAT meaning "female soul" and often viewed as an archaic version of the goddess Hathor. There is no reason to think this was just an earlier name for Isis, although later on she will assume many of the attributes of both BAT and Hathor.

There are other lesser entities; spirits of nature, of the dead and of mourning that seem to be the real precursors of Isis and her sister Nephthys. It is to these that one can point to a more viable ancestor of the goddess, acknowledging that these are minor deities. It would be legitimate to view these entities not as gods at all, but as belonging to another category entirely: that of the spirits or even daemons.

Female avian goddess (dancing?), from Ma'mariya, Nagada II period ca. 3500-3400 BCE. Terracotta, pigment, (29.2 x 14 x 5.7 cm). Brooklyn Museum.

Seth in Plutarch's description, over several disconnected passages, tells us how the god was, in effect, demoted. He could never be killed, but a combination of gods was able to overpower him and permanently place him where he could do no further harm. He endures as a lasting reminder of his evil acts. And a continuous encouragement for mortals not to re-enact his downfall.

SACRIFICE

> "Cannibalism is a predicament of the animistic hunter or gardener, who must live by consuming animals or plants which are essentially persons themselves" (Graeber & Sahlins, *On Kings* p16)

"Thus the weakened and shattered power of Typhon," … still gasps and struggles", so the priesthood must "appease and mollify" which they do by means of "sacrifices". Sacrifice is a very ambiguous thing. Sacrifice brings to mind the ritual slaughter of an animal or, - including in some records - human beings. Although the latter is largely confined to a very remote history of humanity where it is known from archaeological or written records, usually occuring in desperate times. In almost all myths of the world, the gods eat flesh and drank blood. Human beings are even referred to as the "divine cattle" i.e. divine food. Thus is often recorded in religious scripture for the purpose of telling us why we no longer offer such sacrifice. Thus in the famous myth of the Divine Cow-goddess Hathor, she threatens to kill humanity entirely and proceeds to makes a good stab at it. She is diverted from this grisly task with the offer of a substitute that tastes like blood but is in fact beer. You can guess the rest. I hazard an opinion that every culture has a similar story.

The offering of an animal, other than human, is less contentious. The animal offered still shares in some of the characteristics of the god to whom it is offered. The animal is often an avatar of the god, e.g. goats are sacred to the sun god Ra, cats to the goddess Bast, the sacred Ibis to scribal god Thoth, Crocodiles to Sobek or the falcon to Horus. It is a curious double take that one would kill the sacred animal as an offering to the god whom it is thought to symbolise! However, cattle were also offered to all the gods if the moment was appropriate.

With this in mind we can look at the Plutarch's short account of some of the sacrifices offered in connection with Seth. Many of these are clearly of the humiliating variety as when he says "they humiliate and insult [Seth] in certain festivals, jeering at men of ruddy complexion and throwing an ass down a precipice, as the people of Coptos do, because Typhon had a ruddy complexion and was asinine in form."

Much of this is borne out by the archaeological evidence. The ass is the ubiquitous personification of the god Seth. The ritual humiliation was, according to Plutarch, extended to men with red hair; thought to be a physical characteristic of the god. Gwyn Griffiths says that whether the *actual* sacrifice of living red-headed men is involved is, thus far, unproven. He thinks it could equally have been metaphorical, in the sense of "red eyed", and more about deriding a "red-headed" aspect of our personality.

An ancient dream manual, written in the age of Ramses II, provides further analysis of men with a *Sethian* temperament, contrasting it with those of the Horus type.

> "If he drinks a beer, he drinks it to engender strife and turmoil. The redness of the white of his eye is this god. He is one who drinks what he detests. … As for a man who is a drunk, (who) broils, (causes) calumnies, ills and mischief. He drinks beer so as to engender turmoil and disputes … he will take up weapons of warfare . . . before him, a hippopotamus . . . when he perceives on the second day (Gardiner suggests when he wakes up after a drinking bout – which is amusing but more likely to be a reference to a festival) . . . he will not distinguish the married woman from . . . as to any man who opposed him . . . massacres arise in him and he is pleased in the Netherworld. . . He will engender disputes so as to break vessels"

The rest is too fragmentary to make much sense of, but you get the idea. [21]

It may be an admonition to cast out the *drunken* personality, having first manifested it by drinking to excess, a surprisingly common thing to do in Egyptian religious festivals. There is something in this description that reminds me of the "larger than life" personality of King Ramses II, who "though he is a royal kinsman, he has the personality of a man of the people (Rekhyt)." [22]

According to Plutarch, "the people of Busiris and Lycopolis will not use trumpets at all because they make a noise like an ass; and they believe the ass to be in general not a pure, but a demonic beast because of its likeness to Typhon." In Egyptian the word for ass reads "Aa" – and is likely onomatopoeic, representing its braying. In later Gnostic texts the divine formula IAO, which has a similar sound, is said to be an epithet of Typhon.[23] In the PGM "... the god most often employed is IAO, the Jewish god." IAO survives as an important magical utterance where it was central to the magick of the Victorian occult order, the Golden Dawn. One wonders if they might be surprised, even alarmed, at such a provenance.

EATING MAGIC

This is a good moment to discuss the phenomenon of "eating magick", a ubiquitous religious practice, past and present. Indeed, it still is one of the world's most popular ritual acts. Think for a moment of the Catholic Mass in which bread and wine is shared. During Mass, (from the Greek "Messa" meaning barley cake) one is witnessing or participating in what may well be humanity's oldest rite. It was an ancient practice even before the early Christians "appropriated" or adopted it from their Pagan predecessors. It is common to many religions and long may it be so.

Whilst talking about the then popular variety of "eating magick", Plutarch tells us that people attending Egyptian festivals were offered, "round cakes in festivals of the months Payni and Phaophi, [and] as an insult, they stamp on them an image of a tied ass." Elsewhere he says the image is of a male hippopotamus, another common animal form of the same god. With recent discoveries at Hierakonpolis as our guide, we must say that the hippo, male and female, was a symbol of royal prestige from the time of Egypt's earliest dynasties. Is this humiliating or is it, as in the case of the "sacred bread", eaten as a sacrament, like in many of the world's religions, sharing of the body and power of the god? Difficult to say

In H W Fairman's *The Triumph of Horus, An Ancient Egyptian Sacred Drama* published by Batsford in 1974, there is a reconstruction of the entire mystery play compiled from the texts on the walls of the temple of Horus at Edfu. This all dates from the first centuries of the common era but it re-enacts what seems to be an older prototype, dated to Egypt's first dynasty, as depicted in a seal impression from Abydos, where King Den harpoons a hippopotamus.

In the play's third act, a large cake, shaped as a hippopotamus is carried onstage and sliced up, dismembered into multiple portions, which are then laid on the altars of the heavenly company of gods with the words: "Let his foreleg be taken to Busiris, for thy father Osiris Onnophris the triumphant. Consign his ribs to Iyet for Haroeris pre-eminent in Letopolis ... "and so on."

There's no way of knowing whether it was a model cake made of plaster used in the original rite, or if it could have really been eaten. It's entirely likely that the public rite involved some ritual sharing of the offerings. If so it is another example of *eating magick*,

The Triumph of Horus, An Ancient Egyptian Sacred Drama, 1971 performance by Padgate College of Education in Lancaster.

Author photograph from Temple of Horus at Edfu, full text published in Chassinat *Le Temple d'Edfou*, XIII plates DXII & DCXIV.

which at the time of Plutarch's writing, was already an old tradition. For as he says: if the cake is eaten then "they stamp a round sacrificial cake with the figure of a tied up hippopotamus."[24]

Given the popularity of eating magick as a religious activity in the classical world, one might consider whether this was framed as a way of receiving a god's blessing or whether eating was a form of destruction and final absorption of their power? Ptolemaic records contain requests from workers for time off to attend the "Typhonia" for one-and-a-half days before the month of Epiphi (approximate to our May). This information comes from the Heidelberg Festival papyrus, whose translator says that the use of the Dative tense, i.e. "for something", implies "to placate".[25] David Frankfurter discusses graffiti left by ironworkers of Hermonthis at Deir el Bahri, Thebes. Their pilgrimage culminated in the immolation of donkeys.[26] It is not always so clear what their mindset was. The acts are ambiguous, yes some of these accounts of "eating" Seth, seem all about humiliation or even triumphalism. But was there also a paradoxical placation of the god? It all depends on what the celebrant was thinking at the time, and this information isn't always available.

Even Plutarch's account implies that in his day people still venerated the god Seth. In fact the old view that the Seth was somehow "demonised" in this late period or that his cult was in decline has been successfully and repeatedly challenged by new research and discoveries. See for example Eugene Cruz-Uribe's influential paper "Sth Aa Phty 'Seth: god of Power and Might' " for a complete reframing of the old consensus.[27] The 2016

"Demonthings" conference in Swansea University heard several academic speakers talk of the current change in Egyptology's view on this issue. In his commentary on Plutarch, Gwyn Griffiths calls all of these ritual acts the "appeasement of power", that were performed to appease the power of the god who was still a force in the land.

THE BOOK OF OVERCOMING APEP OR APOPHIS

A temple manuscript, originally from Karnak, provides another possible rubric for rites aimed at Seth; although in truth the ritual was actually intended for overcoming Apep. Apep, Apophis, or sometimes even Apopis, is a supernatural entity that emerged during the chaos of Egypt's first Intermediate period between the Old and Middle Kingdoms (c2181-2055BCE). The first reference to the name Apep comes from the tomb of Ankhtifi, a local ruler at Mo'alla, 2100BCE.[28] And indeed occurs in the context of a great famine:

> "... I took care of the towns of Hefat [i.e, Mo'alla] and Hormer at the moment when the sky was clouded and the earth [was parched (in the wind) and when every man would die] of hunger on this sand-bank of Apophis. [The south came] with its people, the north came [with] its children. I reported this... in exchange (?) for my Southern corn and I arranged that this Southern corn (?) made haste; towards the South, It reached the land of Wawat and, in the North, it reached the Thinite Nome. The whole of Upper Egypt was dying of hunger to the point that every man was forced to eat his own children but I, I caused that nobody died of hunger in this nome. I gave a loan of corn to Upper Egypt and (I

gave) Northern corn to Upper Egypt) which was received as a ration. This is certainly not a thing that I have found to have been done by the nomarchs which existed before me; never (indeed), a leader of the army of this nome has done anything of the sort. I cared for the house of Elephantine and for the town of Iat-Negen (Mound of the bulls?) during those years after the towns of Hefat and Hormer had been satisfied. It is not certainly the thing that I found to have been made by my fathers who existed before me. I was like a mountain for Hefat and like a cool shade for Hormer.' Ankhtifi said: 'the whole country has become like starving locusts going some upstream and others downstream [in search of food) : but I never allowed anybody in need to sail from a nome to another one. It is because I am…'"

Painting from tomb of Ankhtifi

The surviving manuscript is dated not later than 312-311BCE in the reign of Alexander IV of Macedon, son of Alexander the Great. Though still a boy, he was technically pharaoh of Egypt from his birth in 323BCE until his assassination in 311BCE. Whilst this book, appears relatively late in the Egyptian timeline, experts agree it was likely based on older rites of a similar nature. In it we could well be seeing the paradigm for all works of magical *execration*.

Reading the extract below, it is easy to see an affinity between Seth and the deity Apep, whom he is often called upon to repel. This could simply be an instance of fighting like with like. The rites contained could easily be reversed to direct them at Seth himself, something that apparently often happened in temple rites.

Although the books themselves were written down at the beginning of Ptolemaic times, similar rites are attested from the first intermediate period between the end of the Old and the establishment of the Middle Kingdoms, a time when things fell apart, and the name of Apep first erupted into the discourse. But it seem likely there were precedents for this kind of magick from even earlier times, for example in the Pyramid texts, a chaotic, demonic serpent entity called 'Imy-nehed.ef ("He who is in the sycamore tree") could menace the deceased, a ghost or "psychonaut", in the Pyramid texts, could equally be protecting them, difficult to say from the context:[29]

On the other hand, despite the late appearance of this book in the timeline, the gods Seth and Apep are clearly distinguishable. Seth invariably appears as the powerful emanation of Ra against

Apep. This in itself is evidence that Seth was never demonised, and was always, to use Cruz-Uribe's words, a "God of Power & Might".[30] Apep is the one who threatens us with non-being at important moments of transition. Seth's inner role is to protect us from complete dissolution in those moments of crisis and magick.

Some scholars say that it provides the model for other execration rites that were used against Seth, in particular at the temples of Horus at Edfu and Hathor at Dendera. We are here invited to believe that Egyptian priests of the late period had an ambiguous relationship with the god Seth. They demonised him by day but were also very conscious of his usefulness in certain situations.

Hence Jacco Dieleman tells us that in the 4th century of our common era, in order to keep Seth's destructive powers ritually at bay, priests manipulated and destroyed small wax dolls or other inanimate objects as magical substitutes for Seth and his group of enemies in the daily temple ritual.

Here is the ritual they used:

> "Seize Seize, O you employees to the orders, Bind, Bind, O you employees to the cords: bound is this vile enemy, Seth, son of Nut, and his associates, who have done evil, who have caused suffering, who have plotted suffering and injustice. The eldest, who was appointed to rule before coming to the world, does not miss this. He made fun of the order of the universal master, of which was told by the One who created that which exists. He created evil before coming into the world, having aroused disorder before his name exists. Do evil to one who has caused evil"[31]

However, Dieleman further reveals how "contrary to the state temple ritual", other rites from The Magical Papyri (PDM xiv 675-94 and PGM XIVc 15-27) "invoke the potentially dangerous powers of Seth, and instead of averting these for the sake of the well being of the country, attempt to direct the destructive energy against a particular individual in a private matter".[32]

This rite, being so important on so many levels, is examined in some detail in my earlier book *Supernatural Assault in Ancient Egypt*, p145-157. It was used to send "Evil Sleep" and if persisted with, could even bring death on the victim. The ritual for sending and also blocking "evil sleep" would be an important magical technique, then as now. (see page 79 below)[33]

All of the above rituals described derive from older paradigms. No doubt copies of them were preserved in temple libraries, some of which may well have dated back to the Middle Kingdom. It is surely no confidence that even the name *Apep* first emerged during the chaotic times of Egypt's first intermediate period that separated the Old and Middle Kingdoms. So we can assume that the temple scribes could do a "cut and paste" job on an older ritual, in the process, substituting the name of Seth for that of Apep. From which we can learn a useful technique of magical "sampling" or "scratching"; take the "best" or most appropriate parts, discard those elements that you don't want or need, and Abracadabra, you have a new hit record.

Edfu in Upper Egypt is the famous cult centre of the god Horus. Many mythological texts there describe the eternal conflict or *contendings* between Horus and Seth. In some accounts Horus & Seth are brothers:

> "I [Thoth] am the son of your son, the seed of your seed, he who separated the two brothers."[34]

But elsewhere Seth is brother to Osiris and Isis, and therefore uncle to Horus, as in this address to Isis from the Pyramid Texts:

> "Thou has come seeking thy brother Osiris, where his brother Seth had cast him on his side." [35]

This is a significant ambiguity or contradiction, and is often cited as evidence that an older story has been edited by the priests, most likely as part of the widespread rewriting to provide an ideological underpinning to the myth of divine kingship.

It has to be said that there are parallels between mythology of Seth and that of Apep, example of which are not difficult to find. Take this passage from a longer spell where the spirit of Apep is seen in the the Thunderstorm:

> "[Thereby] shall Apep, the enemy of Ra, be overthrown in the thunderstorm, and Ra shall shine brightly, and Apep shall be overthrown in very truth". [36]

Elsewhere, notably in the Magical Papyri Seth is also called lord of the storm, although not uniquely so as the epithet is also one of broadly *typhonian* deities such as Bes.

> "O dark's disturber, thunder's bringer, whirlwind,"
> (PGM IV 154-258)

There are several possible explanations for this. Again, it might be yet more evidence of textual manipulation in order to make Seth and Apep *appear* to be the same god. Or it might be more of what I earlier called *fighting fire with fire*: Seth can defeat Apep, because only he has similar powers.

The *Book of Overthrowing Apep* tells us that Apep is prone to roaring: "thereby shall be driven away the roarings[37] of the fiend". Seth is also known to roar. It brings to mind the archaic Indo-European deity Rudra, whose name means "howler". *Goetia*, the Greek term designating the conjuration of demons, also ultimately derives from the word for howl or wail.

We also learn from the *Book of Overthrowing Apep* that he is one of the "red ones". Red is quintessentially also the colour of Seth - "the red ochre god".

GENDER

All classes of venomous snakes and scorpions were ascribed filial connection with Apep, and usually referred to as "sisters" although this in itself implies no actual cosmology.[38] Apophis is a genderless being for it is said of them "you shall not become pregnant, there will be no giving birth for you".[39] The New Kingdom papyrus sometimes known as the *Cairo Calendar* or, as I prefer it, *Almanac of Lucky & Unlucky days* regularly refers to the "Children of Badesh" or of Apophis:

> AKHET (INUNDATION) SECOND MONTH, DAY 25 "it is the day of finding the children of Apophis, wrapped in the archiac way on their sides". [40]

There is another, extraordinary expression that occurs in a long cup divination from the PGM XIV 239-295 line 263-265, for the moon god, Khonsu:

"Even the fury of Apophis and her daughters I summon from their places of punishment, Let him make me answer to every word [about] which I am asking here to-day in truth without falsehood therein." [41]

To finish this section, I draw the reader's attention to the fact that many key elements of this mythological drama of Ra, Horus and Apep, seem to have been transposed into the conflict of Osiris, Horus, and Seth. I've transcribed and edited the book in its entirely and placed it in the appendix. But here is a one fascinating section that has its essence:

THE BOOK OF OVERTHROWING APEP[42]

Here Begins The Book Of Over-Throwing Apep, The Enemy Of Ra, The Enemy Of Un-Nefer (Osiris), Life, Strength, [and] Health [*Be To Him*]! Which Is Recited In The Temple Of Amen-Ra, The Lord Of The Throne Of The Two Lands, The President Of The Apets,[43] Throughout The Day Daily.

I. 2. The Chapter Of Spitting Upon Apep.

Say the [*following*] words:

Be You spat upon, Apep.

Be You spat upon, Apep.

Be You spat upon, Apep.

Be You spit upon, Apep.

Ra rests with his Ka (i.e., double), Per-Aa (i.e., the Pharaoh) rests with his Ka (i.e., double). Ra comes, the mighty one! Ra comes, (3) the victorious one! Ra comes, the exalted one! Ra comes, the one equipped [for battle].

Ra comes with rejoicing, Ra comes in beauty, Ra comes as King of the South, Ra comes as King of the North, Ra comes with divine (4) offerings, Ra comes with triumph, and Per-Aa (i.e., the Pharaoh) shall come. Life, Strength [and] Health [be to him]. You have destroyed for him all his enemies, even as he has over-thrown Apep for you. He has slain for you the fiend Qettu. He ascribes praise to your might. (5) You are adored by him in all your risings wherein you shine upon him, even as he overthrows for you all your enemies throughout each and every day.

[...]

There follows a very interesting passage showing the use of wax dolls or images. It was a common technique within Egyptian magick, and one that seems to have been inherited by the magical practice of later eras. Wax was supposed to be especially appropriate for use in this kind of image magic on account of it being completely consumed in the flames, thus leaving no remnant that could be latched onto by a malign spirit as a vehicle for a return to menace the unwary practitioner.

VI. The Chapter Of Placing Fire Upon Apep.

Say the [*following*] words:

Fire be upon you, O Apep, enemy of Ra. The Eye of Horus has gained the mastery over the accursed soul and shadow of Apep, the burning radiance of the Eye of Horus ate into the enemy (1) of Ra, the burning radiance of the Eye of Horus shall eat into all the enemies of Per-Aa (Pharaoh), Life, Strength, [and] Health [be to him]! both living and dead.

And you shall recite the [*following*] words of power when [the figure of] Apep is put in the fire, and shall say:

Taste You [the fire], perish, O Apep. (2) Get you backwards and retreat, O enemy of Ra, fall headlong, get backwards, retreat, be gone. I have driven you back and have cut you in pieces. Ra triumphs over you, Apep. [Repeat] four times.

Taste you [*the fire*]. [*Repeat*] four times.

(3) Back, Sebau Fiend, destruction be to you. I have heaped fire upon you and I have made you to perish, and I have doomed you to evil. An end and destruction be to you, taste

you the fire, an end to you; you shall have no further being (4). An end and destruction to you, an end to you, taste you [*the fire*] and come to an end. I have caused Apep, the enemy of Ra, to be destroyed. Ra triumphs over you, O Apep.

[*Repeat*] four times.

Per-Aa (Pharaoh) triumphs over his enemies. [Repeat] four times.

Rubric: (5) NOW after [the figure of] Apep has been defiled by you with your left foot four times, You shall say as you stand before Ra with your two arms bent [raised in homage] as soon as he has risen

Ra has triumphed over you, Apep. [*Repeat*] four times.

Ra has made himself to triumph over you, Apep, in very truth.

To effect the destruction of Apep this (i.e., the above) chapter must be recited. It shall be written upon a strip of new papyrus in ink of a green colour, and [recited over] a figure of Apep made of wax (7) whereon his name has been written in ink of a green colour.[44]

The figure shall be laid upon the fire that it may consume the enemy of Ra.

And one shall place a figure of Apep in the fire at daybreak (or, sunrise),

At noon also,

At eventide when Ra heart (8). is in the Land of Life (i.e., the West),

At the sixth hour of the night (i.e., midnight),

At the eighth hour of the day, when evening is about to come

And afterwards at every hour of the day and of the night

On the day of the festival (9).

By day,

By month,

On the sixth day festival each month,

on the fifteenth day festival each month, [full moon]

And likewise every day.

[*Thereby*] shall Apep, the enemy of Ra, be overthrown in the thunderstorm, and Ra shall shine brightly, and Apep shall be overthrown in very truth. (10)

And when the figure of Apep has been burnt in a fire made of khesau[45] herbs, the remains (i.e., ashes) thereof shall be soaked in wine[46] and then thrust firmly into a fire.

And you shall make a repetition of this ceremony at the sixth hour of the night (i.e., midnight), (11) and at daybreak on the fifteenth day of the month (?).

And when the figure of Apep is placed in the fire, one shall spit upon it a very great many times at the beginning of each hour of the day until the shadow comes round. And as for what shall be done after these things, on the sixth day festival (12). each month, at daybreak, You shall place a figure of Apep in the fire, and shall spit upon it, and shall trample it into the dirt with your left foot; thereby shall be driven away the roarings[47] of the fiend "Stinking Face," and you shall make a repetition of this act (13), at daybreak on the fifteenth day of each month; thereby shall Apep be repulsed and hacked in pieces at your Sekti Boat [O Ra]. And you shall make a repetition of this ceremony when lightnings blaze in the eastern pares of the sky, when Ra sets (14) in the Land of Life (i.e., the West), in order that the red ones (i.e., fire-fiends) may not be allowed to come into being in the eastern pares of the sky. And you shall repeat this ceremony many, many times to prevent a rainstorm coming on in the sky, and also to prevent (15) the occurrence of a thunderstorm in the sky. And you shall repeat this ceremony many, many times to [prevent] rain and to make the disk of the sun to shine, [for thereby] shall Apep be overthrown indeed. The doing of these things is a protection to a man on earth and in the (16). Other World (Khertet-Neter), for thereby will power be given unto him to [attain to] dignities which are above him, and he shall be delivered from every evil thing in very truth. May I see [this] happen to me!

For the remainder of this long magical book see the appendix

The ritual was performed in both temples of Amun-Ra at ancient Thebes (Waset), hence the references to the northern and southern apartments; which would be Karnak and Luxor temples respectively. Although our text is very late it seems to be a window into the world of Egypt's first intermediate period, a time of relative chaos between the Old and Middle Kingdoms. The inscription above from the Tomb of Ankhtifi and other sources such as the *Famine Stele* describes those times.

Although many rival warlords competed to achieve hegemony, it was eventually the kings of Waset, (ancient Thebes) - rather appropriately meaning the "place of the Sceptre" - who eventually established themselves with Waset as the capital of a stable realm. The rubric [verses 6-16] says the rite was to be performed several

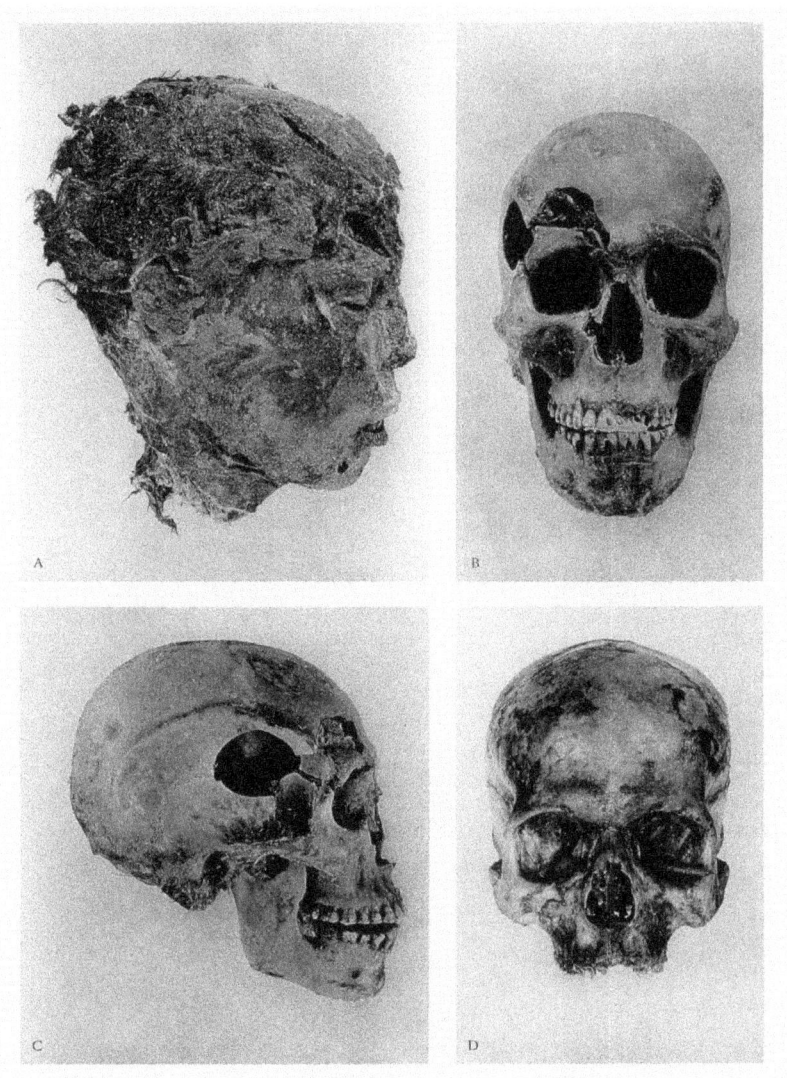

A TO C. BROKEN NOSE AND DEPRESSED FRACTURES OF THE SKULL OVER THE RIGHT EYE AND ON THE RIGHT TEMPLE OF NO. 14. D. THE EBONY TIP OF AN ARROW PUNCTURING THE FLOOR OF THE LEFT ORBIT OF NO. 21. SCALE 1:2

Remains from the Warrior's tomb; a mass grave at Thebes.

times a day. At dawn, noon dusk, midnight (sixth hour of the night) and sometimes throughout the night. The rite also acts as a protection against storms, presumable both those of dust and of rain. If you've ever experienced an Egyptian storm you will understand how elemental and awe-inspiring they are in power. Such storms articulate a metaphorical connection between civil disorder and the biosphere. It is an attractive idea, that social disorder and biosphere disorder are intimately connected. [48]

THE EVIL EYE

Apophis is dangerous to the sun god Ra, and other gods because he has the power of the evil eye, first recorded in a prototype of *Book of the Dead* 108. In the Coffin Texts, it is written:

"I know that mountain of Bahu/
On which heaven rests /
It is a plateau (?), 300 rods (1500 metres) in its length, 120 rods (600 meters) in its breadth./ Sebek,/
lord of Bahu is on the East side of this mountain/
His house is of carnelian /
and there is a snake on the top of that mountain, /
30 cubits (14 meters) in his length; /
3 cubits from his foreside on are a knife/
I know the name of this snake: "who is on his mountain, who is in his flame" is his name. /
Now when it is the time of the evening, he will turn his eye towards Re'. /
A standstill comes about among the crew /
and a great bewilderment during the course. /
Seth will bend himself/

within his reach. "Ah!" he says to him by way of magic. "I stand within your reach! The course of the boat passes off in a regular manner! You who see from afar, /
just close your eye!" /
I have ensnared you - /
I am a robust male! /
Cover your head; /
when you are safe, I am safe! /
I am somebody whose magic is great; /
there has been given (something) to me against you!" /
"What is this?" "Something useful, / O you who creep on your belly" /
… ' etc. [49]

Ra seems to be particularly vulnerable to serpents. *The Book of Overthrowing Apep* is the culmination of a long tradition of such rites. Kousoulis[50] catalogued 36 similar documents, several of which reference the famous myth whereby Isis reveals a morally ambiguous side to her character, when, in order to supplement her already great magical power, she places a venomous snake in the sun god's path:

> "Re has swooned he says "I have trodden on something hot. My heart is afraid, my flesh creeps. The useful member in me obeys me not. "Tell me your name, your mother and me let lay a spell upon you. "I am lion, I am the lion pair, I am the phoenix, which came into being by itself, I am one of millions whose name is unknown. For if the poison go up on high, the Bark of Re will fonder on that spine of Apophis which coils up (/) when it meets the dew' 'flow forth, you scorpion'"[51]

In most instances, the sun-boat encounters a snake at sunset and must do battle daily with an avatar of Apophis, although the name given differs from text to text. The meeting takes place always at twilight, a magical time. The snake has the power to enchant the crew using just the power of his or her eye. Only Seth can withstand him. And the reason Seth can stand up to the snake, although this is nowhere stated in the spell, is because he himself is said to possess a "dreadful" eye. In another version of the spell he lifts up the snake, taking away its power.

MORE OF PLUTARCH'S VERSION OF SETH

Earlier I described how Plutarch wrote of the ancient association between Seth and the lowly ass or donkey. Here he is certainly on solid ground in terms of the native Egyptian tradition: the ass was, and, still is a much abused, beast of burden. The zoologist John Wyatt, who is an expert on the wildlife of Egypt writes that "Donkeys, both wild and tamed, are known for their hardiness, stubbornness, aggressiveness and loudness of voice. Dominant males set up breeding/feeding territories into which they attract groups of females/young which they protect from other males. Dominance, stubbornness, aggressiveness and loudness can all be argued as being features of Seth" (private communication). In mythic texts we are told that Seth assumes the form of an ass when he is forced, as a penance, to carry the barley to the granary. The cut barley crop is the agricultural form of the dead and resurrected god (Osiris) who Seth had earlier murdered. Perhaps this is a metaphorical way of saying Osiris *is* the harvested barley, a recurring theme that had entered into so many aspects of the Osirian myth cycle.

Plutarch also offers an agricultural explanation for Seth's troubled relationship with his consort Nephthys. At the same time it provides a cosmological motive of his primal rage against his brother Osiris. He says, "They give the name Nephthys to the ends of the earth and the regions fringing on mountains and bordering the sea. For this reason they also call her Teleute (The end), and say that she cohabits with Typhon. Whenever the Nile is overflowing, and floods into the outlying regions beyond, they call this the union of Osiris with Nephthys, which is revealed by the sprouting plants."[52]

Thus Nephthys represents the barren land that can nevertheless become fertile when touched by Osiris in the form of the Nile flood. Her adultery is further elaborated by Plutarch: "When Isis found that Osiris had loved and had been intimate with her sister while mistaking her for herself, and saw proof of this in the garland of melilot, which he had left with Nephthys, she searched for the child (for Nephthys had exposed it instantly upon giving birth, in fear of Typhon); and when Isis found it with the help of dogs which had led her on with difficulty and pain, it was reared and became her guard and attendant, being called Anubis. He is said to keep watch over the gods as dogs do over men." [53] However Anubis is never described as the son of Nephthys and Osiris in Egyptian sources, but with the possible exception of the Harris Magical Papyrus where it does say that Anubis is the son of Nephthys; but does not mention his father. Most often Anubis is said to be the son of Isis.

Osiris disappears, or we might say is killed according to Plutarch, in the month named after Hathor called Athyr, third of the season of inundation: "…Osiris disappeared in the month of Athyr, when the etesian winds stop and the Nile utterly recedes, while the land is barred and with the lengthening of the night darkness increases and the power of light is diminished and subdued".[54]

Actually the month Khoiak which follows on after Athyr is very famous for its celebrations in honour of the cult of Osiris at every temple throughout Egypt. This discrepancy must be attributable to the understandable conflicts within the Egyptian virtual year. For further explanation see Richard Parker's thesis on calendars,[55] and its discussion of the transposition of dates from Egypt's archaic lunar to its later solar year. A topic I have explored at length in my indispensable guide, *The Ritual Year in Ancient Egypt*.

"When Isis had recovered Osiris and nurtured Horus, who was becoming strong through exhalations, mists and clouds, Typhon was indeed overcome, but not destroyed; for the goddess who rules the earth did not allow the substance which is opposed to moisture to be completely destroyed, but she was lenient and let it go free wishing the fusion to remain; for the world would not be complete if the fiery element were to cease and disappear ... neither could one reject entirely the tradition that Typhon once ruled the domain of Osiris, since Egypt was then a sea. For this reason many shells can be found to this day in the quarries and the mountains; and all the springs and wells, of which there are many, contain salty and bitter water through stale vestige of the former sea."[56]

Plutarch is surely right in thinking that the native Egyptians had long ago noticed the incidence of geological phenomena associated with the ocean but occuring deep in the desert. Could this be the source of the Exodus story of the parting of the Red Sea? The Theban necropolis is one such arid mountain range whose sediments are all too obvious, including strata high up in the mountains that yield seashells. Some modern commentators have doubted the association between Seth and the dea, despite several different texts referring to it. For example is another from the collection of ancient spells published by J. F. Borghouts:

> "The raging of Seth is against the 'Akhu demon', the grudging of Ba'al is against you. The raging of the thunderstorm - while it thirsts after the water in heaven ... then you will taste the things the sea tasted through his hand"[57]

Borghouts and others think this spell reveals Canaanite (modern Lebanon) influence, principally the myth of Ba'al and his battle with the sea. It is true that the iconography of Ba'al often does resemble that of Seth.

Baal imitating Seth as he smites a triton –
[magical gem 21/7 *Ibiza* no. 73 (Ibiza 3650)]

Borghouts' collection of magical texts includes many old healing spells and formulae. Notably here is the appearance of Egyptian Seth in a *benign* capacity, against the *Akhw* demon, here used in the sense of a disease entity. These spells are quite early, perhaps within the so-called second intermediate period (c1640-1532BCE). This was a time of instability. when a strong or unified government of the whole region was lacking and political power was divided amongst a number of rival dynasties. One of these is famously referred to as the Hyksos. The ancient historian Manetho called them Hiksos "the Shepherds" but the Egyptian expression is Heqw khasut (*ḥK3w- ḫ33wt*). meaning "rulers of foreign countries". This implies they were rulers, mainly based in the eastern delta region, who had infiltrated or invaded Egypt. I mention this as for some it provides a ready explanation for supposed non-Egyptian elements in texts such as those we are about to discuss.

The spell begins with the typical Egyptian mythological preamble, known by Egyptologists as a "Historiola". This serves as the explanations of the god Seth's particular efficacy against the Akhw demons:

> "The raging of Seth is against the 'akhu-demon, the grudging of Ba'al is against you! The raging of the thunder storm – while it thirsts after the water in heaven, is against you" Then he will make an end of the violence, [having laid his arms on you.] Then you will taste the things the Sea tasted through his hand. Then the [lion] will make his approach [to you], Baal will hit you with the pine-tree that is in his hand, He will treat you as the pine wood spears that are in his hand!" (Borghouts 1978: 19)

The interchanging of the name of Seth with Canaanite deity Ba'al places this text within the Hyksos realm for it was exactly they who made Seth lord of their capital at Avaris in the Delta, combining his mythology with that of the Syrian storm god Hadad. Although Seth was also known as "Lord of the Storm" in the earlier Pyramid age, as in Pyramid text 261:

> "Address to the spirit as it leaves the burial chamber. The storm-lord, the one with spittle in his vicinity, Seth – he bears you: he is the one who bears Atum" [58]

A non-Egyptian element is said to be exemplified in the line "Then you will taste the things the Sea tasted though his hand". Similar sentiments are expressed in several of these spells, notably number 56: *A Conjuration of the Asiatic Disease* (*t-n.t 3ᶜm.w*) with the line: "Seth conjured the Great Green (sea)" i.e. the Mediterranean. Seth is usually considered an upper Egyptian god with no cult centres anywhere near the Mediterranean.

Borghouts thinks this can only be an Egyptian version of Canaanite myth of the conflict of sea god Yam and Ba'al imitating Seth. But here Hans Goedicke has an interesting rival theory to explain the unusual connection between Seth and the Mediterranean. During the Hyksos period, Seth, the mostly Upper Egyptian god, acquired a new cult centre at Avaris in the Delta. This is also the period of increased seismic activity at Thera, which eventually culminated in the massive conflagration during the reign of Hatshepsut. Some say this is the origin of the Myth of the End of Atlantis. It was certainly the end of the Minoan Thassalocracy and cult. This association between Seth, the water and the sea also finds expression in the spells of the Graeco-Egyptian Magical Papyri:

"Shaker of rocks, wall trembler, boiler of *The waves, disturber of the sea's great depth,*" (PGM IV 154-258)

This entire spell goes on to include a Typhonian initiation, divination, and daily rite discussed in our appendix below on pathways to Seth.

When the Thera supervolcano erupted, the resulting tsunami engulfed the Egyptian delta but stopped short of Avaris, protected, one might say, by the power of Seth. Could this be the origin of his new epithet and power over the Mediterranean?

The dislocation caused by this tsunami is the likely cause of the epidemics noted in records of the time, including the Bubonic Plague. Hittite sources show that plague was endemic during the time of Akhenaten and the foundation of his new city may have been an attempt offer a sanctuary to the elite, away from centres of contagion. The god Seth was no doubt also invoked to counteract this wave of disease and chaos especially as more naturalistic measures proved of no use.

THE CORN MUMMY

"Everyone knows that among all the people of antiquity the Egyptians have the strangest uses of the materials of perfumery ... and also are the most peculiar in their uses of the most common of products" (D. H. Aufrère)

There's an account of the Khoiak festivals carved onto walls of the Osiris shrine on the roof at the temple of Hathor at Denderah. Similar rites were celebrated at every major temple in Egypt. Thus included the newly rediscovered sunken city of Thonis-Heracleion, which, rather like Pompeii, has preserved many cultic objects from this festival (see various works by underwater archaeologist Frank Goddio, especially *Sunken Cities*).[59]

Plutarch's contention that[60] "the death of Osiris occurred on the 17th (of the lunar month) when the full moon is most obliviously waning", seems to work. Actually the entire passion of Osiris is played out over the complete cycle of the moon. And in this holy month of Khoiak, approximately October in our modern calendar, important events happen on the 12th & the 16th day, when the sun and moon can appear together in the sky and when cult rites were enacted all over Egypt.

Here we find one of most important magical techniques bequeathed to us by antiquity. It's a rite than we can and many do still replicate in some form and is an instance of the highly important magick of statues. In this ritual sequence two small statuettes, each the approximate length of one's forearm (a cubit); are prepared in parallel over the course of the month. The two figures are Osiris-Vegetans and Osiris-Sokar.

Starting from the new moon, earth and water - the material for the Osiris Vegetans or germinating figure of Osiris are placed into a small mummiform planter. I use a small metal mummiform pencil case obtained from the British Museum shop. The seeds need darkness to germinate but should be ready to be a "corn mummy" by the appropriate day, in this case the 12th. Now exposed to sunlight, allow the corn mummy to continue germinating until the 22nd day, when in olden times it participated in a nautical festival on the river in which, Strabo wrote that, 34 papyrus boats took part, illuminated by 365 lamps, presumably, then, a night-time festival.

Parallel to this is a rite to Osiris-Sokar, who we might consider as an older form or precursor of Osiris. Sokar was the god of dead. Some say that this part of the ritual may not originally have had any association with Osiris but could be of the cult of Ptah, Re or even moon god Khonsu.

In both instances we see a connection being made between death and fertility. This Osiris-Sokar rite requires the construction of a second corn mummy but using a different technique. This mummy is also made on the 15th or full moon day; but now 14 different components are ritually prepared, each symbolising different parts of the dismembered god. They are first carefully measured out into 14 different containers, which included things such as incense, precious stones and earths, with special rites for each substance.

The recipe for the "precious unguent" as carved on the wall of the chamber of the temple of Edfu, known by Egyptologists as the *Laboratory*.

> "A location where the recipes for various unguents and perfumes used in the temple were precisely described – was common to all places supposed to have have one of the pieces of Osiris' body."

This following recipe describes the 14 parts. Unless otherwise stated, One part of each, actually 1 hin unit of liquid measure is equivalent to approximately 0.46 litres.[61] As this would make for quite a heavy mummy I would use smaller amounts but keep the same proportions. I've not done this in truth yet but occurs to me this is a potentially combustible mixture and appropriate safetly precautions will need to be in place, including fire control. Make a two part mold from plaster using a model of Osiris as a marquette. Calculate the final volume by measuring the displacement when submerged in water. For example, if the final volume is two litres, this divided into 14 would be approximately 143ml for each part: a much more manageable size! The recipe is as follows:

1. Bitumen, ground to perfection
2. Vegetable tar (a by-product the fir tree), then put on the heat to cook

add

3. Fine lotus essence, 1st quality
4. Frankincense, of 1st quality
5. Fine oil, (castor oil?)
6. Wax,

with

7. Fresh turpentine resin,
8. Dry turpentine resin
9. Extract of carob bean,
10. Aromatic Herbs and spices mixed in wine, 1/2 measure
11. Fine oil (possible Moringa or Algan)
12. True metals and minerals crushed into a very fine power Spread with
13. Honey

and incorporate with

14. Dry frankincense.

Assemble into one mass & apply on the day of the internment in [in the mould]

Edfu "Laboratory" Room Z

"The mixture was cooked and formed a blackish liquid with a predominant odour of bitumen." [62]

After the component have been combined together they are kneaded into an egg, which is kept moist inside a special reliquary made of sycamore gilded with silver. On the 16th day it is pressed into a two-part mould.

This mummy, being still in construction, could not have participated in the boat festival mentioned in connection with the Osiris *Vegetans*. The egg is very suggestive of an unborn embryo. It is my contention that it is this object that is referred to as "headless", in for example the rubric from Denderah transcribed below. The theme of headlessness and the unborn, are part of the complex, astronomical and metaphysical mysteries of this cult, many elements of which far predate the emergence of the cult of Osiris.

One might expect Osiris to be dismembered into 15 rather than 14 parts, 15 being the number of days as counted in the original Egyptians lunar half month, rather than the later lunar days of the Greek astronomical schema. If there were a "missing" component to the corn-mummy, this would reiterate the fact that in the myth, one of the Osiris parts was never recovered; his

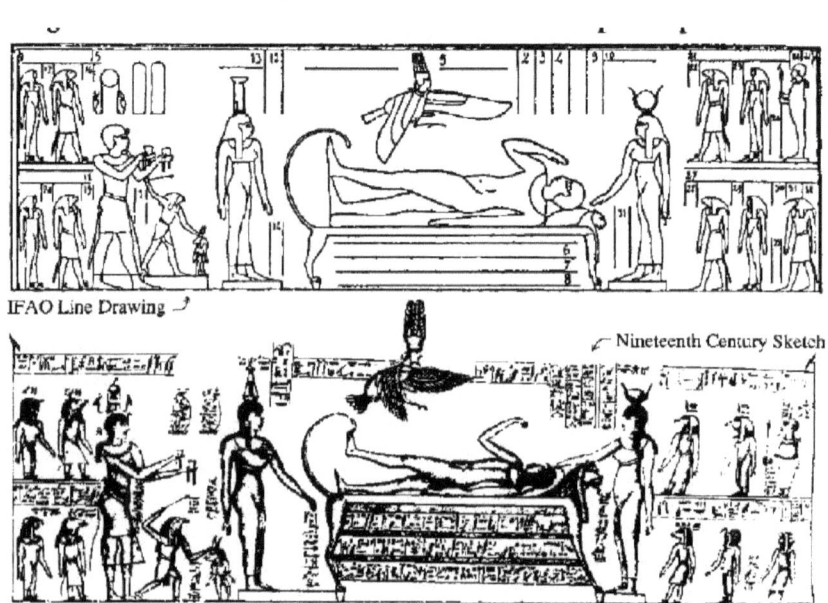

Ritual from Opet attached to Temple of Khonsu, Karnak

phallus, eaten by the Oxyrhinchus fish. The goddess Isis was able to reconstitute it by magick.

This might also explain the remarkable erotic interchange between Ra and Osiris in the Temple of Opet (revival of Osiris) at Karnak. The original was mutilated by Victorian archaeologists. Osiris receives his missing part, the phallus from the sun god Ra. Sometimes it is his head he received although here some sort of euphemism or correspondence may be meant.

Meeks notes that in the famous Denderah account of this ritual, the "corn mummy" borne in the hollow plinth of a gilded wooden statue of the Cow goddess is said to be headless:

> "Concerning the cow "bearer" (remenit), she is made of sycamore wood covered in gold. A [corn] mummy with no head is inside, the venerated recipient; is a cubit in length. There are two mice on the plinth of gilded wood beneath her. It is a cubit long. A table of offerings is placed in front of her. She has a scarab on the top and a covering of sai [fabric], the Atef crown on her head & an Usekh collar of flowers & lapis lazuli" [63]

At the culmination of the festivities on the 30th day of the month, which would be Halloween in later ritual years, the corn mummy from the previous year is moved from the "upper" to the "lower" tomb. Finally a Djed pillar, a stylised tree, is raised, representing stability and resurrection. This is a very ancient ritual act, the raising of a pillar or pole of some kind. Some have suggested this kind of act is recognisable in one of the oldest ritual sites thus far discovered: Gobekli tepe in Anatolia.

ASTRONOMICAL ASSOCIATIONS

Plutarch writes that, "[Seth] Typhon [is considered] to be the solar and Osiris the lunar world ... for this reason the Egyptians call Typhon Seth, which denotes 'oppressive and compulsive' ". If anything, native sources would place things the other way around. Seth is one of several lunar deities in Egypt, most often associated with the full moon. Although there is an interesting aspect to the mysteries of Osiris where he is a headless god, which seems to be connected to the dark period of the new moon.

Plutarch, gets even more technical when he says[64] that some astronomers "give the name Typhon to the shadow of the earth into which they believe the moon falls and so suffers eclipse ... The moon herself in turn obscures the sun on the thirtieth of the month [the new moon] and removes it from sight, yet does not completely obliterate it, no more than Isis did Typhon".[65] There is an allusion here to the myth given in the *Contendings of Horus & Seth*[66] whereby Isis throws a weapon to Seth that he might not be defenceless against Horus, thus preventing his annihilation. Just as in the myth of Apep, enemies are never completely destroyed, if only to preserve the pretext for cathartic rage. Isis is beheaded by her son Horus for her troubles and in turn receives a replacement head, that of the cow, hence her appearance as Hathor. This is a complex ritual/symbolic play here on the theme of headlessness – a glimpse of the deep inner mysteries of the cult. Gwyn Griffith has identified the name of this shadow that causes the lunar and solar eclipses from Greek astronomers as the river Styx or *Road to Hades*.

This story, differs slightly from native sources, but does seem to be a faithful reflection of Seth as the power of darkness, who with his ancient brother Horus can represents the waxing and waning of the lunar cycle. One might also detect a "dualistic" interpretation of the universe at play here, good and evil, light and dark, which together produce a pleasing result. According to Griffith, most Egyptologists concur in seeing the myth as representing the more frequent event of the waxing and waning of the moon. Although there is in fact no decisive text available to prove this, but there are enough references to lunar phenomena, to make this interpretation a reasonable certainty.[67] See for example:

> BOTD spell 80
> "I have carried away the darkness by my power. I have filled the eye with what was lacking in it, before the fifteenth (full moon) day of the festival had come." quoted in Gwyn Griffiths *Conflict of Horus & Seth*.

Gwyn Griffiths warns us that there is an alternative version of this same text where the eye is filled on the sixth day of the lunar month, another important day in the Egyptian calendar, after first crescent day when the moon is visible in the sky. [68]

Furthermore native Egyptian texts often do say that Seth bears the power of darkness which can threaten both sun and moon; "I am the son, Seth, who causes (or clears) the turbulence of the storm, circling within the horizon of the sky, like the crooked god. That is his desire."[69] This particular spell is actually aimed at

Apophis, but the verse demonstrates an identification of the archfiend with Seth, like several other texts.

Thus many apotropaic rites to counter Seth's dark nature, incorporate lighting fires or removing that which blocks vision in order to allow the light to shine, as in the ubiquitous temple liturgy, when a bolt is drawn opening the door to the shrine, with the words: "The finger of Seth is removed from the eye of Horus. It is well."[70]

It is possible to understand this duality from a neo-Platonic perspective, as shown by Plutarch when he writes that, "The concord of the cosmos is caused by opposite tensions, just like that of lyre and a bow", [71] and according to Euripides, "the good and bad could not appear apart, and a certain mingling gives a goodly poise". Platonism, and neo-Platonism are popular tools for interpreting the Egyptian mindset, that many would accept as being close to the Egyptian's own view, perhaps even derived from native sources (see for instance Jan Assman's: *Moses the Egyptian*). Randy Conner, who has a background in the study of African religions, finds Platonism a false friend in this project, for example that from the perspective of many African religions, the magick that resides in the heart of every statue, makes it a unique living thing and not merely a participate in an abstract "form" of the statue. [72]

Plutarch tells us that "nothing comes into being without a cause, and if good could not provide the cause of evil, then nature must contain in itself the creation and origin of evil as well as good". A very clever argument, which has been used to, amongst other things, prove that "the all-father" (Amun-Ra), if he is able to create male and female beings, must in reality also be both male and female. And the god Seth, as an emanation of Amun-Ra, is an externalisation of the creator god's aggressive tendencies, done to serve a particular end: opposing an equally violent and chaotic force, known from the end of Old Kingdom as Apophis. Although it might be going too far to assume that Apophis is also some aspect of the All-Father, although this would be the logical conclusion of this line of reasoning. As far as I know, Apophis is *sui generis*, the principle of absolute evil, that came into the Egyptian world, when things got really bad and began to fall apart. Perhaps Apophis belongs to an older strata of belief, when monsters roamed the earth, that received offerings not through love but from a deep-seated need to propitiate them?

Plutarch encourages us to apply additional ideas that he ascribes to Chaldeans, the Hellenistic designation for Persia-Babylonia. The famous "oracles" emerged or were compiled in Alexandria in late antiquity, the last great book of the Pagan world, and very much of Plutarch's time.[73]

If we acknowledge Alexandrian neo-Platonism, was one of several Egyptian philosophies with no compelling reason why it should be the only one view in circulation. Think of India which at this time acknowledged the existence of at least six *darshana* or philosophical systems or *views*.

"The Chaldeans," as Plutarch tells it,[74] "aver that of the planets, which they call the gods presiding at birth, two are beneficent and two maleficent, the other three … sharing both nature." In Egyptian religious astronomy, the correspondence between the gods and planets is thus:

Sun (Amun-Ra)
Moon (Khonsu)
Mars (Horus the red $ḥr$-$d3$)
Mercury (Seth)
Venus (Osiris "Star who crosses")
Saturn (Horus bull of the sky $ḥr$-$k3,pt$))
Jupiter (Horus who rules two lands)

Of these, Mercury (Seth) and the Moon (Khonsu) could be malign, the Sun (Amun-Ra) and Venus (benign), leaving Saturn, Mars and Jupiter, and these last three were viewed by Egyptians as different forms of Horus, sharing both natures, thus the native Egyptian mythology is compatible with the Chaldean view.

Plutarch is on familiar ground when he acknowledges the long-standing connection between Seth and the constellation of The Bear, or Ursa Major.

Plutarch also says that "Typhon is the element of the soul which is passionate, akin to the Titans, without reason, and brutish, and the element of the corporeal which is subject to death, disease and confusion through bad seasons, imperfect coalescence of air, eclipses of the sun, and the disappearance of the moon, which are all in the manner of sallies and rebellions by Typhon; for it denotes the overpowering and violent, it denotes frequent return and over-leaping". [75]

His views do have backing from Egyptian sources, some of which I discussed in my book *Supernatural Assault in Ancient Egypt*, where I attempted to reconstruct a proto-Egyptian psychology, a science of the soul if you like, based on fragmentary remains of a New Kingdom dream manual, one of several that have survived the ravages of time. In this we can say that the gods Horus and Seth provide two models of maleness, Horus the ideal, but Seth, less than ideal, but not uncommon, as in "the redness of his eye":

"If he drinks a beer, he drinks it to engender strife and turmoil. The redness of the white of his eye is this god. He is one who drinks what he detests."

He is beloved of women through the greatness of his loving them. He likes women and consequently they like him.

"Though he is a royal kinsman, he has the personality of a man of the people (the Rekhyt)."

" . . . he would not descend unto the west, but is placed in the desert as a prey to rapacious birds . . ."

"As for a man who is a drunk, (who) broils, (causes) calumnies, ills and mischief. He drinks beer so as to engender turmoil and disputes . . . he will take up weapons of warfare . . . before him, a hippopotamus . . . when he perceives on the second day (Gardiner, the translator and commentator of this text, suggests when he wakes up after a drinking bout;

which we cannot help being amused by such a thought although in truth it is also likely to be a reference to waking after a religious festival) . . . he will not distinguish the married woman from . . . as to any man who opposed him . . . massacres arise in him and he is pleased in the Netherworld. . . He will engender disputes so as to break vessels" - The rest is too fragmentary to make much sense of, but you get the idea.[76]

It is noteworthy to see the word "Rekhyt" here, denoting the common people, obviously this is a significant attribute of Seth, revealing some proletarian sympathies perhaps. In some ways, all this could be a sketch of the famous King Ramses II – who was apparently a red head, with a strong constitution that enabled him to live into his one-hundredth year.

Horus and Seth are famous for their conflict with each other. From Plutarch we are grateful for passing on this delightful story of how he had heard of a "statue of Horus in Coptos that holds the genitals of Typhon in one hand and they relate that Hermes, having ripped out the sinews of Typhon, used them as lyre strings, claiming that this shows how reason regulated the universe and made it harmonious out of discordant parts; [thus] did not wipe out the destructive elements, they aver, but maimed its power."[77] Gwyn-Griffith thinks this story betrays a purely Greek influence and concern about the mythic origins of Hermes' lyre.

But there is indeed a shrine to Horus, Isis and Min at Koptos, although thus far no such statue has come to light. In Ptolemaic times, Osiris was often worshipped in the form of Dionysus, a

god also famous for his lyre, so perhaps Plutarch is helping us to remember this. The Roman emperor Nero, also a lyre strummer, appears on a sandstone stele making an offering to Min, whilst behind him Horus is slaying some unseen creature, an image of the god as avenger of his father as shown at Edfu.[78] The inscription reads: "Live Horus, the warrior, smiting the foreign countries, Nero Caesar has made his monument for his father Min-Ra". As Seth is sometimes said to be the personification of foreigners, perhaps there is some corroboration here? The image before Horus is usually interpreted as a sloping ramp leading to the shrine but perhaps if a traveller, unaccustomed to the conventions of Ptolemaic art saw this, they might interpret as a lyre?

The inner meaning of names was obviously something important to Plutarch judging by the many times he offers an etymology of Seth. Egyptologist Te Velde approves, believing, as he does, that Plutarch is recording authentic understandings of his time: "Typhon, as we already said[79] is called Seth, Bebon and Smu, names that try to express some violent and hindering restraint or opposition or turning back. They still call the loadstone (magnetic oxide of iron) 'the bone of Horus' and iron 'the bone of Typhon' as Manetho records" ...[80] This association between Seth and "iron from the sky" is ancient and attested from native sources.

Iron is heavy and by association, Plutarch implies that Typhon's nature is sluggish. and therefore repelled by a livelier energy. Hence "they say that with the sistrum they repel and ward off Typhon, meaning that when decay confines and restricts nature, the power of creation sets her free and restores her by means of movement."[81]

Plutarch's uses Platonic language, which has a strong moral emphasis – Typhon is without measure and order. Therefore "we should not be wrong if we simply ascribed to Typhon whatever in these things is without measure and order through excess or deficiency, whilst venerating and honouring the well ordered, the good and the useful as the work of Isis and such things as the image, the imitation and reason (logos) of Osiris." [82]

Ovid,[83] was one of many Greek poets who connected the Typhon with Egypt, the place where the gods supposedly fled in fear of him, disguising themselves as animals. This aspect of Egyptian religion fascinated the Greeks. But Plutarch rejects all of this explanation and offers another: "The story that the gods changed into these animals in fear of Typhon, as though hiding themselves in the bodies of ibises, dogs and hawks, surpasses all childish marvels and fairy-tales; and the ideas that the souls of the dead which survive then achieve rebirth in these animals only, is equally incredible." [84]

Plutarch contends that an animal deity is all about how conflict was managed and channelled in Egyptian society, how it could be deflected from the ruling elite by a strategy of divide and rule. So for example, he says "the Oxyrhynchites, when the Cynopolitans ate the Oxyrhynchus fish, seized a dog and after offering it in sacrifice, devoured it as a sacrificial meat, as a result they went to war."

By saying that Typhon's own soul was assigned to these animals, the myth would appear to indicate symbolically that every irrational and bestial thing is connected to, and participates in, the "evil daemon. It is really to appease and assuage him that they respect and honour these animals. If a great and severe drought arises which brings with it in large measure either of pernicious desires or unexpected and strange misfortunes, then the priests lead aside, in conditions of darkness, silence and secrecy, certain of the animals honoured; and at first they threaten and frighten them; and if the drought continues, they consecrate and slay them, intending this as a sort of punishment of the daemon or otherwise as a great expiation." [85]

This seems a mean trick but this spiritual *transaction* is actually quite common in Egyptian religion. The threatening of a deity with the withholding of cult offerings in the event of adverse conditions or even a semi-secret technique called *diabole*. Appropriate cult animals were sacrificed as an antagonistic act in order to provoke the presiding deity to take its revenge. This was done in the belief that such revenge would not fall on the person making the sacrifice, but rather on someone who is falsely accused of making such a sacrifice. Perhaps this could be considered as of the earliest examples of "false flag" and "black operations"? A great depiction of this kind of dynamic can be seen in the Jacques Tourneur film, "Night of the Demon".

Spell to cause evil sleep[86]
PDM xiv 675-94 [PGM XIVc 15-27]

The rite was to be completed twice a day, at sunrise and sunset. It is repeated over four days causing the victim to suffer from evil sleep - 'nektek bin' (*nktk bin*). If the process were continued for seven days, the victim would die (this later feature is written in code for obvious reasons).

The spell invokes Seth-Typhon to accomplish its aim using a technique known in the classical times as a diabolè–literally that which 'tears apart' as opposed to the symbolic–'that which unites'. The appropriate god is provoked or antagonised even desecrated until he or she becomes sufficiently angry that they send a 'demonic' emissary to trouble the victim in their sleep.

Instructions:

While facing the rising or setting sun, the practitioner should place the head of a donkey between his feet and position his right *hand* in front of, and his left hand behind, the animal's head. While he is seated on his heels above the head, he has to recite the invocation. Before starting the rite, he has to anoint his right foot with yellow ochre from Syria, his left foot and soles with clay, and to put donkey's blood on one of his hands and the two corners of his mouth. As a phylactery, he should bind a thread of palm fibre to his hand and a piece of male palm fibre to the head and phallus. The accompanying Greek invocation runs as follows:

> I call upon you who are in the empty air,
> You who are terrible, invisible, almighty, a god of gods,
> You who cause destruction and desolation,
> You who hate a stable household,
> You who were driven out of Egypt and have roamed foreign lands,
> You who shatter everything and are not defeated.
> I call upon you, Typhon <u>Seth</u>;
> I command your prophetic powers because
> I call upon your authoritative name,
> to which you cannot refuse to listen,
> then some barbarous names of power including:
> IÔ erbÊth IÔ pakerbÊth IÔ bolchosÊth etc
> Come to me and go and strike down him, NN, (or her, NN) with chills and fever. That very person has wronged me and he (or she) has spilled the blood of Typhon in his own (or her own) house. For this reason I am doing this (add the usual ie more details in your own words)

The rite and the invocation are linked together through the Egyptian god Seth, who was identified, at the latest from the fifth century BCE onwards, with the Greek deity Typhon, whom Zeus had punished for insurrection by throwing him into the Tartarus. The rite evokes a connection with Seth by means of the manipulation of the head and blood of a donkey, which animal was the symbol *par excellence* of the god Seth in Egyptian temple ritual throughout the Late and Greco-Roman period.

The reversed nature of the rite manifests itself most explicitly in the donkey's head. According to an account of Herodotus, "Egyptian priests never offered an animal's head up to the god, but cursed it and took it outside the sacred precinct of the temple."

> "After leading the marked beast to the altar where they [Egyptian priests] will sacrifice it, they kindle a fire; then they pour wine on the altar over the victim and call upon the god; then they cut its throat, and having done so sever the head from the body. They flay the carcass of the victim, then invoke many curses on its head, which they carry away. Where there is a market, and Greek traders in it, the head is taken to the market and sold; where there are no Greeks, it is thrown into the river. The imprecation, which they utter over the heads, is that whatever ill threatens those who sacrifice, or the whole of Egypt, fall upon that head. In respect of the heads of sacrificed beasts and the libation of wine, the practice of all Egyptians is the same in all sacrifices; and from this ordinance no Egyptian will taste of the head of anything that had life."   [Herodotus, *The Histories*, II, 39]

"By making use of the head of a donkey, the rite does not only establish a close relationship with Seth, but also it defines itself as a rite opposed to the rules of regular temple ritual, which is in accord with Seth's role as an enemy to the ordered world. When the practitioner applies the donkey's blood to one of his hands, he trespasses in the same way another rule of Egyptian temple ritual. Because blood was seen as impure, the flowing of the sacrificial victim's blood symbolized the triumph over enemies in regular temple ritual. In this particular case, the practitioner does not cast the blood away, but smears it on his hand and, in the act, identifies with the enemies by way of contiguity."

"Next to Seth, the rite is also concerned with the sun god Ra, since the invocation has to be recited to the sun, while the practitioner faces the rising and setting sun disk. Daybreak and evening were probably considered opportune moments for this rite, because they are the beginning and end of the sun god's nightly travel through the underworld, where he has to enter into battle with the forces of chaos and evil, who attempt to bring the sun boat to a standstill in their effort to subdue the forces of creation and rejuvenation. By reciting at these critical moments between light and darkness, the practitioner takes full advantage of the intensified activity of the forces of disorder. More-over, according to pharaonic sun theology, the god Seth, part of the sun boat's crew as a servant to Re, exerted his destructive powers now to combat the snake Apophis, the sun god's arch-rival in the underworld. Seth and the sun god were consequently believed to be in each other's presence at these moments."

"The Greek invocation develops the Sethian elements of the rite further by calling the deity the god of cosmic upheaval, who is hostile to the social order and dwells in foreign countries. As outsider to the divine pantheon, the social world and the land of Egypt, he is the appropriate candidate to take up the anti-social task. In the final lines of the invocation, the practitioner prompts the deity to come to his aid by accusing the victim of having 'spilled the blood of Typhon in his own (or her own) house' (line 19-20)." [87]

As the ancients knew only too well, in the right hands, even a poison can become a medicine and vice versa. Kasia Szpakowska writes with great insight in *Behind closed eyes : Dreams and nightmares in the ancient world view* that "a dream is something seen not done" and is more like a vision, spectacle or memory. The action occurs in a special realm, similar or identical to the otherworld, where spirits and the dead also reside. Although Szpakowska does not discuss the kind of dream sending evidenced in this particular spell, this is a very important insight. The adept Miryam Devi has identified what could be a problem in the mechanics of ritual here and it is that, on the face of it, the ritual would almost certainly give the *sender* bad dreams but it's not obvious how this would have any effect on the intended *victim*. The answer may lie in the intention or belief of the magician who devised and sold the spell in the first place. He or she almost certainly did beleive that the bad dreams of the sender would generate a vision that the victim could not help but also see. So as the case of what we call the *placebo* effect, it is the self-belief of the physician that makes the *medicine* work.

The Seven Spells or Utterances of Nekhbet

Plutarch's descriptions in his dialogue *On Isis & Osiris*, and incidentally also of Seth, often leads us into some very taboo territory. I'm thinking of where he ventures into the controversial area of human sacrifice. What Plutarch reveals is really only hearsay, stories he has heard, wherein he reveals sacrifice in its most savage and primitive form.

Memories recorded via myth imply that pretty much every culture of the Near East, where they had once practised human sacrifice, record the point when they stopped doing so. They often framed this as an instruction from their god or gods. In its stead they usually substitute perhaps a bodily modification such as circumcision or, more commonly, an animal sacrifice.

Ancient Nekheb, Greek Eileithyia, or Ilithyia, Modern Elkab.
A section of enormous mudbrick wall surrounding the ancient city.

Thus, some of us learnt in "Sunday school", how Abraham set out to sacrifice his first-born Isaac but was stopped from doing so at the last moment when god instructs him to instead sacrifice a Ram.

In Egypt the corresponding "polemic", if that is what it is, could be found in the *Story of the Heavenly Cow*, and the blood lust of goddess Hathor, or in some later versions of the myth, the lion goddess Sekhmet. Her rage at the insult to the All-father Ra, in which she sets out to slaughter of the "human cattle", is only sublimated when she is induced to drink as much beer as she can hold, which is a lot. To this day, votive offerings of beer are flavoured with red ochre, whose metallic tang is so reminiscent of blood. Experts assume that human sacrifice did occur in archaic Egypt and is known to have persisted in special circumstances, usually in what we might call conflict zones or occasionally via outbreaks of communal violence aimed at the people of Seth, who became the victims on the altars of the antagonistic god.

Thus in Plutarch one reads how: "In Eileithouias-polis they used to burn men alive, as Manetho has recorded, calling them Typhonians, and they used to remove and scatter their ashes with winnowing fans. But this was done openly and at a fixed time, in the dog days."[88] The dog days are the time in the hot summer months commencing with the dawn rising of Sirius, the most sultry and uncomfortable time of the year in Northern Climes and indeed especially so in Upper Egypt. It would be a time when the unsavoury power of Seth were most apparent, hence the idea of punishing his "people".

Eileithyia, or Ilithyia after whom the Greeks named this Egyptian settlement, was the goddess of childbirth and midwifery. The Native name would be **Nekheb** from Nehbet the white vulture goddess, hence the modern town of Elkab, which is same name expressed in Arabic. The vulture as a hieroglyphic sign means mother, and as a goddess she is indeed associated with childbirth.

She is also a powerful protector of Egypt's dangerous southern border and it is in this aspect that the story of the Typhonian sacrifice likely arises. Nehbet, Goddess of the south, was identified with Selene by Greeks.

ιαʹ. Τί γῦπα γράφοντες δηλοῦσι.

Exploring Elkab &
pre-historic semiology

The author taking a rest in the shade, "Rock of the Vultures"

View west into the Wadi Hilal

Prehistoric pictogrammes of donkeys at Elkab

The discoveries at Elkab are concentrated at the mouth of Wadi Hilal. The ancient flood waters excavated this channel between the Nile and the Red sea at Quseer. These waters must have been mighty and sustained. Only two small outcrops or bergs of very hard rock remain.

This is the "Rock of the Vultures" which we must consider the original and source of the whole area's association with Nekhbet, the ancient vulture goddess, who is titular goddess of upper Egypt, the Nile valley and this magical desert spur.

Over 600 small votive inscriptions are documented here – some prehistoric, some Islamic but a great many from the very early Egyptian old kingdom, principally the sixth dynasty. They are short biographies of the priests of the goddess Nekhbet.

The modern discoverers of these texts wondered where the last resting place of these people might be. It was not long after this that the massive rock necropolis and other ancient cemeteries were located nearby in the cliffs that flank the wadi.

Unfinished antithetical image of Imhotep, architect of Djoser's pyramid or devotee of, from El kab, identified by characteristic skull cap.

There are hundreds of votive inscriptions on the rock, from prehistoric to pharaonic in cursive hieroglyphs even to Arabic.

The sun gives the hard rock berg a black surface that can be pecked away to leave these prehistoric designs, including gazelles, cows, and canids. There are symbolic boats identical to those found in the ancient tombs nearby, including the famous painted tomb at Hierakonpolis.

Thus far, evidence of human sacrifice has not been found in this location although it was a *conflict zone*, connected with the "last stand" of Egypt's final native king, Nectanebo II. So once again Plutarch has guided us to what is today a fascinating site in Upper Egypt, where groundbreaking archaeological excavations continue to yield fascinating evidence of cult behaviour related to the god Seth and the vulture goddess Nekheb.

THE SEVEN SERPENTS & THEIR UTTERANCES

The seven utterances of a god become other gods. We see this pattern in several Egyptian monuments and it is an idea that finds its way in the Greco-Egyptian Magical Papyri (PGM).[89] The excavation of the temple that must have dominated the interior of the citadel revealed a remarkable piece of Sethian themed battle magic. It also seems to be an instance of an important grouping of serpent demons, who are closely related to Seth. I would remind the reader of the number of times the sevenfold cluster of components arises in connection with the God Seth, whose constellation is, after all, the sevenfold Ursa Major, the Starry Plough. Working this in ritual has shown this to be the Egyptian equivalent, perhaps even source of the seven headed dragons that prowl or are widely remembered in the universal mythos. It is the serpent in each of the following tableau on which one should focus as the core, the 'riders' being there to explicate its character.

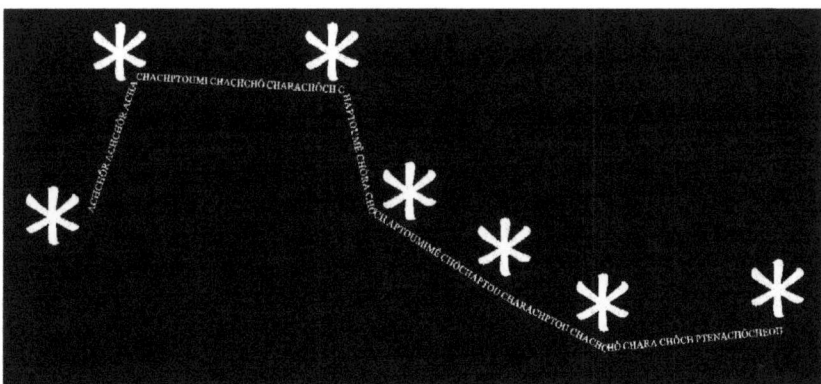

I've written about this, most recently in *Phi-Neter: power of the Egyptian Gods* where I analysed the seven signs of deliverance in the Greco-Egyptian magical papyri and their possible iteration in the Arabic magick as the seven seals, shown here:

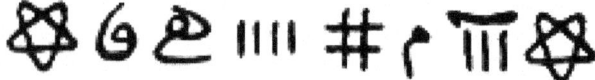

This rite I am about to describe exists is several versions although that at Elkab seems the most complete. Others are to be found in the temples of Edfu, Philae and Denderah.[90] This in itself is rather remarkable, as each of these three shrines has strong sectarian associations with the deities Horus, Isis and Hathor; respectively. All three of these deities could be thought of as the enemy of Seth. These temples are all late period Ptolemaic constructions, although built on foundations of older temples. There is here, incidentally, strong counter evidence to the widespread belief that the cult of Seth experienced a decline in status as Egypt's history unfolded, especially in the late period; close examination of new evidence shows the situation to have been much more complex.

The Belgium Egyptologist Jean Capart discovered a crypt at Elkab during his mission to excavate the citadel in the dig seasons of 1937-1940, immediately prior to the second world war.[91] The temple of Nekhbet is situated on a prehistoric mound, enclosed by massive mud brick walls that surround the sacred precinct and the associated township. (see earlier picture)

The seven utterances of Nekhbet are to be found on the west wall of the crypt in the most recent part of the sanctuary. The blocks are marked with the cartouche of Saitic warrior king

Psammetichus I ("Psamtik"). This king won his country's independence from Assyria. His name was later replaced with that of Amasis II, who built the crypt. It faces east to the mouth of Wadi Hillal, an important gateway to the Nile from the Red Sea, approximately 80km south of Luxor. There is another spell connected with this king that also has strong Sethian associations (see page 203)

The necropolis of the city is situated nearby in the cliffs of this wadi, and has thus far yielded tombs from all periods, the oldest pharaonic tombs from the XIth dynasty of Teta and Papi are located there but some are even older, prehistoric.

A few kilometres into the wadi is what must surely be the original sanctuary of the Vulture goddess, the "rock of the vultures" which is covered with inscriptions dating from modern times back into the prehistoric age. Even here we can detect an ancient association between the vulture goddess and Seth, who appears in the form of an ass or donkey; several extremely ancient pictograms of which are inscribed in the same rock.

The seven utterances of Nekhbet, as shown in the freeze overleaf, are the rubrik of a "typhonian" ritual of defensive magic, with the intention of repelling external attack from Egypt's vulnerable borders. The "grimoire" is to be read from left to right:

Reconstruction of the eastern wall of the crypt from Capart's publication.

THE TEXT

1. [Seth] Aa pehti, "great of strength, the 1st arrow of Nekhbet, save the king from the slaughterers of Sekhmet".

2. To the twins Horus-Seth, Abductor of the heart that pleases and the Unique.

"Health to you, of powerful sight, criminal master who makes massacres, save the King from any wound, (give him protection against) your impure followers. For you are the unique, protector the gods."

3. "Master of the tent - the one who does not listen."

"Oh grand god, master of eternity, with the terrible face, of which none cannot deflect the harm, master of prestige, great are your roars, putting terror into the heart of the gods, save King Psamtik from any sickness during the course of the year."

4. "Redden face, whose face is inflamed, scratching with your nails."

"Salutation to you, grand god ... powerful, whose power projects as far as you will it, (master of terror), the strongest, the executioner when comes on the day of the slaughter. Save the son of the sun Psamtik. Save him from any wound, caused by thy flame; you are the son of Sekhmet during the season where she dominates, you are Khonsu, the joyous, son of Bast."

5. "The one that is in the papyrus bush in the midst of the Nile making carnage."

"Salutation to you, of the sacred forms, salutations to you mysterious master, who makes wounds, creates disorder and produces ruin; put your heart to the task and save the pharaoh from the wicked."

6. "Creator of disorder (in the middle of your redness)."

"Salutations to you, sole generator of forms, great bull, master of the inundation (?) ... of which we ignore the surge (?) coming under the form of wind without being seen; let us go, save the pharaoh."

7. "Red bull, generator of trouble" …

"Salutation to you the very strong, maker of warfare, master of the axe, with the piercing arm, repelling the enemy from the prow of the barque of Ra, protect you the pharaoh"

"Nekhbet, the white of Nekhen, with the raised talons of iron … the progenitor of the gods, mistress of the palace of the south. Commands my seven messengers to make it so."

Discussion (translated from Jean Capart 1940s essay)[92]

The first utterance (upper register) is addressed to a spirit with the head of a crocodile and holds in both hands a sharp sword. The corresponding figure at Edfu is lion headed, at Philae similar but is armed with an iron tipped wooden stake. At Denderah the mutilated figure carries two swords.

The name of this figure is Aa pehti, "great of strength", which is the standard epithet of Seth. The corresponding figure at Edfu is identically named whilst that at Denderah remains unnamed, no doubt out of respect for Osiris in whose chamber it is located. Philae provides an important detail, calling this figure "The 1st arrow of Nekhbet". And indeed at the extreme right of the tableau at Elkab, Nekhbet can be seen with her bow and a handful of arrows. At Philae the composite, deity Tutu, "great of strength, vigorous, son of Neith" is substituted. Tutu has a lot in common with Seth, being the popular guardian for his devotees from demons, especially those responsible for evil sleep. Evil sleep, discussed earlier, is known from the magical papyri to result from magical attack.

Seth obeys the commands of Nekhbet in these Elkab inscriptions, the oldest of all the examples; principally he saves the king from the "slaughterers of Sekhmet". These are demons that cause disease, especially plague. They are also messengers of the gods.

The second utterance (lower register)
Spoken to two bull headed spirits who face each other with hands clasped. They could be locked in the same kind of paired dance shown elsewhere on tomb carvings. In the Denderah variant they each hold a knife. Called "The Abductor of the heart that pleases" and "The Unique" – these are twins, most likely, given the context, Horus and Seth although Montou-Seth is a possibility or perhaps Khonsu, a deity also shown in this form.

Image of paired dancers Deir El Gebrawi.

They say: "Health to you, of powerful sight, criminal master who makes massacres, save the King from any wound, (protect against) your impure, for you are the unique, protector the gods."

However, it seems we must consider that the two gods as forming a unity because Edfu, in the general title of genie, declares formally that they are one among the seven. We shall come back to this later; however it is necessary, now, to be aware that the series encompasses Seth at the head, followed by six genies, of which the five are explicitly shown riding serpents, a form, familiar as decans from the astro-religious texts. Various characters, which guard them and control them, accompany these, of which the name, in Denderah, will always be written with the sign of the serpent, but it would be false to consider them as separate entities.

The third utterance is addressing itself to a genie, "the master of the tent (determinative indicates this was made of leather) Edfu, Philae and Denderah write this as fabric. The "the one who does not listen" – who rides on the back of the serpent is a hawk headed genie at Elkab, whereas at Philae and Denderah its head is that of a lion. " oh grand god, master of eternity, with the terrible face, of which we cannot deflect the harm, master of prestige, great are your roars, putting terror is into the heart of the gods, save King Psamtik from any sickness during the course of the year."

The fourth utterance in the lower register and the scene that is related to it shows a *serpent* whose name is "redden face, scratching with your nails". More can be restored from variants at Philae and Denderah "his face is inflamed". Edfu employs an interesting hieroglyphic rebus to express the same idea: a face encircled by little points of fire. The text beneath the head of the serpent reads: "salutation to you, grand god ... powerful, as far as he wants, (master of terror), the strongest, the executioner when he comes on the day of the slaughter, save the son of the sun Psamtik". Our version is very brief, Philae has more, making an interesting assimilation of several other gods: "save him from any wound, caused by thy flame; you are the son of Sekhmet during the year where she dominates, you Khonsu, the joyous, son of Bast". The joyous is an epithet most commonly known from the deities centre at Thebes.

This fourth serpent entity, bears two gods upon his back, facing each other and holding hands. The first has the head of a lion, the other one that of a falcon. Behind, march two baboons. At Edfu these gods are both lion headed. At Philae a lion is placed below the serpent and the baboon is above. At Denderah it is a monkey and a jackal.

The fifth utterance is the most important because in it appears the figure of the king whom the genies are charged to preserve from all danger. Its name is "the one that is in the papyrus bush making carnage." Or "in the Nile" The diverse versions are, for the first part; Edfu, Philae & Denderah. The determinative shows a hippo, even thought the image is of a serpent that also has claws!

The serpent supports the full weight on his neck of the pharaoh with the double crown, holding a flower or papyri. Behind him is a god with the head of a jackal holding the same object, is the third rider who has a disk instead of a head; finally we see, seated in the air, wrapped in a protective shroud, with the head of the Seth animal. At Edfu, this last one has the head of a hare, well known, as a figure painted inside coffins.

The Denderah version seems to have messed everything up. There is no serpent and the first two figures are replaced by the repetition of the coupled gods, with the head of a bull, face to face. Then comes a standing man, with a beard and a headband; he holds a serpent that replaces the one that should have been on the ground. The last five are images are of serpents – always written with determinative of the serpent. The shrouded god must have had the head of a hare but has been mutilated.

The sixth utterance (lower register) accompanies a winged serpent called "creator of disorder (in the middle of his redness". The incomplete text says: "salutations to you, sole generator of forms, great bull, master of the inundation (?) … of which we ignore the surge (?) coming under the form of wind without being seen; let us go, save the pharaoh."

Two divinities are standing on the winged serpent, both having the head of the Seth animal. A serpent elevates itself from the ground toward the first genie, which seizes it by the neck. At Philae heads of hares replace those of Seth. At Edfu, the great winged serpent has two pairs of wings and a smaller serpent rises on the extremity of its tail. Denderah is similar except that the gods have heads of bulls and are armed with knives; they face each other, hands clasped, perhaps in a dance.

The seventh utterance addresses to the serpent as "The red bull, generator of trouble". The text between the feet of the two divinities standing on the snake is in raised relief; which differs from the remainder of the inscription, as the engraver must have forgotten the formula for protection. It has been corrected to "Salutation to you the very strong, maker of warfare, creator (here Denderah has written "adversaries" master of the axe, with the piercing arm, repelling the enemy from the prow of the barque of Ra, protect you the pharaoh)"

The restitution of the text of these seven utterances has been made possible by the discovery, in the foundations of the central sanctuary of the great temple, of the block that is missing in the crypt. We also have the title of the goddess. Upon the serpent called "the red bull" there are two gods with the head of Seth standing facing face to face. The head of the second is found also on the block:

At Philae there is also a great serpent with raised head; upon its tail there is a Seth – meanwhile another one, hand raised, seems to lift the serpent. At Edfu the Seth placed on the serpent holds a knife; the other is standing across the serpent, is seizing it by the neck. At Denderah two gods with the head of a bull are facing each other; the one on the right is holding the serpent by the neck and a knife. When the crypt was made, some parts of the scene were missing but they were completed by paint in black ink. Of the goddess only the feet remain; the body was redone quickly and without giving it the exact proportions. In the vertical line someone wrote "Nekhbet, the white of Nekhen, mistress of the sky, mistress of the two lands."

The original text was more complete and interesting "Nekhbet, the white of Nekhen, with the raised talons of iron ... the progenitor of the gods, mistress of the palace of the south."

Such is the general analysis of the picture. Nekhbet the great goddess of the south, dispatches seven of her messengers, to whom she addresses seven utterances defining their mission. This will be, contrary to their nature, for they must focus all their energy on the protection of the king. The king might be exposed to disease, to wounds and to dangers of all kinds. Thus the god Seth and the Sethian forms keep guard, like a military patrol, mobilised to protect him on the front line. As Edfu further clarifies: "they are here to safeguard the members of the king" but Edfu, in a text sadly mutilated, described the group of seven spirits or genies and presents them as being really part of the entourage of the great goddess Nekhab.

> "There are the seven manifestation (*Chronicle of Egypt*) of, the seven rebels of Wosret (the powerful), the great butchers of the mother of the living gods, servitors that accompany the goddess with the white crown. Seth is in front of her, followed by his brothers making a total of seven butchers that belong to him … the day of all feasts of the calendar when the liturgy is celebrated"[92]

At Philae, the picture with the genies is surmounted on the top left by the figures of Horus, Thoth, and of Tutu, son of Neith. To the right there is a seated lion "mahes". At Elkab seated lions called "Horus who pushed back the harm" are also found. At Edfu, as in Philae, the seven genies of Nekhbet are posted on the right and on the left of the door that the king will cross during the ceremony. It is curious to note that even at Denderah these guards are located in the chapel of the dead Osiris. Perhaps this is the reason it was been necessary to disguise somehow the Sethian genie, replacing the heads of Seth by those of the hare or the bull. But the strongest of them, who marches at the front, retains his usual head, although this was later mutilated.

In Elkab, we do not know exactly in which context the genies were employed due to as yet undiscovered accompanying text. The Persian invasion provoked destruction of the temple of the protective goddess of Upper Egypt, situated at mouth of the Wadi Hilal, hence her epithet mistress of the valley mouth. Jean Capart, the archaeologist who made these discoveries, was never able to find the remainder of the text and to tell the whole story of Nekhbet, of Seth, of Thoth and his baboons, and of the flame.

As a ritual of protection it has a good pedigree. The present author has used it once thus far with some success. I'm also reinterating what I wrote at the beginning concerning the significance of this as the Egyptian equivalent, perhaps even source, of the seven headed dragons mythos. It is the serpent in each of tableau which was the focus of a gnostic rite, where the "riders" help to understand its nature.

Could it also be to this that Plutarch was referring where he talks about secret consecrations of animals at Elkab in which they were honoured in mysterious ways, "which occurs at irregular times and relate to casual events, the majority know nothing of them, except when they enact burial ceremonies and display some of the other animals and in the presence of all bury them together, believing that thus they cause vexation to Typhon and lessen his pleasure."[93]

Plutarch gives the impression here that apart from a few well-known examples such as the goat for Amun and baboon for Thoth, most other animals in Egypt were assigned to Typhon. The correspondences between gods and animals is a lot more complex than he makes out, even so, those animals with clear Typhonian associations, such as the donkey, or the Oxyrhynchus fish, were used in many hostile rituals, described above as Diabole, in which the totem is punished as a way of provoking or deriding Seth.

King Psamtek's success in expelling the Persians was not to last. It therefore fell to Nectanebo II, Egypt's last native king, to face another invasion, that despite all his best efforts, including magick, he eventually lost after a long struggle against the Persians, although not before his powerful battle magick had done them much damage. According to the *Alexander Romance*, he left Egypt and became a jobbing magical specialist in the court of Philip of Macedon; secretly fathering the child who would become Alexander the Great, the nemesis of the Persian Empire, from which he would eventually "liberate" Egypt.[94]

Reconstructed image of Goddess Nekhbet, the white of Nekhen, with the raised talons of iron … the progenitor of the gods, mistress of the palace of the south.

Chapter Two
Modern views of Seth:
The Nagada Hypothesis

PLUTARCH'S INFLUENCE ON MODERN RELIGION

As this book is about Egyptian Seth in a modern context I am going to backtrack a little to examine some characteristics of the Church of Satan, whose origins in the 1960s American milieu I described earlier. This Church arguably contributed a great deal to the character of a postmodern Temple of Set, which was founded by Michael Aquino, one of its leading members.

Unlike earlier "occult" organisations, this Church of Satan seems to possess an overtly political as well as magical agenda. This whole issue of politics and the occult is quite complex and controversial. It's probably unwise to try to identify the typical political profile of the occultist. I already mentioned the socialist Gerald Massey, whose writings still exert an influence over the occult world. From the period of what is known as the occult revival in the late 19th century it is possible to identify liberal views and their opposite within the same organisations. Take for an example the Theosophical Society, founded in 1875, one of its early leaders, Annie Besant, is still viewed as a heroine of the fledging trade union movement, a leader of the crucial "match-girls" strike for a safer working environment at the Bryant & May match factory. She was also a campaigner for birth control. At the same time the Theosophical society promulgated an elaborate theory of race from which many later racialist movements drew some inspiration. It's co-founder, H P Blatvatsky claimed to be one of Garibaldi's "Red Shirts" although she could also be socially conservative and was opposed to birth control.

The Church of Satan was not backward at coming forward on this. They were politically of the right; they eschewed earlier literary conventions, and acquired a political dimension against liberalism. Michael Aquino, during his time as a leading member of the church of Satan wrote "A Grotto (the Church's equivalent of a lodge) is an autocracy not a democracy" or more worryingly "There is nothing in the Nazi philosophy that conflicts with the basic desires of the human personality."[95]

Both groups, the Church of Satan and The Temple of Set could be considered elitist, and, it has to be said like several other occult sodalities, are proud of their elitism. In an article by Michael Aquino, where he is channelling his agatho (noble) daemon writes "I seek my elect and none other ... and I think not of those who think not of me".[96]

I'd say they are also deeply pessimistic about human nature as instanced in this quote, again from Michael Aquino:[97]

> "As you become an adept in LBM (Lesser Black Magick), you will be tempted to use it for all manner of personal gratification. The more skilled you are, the more you will be inclined to think that you can get away with almost anything. The governing factor is not whether you can or can't but rather whether your consciously determined ethics allow you

to. As you going to direct your life independently of morals, codes and customs imposed upon you by the politics and propaganda of society, you will have to assume the responsibility for your own ethics. Only if you are known to be a strictly ethical individual will your rejection of social norms be tolerated. Otherwise you will be ostracised and probably persecuted by society."

Then follows a long, reasonable and informed discussion of ethical theories from Plato to Nato. On Egypt he writes:

"The Ancient Egyptians perceived the Universe as actively controlled by conscious natural principles or 'gods' (neteru in hieroglyphic) To the Egyptian, all of 'nature' (derived from neteru) was alive and the direct consequence of the wills of the neteru. Nature was intelligible not just through inanimate, automatic, general regularities, which could be discovered via observation but also through connections and associations between things and events perceived in the human mind. There was no distinction between 'reality" and 'appearance'; 'any thing capable of exerting an effect upon the mind thereby existed. Just and virtue were sought in the manifestations of beauty, symmetry and harmony, and were personified by the goddess Ma'at." [98]

At the same time Zeena La Vey says in a preface to her father Anton's *The Satanic Witch* that the book is "a guide to selective breeding, a manual of eugenics - the lost science of preserving the able-bodied and able-minded while controlling the surplus population of the weak and incompetent.".[99] Although given the penchant of occultists for black humour, it is always possible to interpret this as a joke, although perhaps not a funny one.

Elsewhere Michael Aquino quotes Anton LeVey as saying "Satanism is Americanism in its purest form."[100] But as he never defines "Americanism", what is meant by this? It could be a range of political ideals including self-government, equal opportunity, freedom of speech, and a belief in progress. It can also encompass American exceptionalism, a sense of "manifested destiny" which can set its aims above those of other peoples. Controversially the Ku Klux Klan also espoused Americanism, adding to it to what they saw as Protestant values and idea of racial purity and white supremacy.

For LaVey and his disciples "Satan was a symbolic standard bearer for social criticism and affirmation of individual license" as expressed in their celebrated maxim "indulgence instead of Abstinence".[101]

Elsewhere they also wrote that "Might is Right", perhaps believing this to be the way of the world, with resistance being futile, one may as well live with it, love it even.[102]

I could go on but perhaps you get the picture, and unlike myself, many might find themselves agreeing with these sentiments. Wherever you, the reader, stand on this, it's surely true that the Church of Satan really did stand out as being the antithesis to the politics and social mores of their fellow San Francisco parishioners during its famous "summer of love".

Let's remind ourselves how it was for America: a time of cultural renaissance, which incubated some of the most radical social reforms of modern times. It also coincided with the end of the long Vietnam War, in which Michael Aquino had done his military service. This conflict divided America in a way it had not been since its civil war of the 1860s. Future US President Bill Clinton described it as an immoral and unnecessary war. He in turn is criticized as a "draft dodger" although it's a moot point, taking advantage of his well connected friends, to serve his time in the ROTC rather than leave for Canada or go to prison.

It was a time during which the pillars of western social mores were definitely shaken by such things as abortion law reform, divorce, and decriminalisation of homosexuality. It is the present author's firm conviction that the whole rotten edifice needed to be shaken up.

But if the famous summer of love was in the air, the Church of Satan did not or would not join in and, if anything, was part of the Counter Reformation. This is important for our study because it effects the way people came to see Satan and Seth; who, for a while, became the standard bearer of a political religion of the right.

But it has to be said, at this point the influence of what we might call the Sethian archetype was not much. Although in the Church of Satan, Seth was playing a significantly larger role than he had in earlier occult societies, he was still not central or unique. It might be, and this is certainly my view, that over time, its adoption had unexpected consequences. There is perhaps some indication that the crude views of his new devotees are reformed or change as the energy of the god begins to work its magick.

One area in which he did have a newly recognised role was in the organisation's attempts to construct a ritual calendar. Because ritual calendars are a special interest of mine, I found my attention drawn to how this was handled with the Church. The Wiccan "wheel of the year", a cycle of eight festivals spaced at regular intervals is the most famous example of a reconstructed Wiccan ritual calendar. I find ritual calendars transformative tools, they can be arcane but also surprising fecund generators of magical knowledge, a feature often overlooked.

It is now commonly agreed that the original basis of the ritual year lay in observations of the movements of the stars and heavenly bodies. The spectacle of the night sky was almost certainly humanity's earliest teacher. Look deeper at ancient mythology from almost any culture and one will soon discover it has strong, unbreakable connections to the observation of the night sky.

For example, the annual cycle, the rise and fall of the constellation Orion lends itself to an interpretation in the form of a story of a dying and resurrecting god. This spectacular constellation is easily recognised, and must always have attracted the attention of early star gazers, from its appearance in the sky, rising higher and higher in the east over a period of time, but then descending into the west to enter the Underworld when it is completely absent from the night sky for many months. This must have caught the attention of our ancestors who were no doubt spurred to try to explain what was going on. Thus we have corresponding myths of rising and falling gods such as Osiris and later Jesus, who seem to reiterate this natural phenomenon.

Ritual calendars grow from these stories and are a way of re-enacting the ancient Sky religion in one's own life. To their credit, the Church of Satan recognised this and made their own efforts to reconstruct something appropriate. Consequently Set was allotted the important role as "opener of the year", beginning on the winter solstice, 22nd December. The month was dedicated to Set(h) as the "Lord of the Wasteland".[103]

In any religion the period around the New Year will always have a special significance, whether it represents the last of the old and/or the first of the new. Ancient ritual calendars were *Theophoric*, that is to say, many, if not all months was sacred to a particular god or goddess, the month names literally "held" or "carried" them. This relationship has become obscured by the later Roman reframing or reform of the calendar we still use.

(1) March/Mars,
(2) April/Aphrodite,
(3) May/Maia,
(4) June/Juno all of which have connections with deities.
But after this point the names of Roman emperors are substituted thus:
(5) July (Julius Caesar),

(6) August (Augustus), this is then the following by mundane numbers, in Latin:

(7) September,

(8) October,

(9) November,

(10) December,

(11) January/Janus,

(12) February/Purification followed by the intercalaris. Hence after the Norman invasion of Britain, their calendar replaced the Saxon month name of Easter with April, which is Latin for second [month].

Michael Aquino, like many before him, obviously struggled with this task of constructing a new version of the calendar for his Church, and acknowledged that a more authentic calendar should have been opened by Set(h) on the summer solstice.[104]

The *Book of Abramelin the Mage*, which since the Victorian occult revival has had a special status among advanced occultists in the west, provided them with another aspect of the ritual year. This book contains an elaborate demonology or hierarchy of the infernal realms, at the top of which are said to be four princes, Satan, Lucifer, Belial, and Leviathan. These were allocated on a rather arbitrary basis to the four season of summer, spring, autumn and winter respectively.

Other than the appearance of the god Seth in the calendar, there was in the Church of Satan one "Grotto" i.e. lodge, named after Typhon, the Greek equivalent of Seth.[105] Incidentally my monograph *The Ritual Year in Ancient Egypt* is the fruit of my own research in Egyptian calendrics and presents a working version of a calendar from both an Osirian and Sethian point of view. [106]

THE REVELATION

Returning to the moment in 1974 and the advent of the modern Temple of Seth and, almost simultaneously, Kenneth Grant's Typhonian Order/Ordo Templi Orientis. We see a significant shift in esoteric lore. Both organisations are about to recast Seth in a role he had not occupied in an esoteric grouping for several millennia, perhaps never before. I would argue that this changed must have been part of the spirit of the age, what Hegel would have called the "Zeitgeist". I say this because two independent intellectual domains seem to have arrived at the insight at near enough the same moment in time. Michael Aquino, writing in 2010, records how in 1974 his attention was drawn, as we mentioned earlier, to two new academic books.

Of all the many books published on Egyptology one couldn't think of two others that have been as influential to not only Egyptologists and scholars, but also as it turns out, and almost certainly unbeknownst to their respective authors, hugely influential in the world of the occult. There is no doubt in my mind that they acted as catalysts that brought about Michael Aquino's shift in allegiance from Satan to Seth. These two influential books we already referred to several times, but here they are again in full:

J Gwyn Griffiths (1960) *The Conflict of Horus & Seth: a study in an ancient mythology from Egyptian and Classical sources*, LUP.

H Te Velde (1967) *Seth, God of Confusion: A study of his role in Egyptian Mythology and Religion*, Brill.

We have already said how in academic terms they are groundbreaking books. The study of the hugely important Sethian archetype had until the 1960s been largely neglected. This also explains the absence of the deity in much pre-1960s "demonology".

The theories of both authors brought them into intellectual conflict with each other due to some important differences in approach. Even so they were aware of each's significance in terms of the historic record, both contributing such a great deal to the change in public awareness of the god Seth. Te Velde devoted a chapter in his book to the discussion of Gwyn Griffiths' earlier work and theories, commenting, "this lucidly written and excellently documented work deserves much appreciation."[107]

Naturally it fell to Gwyn Griffiths to review his younger colleague's work and welcomed Te Velde's addition to the field and acknowledges how even when strongly disagreeing with other scholars (notably himself), he does so without rancour.[108] Since the publication of his PhD thesis Te Velde has won respect as the leading authority on Seth, as well as on the related topics of demonology and the darker byways of Egypt.[109] So hopefully that is enough for you to see that these are no ordinary academic monographs but really opinion changing. The fact that they were read and assimilated by occultists, who would mostly be dismissed as cranks by the academic authors themselves, shows that that neo-pagan practitioner's reading habits often are ahead of the curve.

Actually the occultist Michael Aquino was awarded a PhD in political science from the University of California in 1980, and is a military intelligence officer as well as an intelligent researcher and reader. In his own account he records that his attention was drawn to both of the above books by John A Ferro, a senior VI degree member of the Church of Satan who also happened to be a history lecturer at the University of San Francisco. [110]

In 1974 Michael Aquino and John Ferro embarked on an extended correspondence concerning magical history. It was during this exchange, recorded in chapter 33 of Aquino's long memoir *The Church of Satan*, that Ferro introduced him to the works of Gwyn Griffiths and Te Velde.[111] Aquino says that up until then his principle sources on Egyptian culture were Pierre Montet who excavated the old Hiksos capital at Tanis, and discovered the first traces of the ancient city of Ramses II known as Piramesse. Montet wrote several important books including *Lives of the Pharaohs*. Aquino also relied on Heinrich Brugsche (1827-1894), one of the all time greats of Egyptology, whose careful dissections of Egyptian culture are still key source books. He also read Walter Fairservis, the accomplished "finder of ancient cities" more well known for his work in India on the Indus valley civilisation. Fairservis also made important discoveries in Egypt, at Hierakonpolis (Citadel of the Hawk) and Abydos.

The raison d'etre of the correspondence was a discussion of Cecil B De Mille's *The Ten Commandments*. This famous movie follows the conventional casting of 19th dynasty king Ramses II, played by Yul Brynner, as the villainous, hard-hearted pharaoh who will not let Moses' "people go". The father of Ramses II's, King Sety I ("He of Set") also features in the film.

This in itself would make an interesting digression, with much to say about the relationship between Egyptian Seth and Hebrew Yahweh. It's worth looking at books such as John Ward's *The Exodus Reality* for an examination of the field and some explanation of why the pharaoh of the Exodus cannot be those proposed by Hollywood–neither Sety I nor Ramses the great or indeed any of that 19th dynasty, they were usually thought to be too late in the historical timeline, with Israel being already established before they lived. It has to be earlier, more likely Moses is to be found among the 18th dynasty founders of the New Kingdom, the Thutmosids "Born of Thoth" who battled with and eventually expelled the Hyksos. They are to us the most famous of all Egyptian rulers whose names include Ahmose, Amenhotep, Queen Hatshepsut, Akkenaten and Tutankamun. As I write some new research has been published based on an analysis of early eclipses. This sets a firm date for the reign of Ramses II as 1276-1210BCE. The evidence would also have him as a near contemporary of Joshua, the first king of Israel after the Exodus.[112]

Michael Aquino's correspondent John Ferro corrected his historical summary and recommended two books he had himself just acquired: Gwyn Griffiths and Te Velde. He added that "Griffiths

… contends that the Horus-Seth myth, unlike that of Osiris, had an historical and political origin, i.e. the unification of the two lands into a single kingdom under Menes." The name "Menes" does not occur in any native Egyptian king lists until the writing of Egyptian historian Manetho, when the Greek Ptolemies ruled the land, ie thousands of years after he was supposed to have lived. Even so many authorities identify Menes as king Narmer. Narmer was a very early Egyptian King known mostly from the ceremonial make-up palette that bears his name. This wonderful treasure was made to commemorate his struggle to unite competing tribes under his rule. One of those competing tribes might, according to the theory, be that of the people of Seth.

King Narmer, founder of 1st dynasty, palette from foundation deposit at Nekhen/Hierakonpolis, "Citadel of the Hawk"

"The other study", continues Ferro, " … repudiates Griffiths' thesis with some impressive evidence and argumentation. However I found it most engrossing in regard to the extended discussion of Seth, as *the personified embodiment of refusal to submit to rules and arbitrary distinctions, the principle of indulgence, intemperance, and undifferentiated sexual activity,* e.g. his [sexual] advances to Isis and his [homosexual] assault on his nephew [Horus]."[113] [My emphasis] It is a moot point as to whether this is a fair summary of Te Velde's view; even so it does neatly demonstrate the possible significance to all of us, of the "Sethian" archetype in one form or another.

In other words these two academic books encapsulate two rival theories about the origins and indeed nature of the God Seth. The modern temple of Seth and, to be fair, many other readers have tended to follow Te Velde's interpretation ever since its first publication in 1967. One might say Te Velde achieved intellectual hegemony in the field of Sethian interpretation, until fairly recently, when the tide of scholarly opinion began to turn back to the earlier ideas of Gwyn Griffiths, and adopted what is, in my opinion, a more nuanced view.

Furthermore, if Ferro's précis is accurate, then it leads to the rather surprising conclusion that the origin of the Temple of Set's theology and philosophy is to be found in the pages of Te Velde's academic monograph.[114] The character of Seth that emerges in TOS seems to be essentially a *continuation* of Satan as promulgated by the Church of Satan. There is a change of name but in essence they are the same, at least in that first generation. It has of course evolved and continued to change in the several decades since it was first adumbrated. We therefore need to discuss this in some detail to see how much the historical studies helped form or validate this archetype and whether it is really a post modern "ideal" projected onto the actual god. This is assuming that the characterisation of Seth that comes to us from academic study is itself accurate, and what aspects of it are assimilated by the practitioners of the Temple of Set, whether they select academic views when and where they agree with existing presuppositions. Or indeed the opposite . . . [115]

THE NAGADA HYPOTHESIS

This is the designation I suggest for the view of Seth based on Gwyn-Griffiths book *The Conflict of Horus & Seth* already mentioned plus several newer studies. Seth is a complex and fascinating deity, his story stretching back into prehistory. Gwyn Griffiths offers several sub-versions of his own thesis, these include feminist or sexual-political interpretations, as conflicts between matrilineal Sethian culture and the rise of the more patriarchal Horus kings. There is also a geo-political, or tribal conflict, theory and even a Jungian interpretation based on the importance of the shadow.

Among the oldest sources for the study of Egyptian mythology are the texts inscribed on the walls of 5th & 6th dynasty pyramid tombs, the earliest being Unas (2356-2323BCE), the most recent Pepy II (2246-2152 BCE).[116] Pepy's name may indicate some the Sethian sympathies, detectible among these Kings of the early dynasties. It could be translated as "strider" (from verb Ppy) which on the face of it does not seem particularly Sethian until one compares it with that of Hiksos king Apophis, (A-ppy) whose name could mean "true of voice" or possible "loud voice" like the roar of the Hippo perhaps? The Hippo was an animal of royal prestige, and although difficult to prove 100%, was likely seen as an avatar of Seth.

The tomb of King Peribsen, a 2nd dynasty king buried at Abydos expresses a more overt allegiance to Seth. Inside two pillar-form steles mark the entrance. One of these is displayed in the British Museum. Although some of it was effaced in later times, if you look carefully you can just see how in the topmost register bears an image of Seth.

Tomb stele of King Peribsen/Khasekhem
from Petrie "Royal Tombs of the early dynasties" II 33 plxxxi

To date, the Pyramid Texts are among the earliest examples of extensive religious literature found anywhere in the world. These are complex texts, a compendium and palimpsest of earlier stories and narratives, recording views from an implicitly oral and written tradition, now lost. The key thing to remember is that an awful lot of things happened in Egypt before being mythologized in stone. Our knowledge of this relies on archaeological remains, short "proto" hieroglyphic inscriptions, tombs, settlements, temples and images of gods.

So for example, it is a perhaps an unsettling fact that there is little or no such evidence of Egypt's most famous god Osiris before the time that his name first appears in the Pyramid Texts. Contrast this with the evidence of other gods, including Seth, Neith, Hathor and Horus, whose archaeological traces and images are quite common in the older period before the Pyramid Texts were recorded in stone. The Peribsen stele above being a good example of this, occurring as it does before the pyramids. We have to keep in mind that in the absence of long written theological descriptions of these gods, their naming is based on a projection backwards from material of later times. So for example we know that in the time of Ramses, the hippo was an avatar of Seth, so we induce that the hippos of earlier times were also thus. But this is an assumption, it is feasible that a new meaning has been added to an old symbol and an old one reframed or taken away. This happened all the time in Egypt's records.

We could assume that Osiris and his cult originated at the same time, or perhaps a little before the writing of the Pyramid Texts.

His mythology appropriates or assimilates that of older times, as is obvious from the several contradictions in his narrative. These visible "cracks" or seams in the narrative often involve the god Seth. We've already quoted two examples above where Seth sometimes appears as the older "uncle" to Horus and sometimes as his younger brother!

Our task, whether as historian or amateur Egyptologist, is to deconstruct the various layers of myth. The Nagada Hypothesis recognises an archaic myth of Horus and his brother Seth. This is the myth of an ancient "Elysium" on which Te Velde casts so much doubt. He felt the evidence at the time he wrote was just too thin on the ground to justify such a reconstruction. He found it entirely possible that the "wicked" Seth of the Pyramid Texts was how it always was.

So we have the later all-encompassing myth known as the Osiris legend. In the Osiris legend, this god of fertility (sex) and the dead (death) is murdered by his jealous twin brother Seth. This legend is often viewed as a theological "theory"– an entire religious system and hierarchical relationship between an all-encompassing pantheon of gods. Isis, his sister and wife, contrives through her magical prowess to revive the dead Osiris and from him conceive a child and heir, Horus. Perhaps because of the unorthodox conception of Horus, doubts arise as to his legitimacy.

Horus, who as a weakling child - another likely allusion to his unorthodox conception - must be protected by his mother Isis until he matures. Fully-grown and now powerful, he challenges

Seth, the usurper uncle, first in the law courts, but also by a continuous battle of wits, until eventually he is vindicated before the tribunal of the gods. Violence is inevitable and the two gods fight in truth, inflicting grievous wounds, loaded with symbolism: Seth blinds Horus and Horus castrates Seth. It seems likely such wounds were a common enough fallout or consequence of ancient battle; but they are also providing us with powerful metaphors of the human character, one speaks of someone being blind or lacking balls or being emasculated.

All of this is more or less familiar, embedded as it is in our own intellectual history. It is for example the myth of divine kingship that we see played out in Shakespeare's brilliant tragedy *Hamlet*.

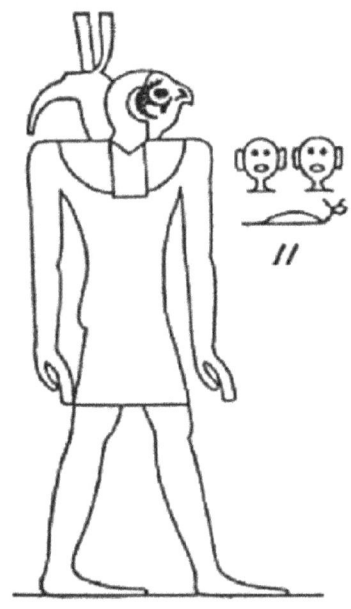

Horseth, from Book of Gates

Another myth of Horus and Seth seems to stem from an older layer of mythology, so old it has no clear beginning or "lost in the mists of time" to use Te Velde's locution. In these strata one need hardly mention the name of Horus without having to also name Seth in the next breath. They are indissolubly linked, their names always occurring as a couple and always in the order, first Horus, then Seth. So important is this connection that we might consider them as one hybrid entity–known in the record as Horseth.

Gwyn Griffiths, with an abundance of scholarly gifts, did the careful detective work, that enabled him to conclude the "independence and *priority* of the Horus [and Seth] myth," which he thought could be demonstrated by analysis of the sequence of Pyramid Texts alone. Quoting Faulkner, he notes that placed in their correct sequence, the number of references to the Osirian legend increases the further one moves through the sequence, less in the beginning, more as one moves forward in the timeline. This seems to mirror the spread of the worship of Osiris which took place in the second half of the sixth dynasty.[117] Thus references to the quarrel of Horus and Seth, without any mention of Osiris, are more common in the earlier pyramids of Wenis and Teti than they are in the three later ones of Pepi I, Merenre, and Pepi II, though the differences are subtle. But it does show how the Pyramid texts document the story of the beginning and subsequent progress of the Osirian religion.

Gwyn Griffiths clearly favoured the historical-political view, championed by generations of earlier, eminent scholars, including his own teachers. In this view the conflict between Horus and

Seth arose because of an ancient war between two rival tribes. This conflict involved much savagery, from divine, and, presumably human protagonists. We've already described how Horus loses an eye in the fighting and Seth is emasculated.[118] This is the "Nagada hypothesis", which I've named after the modern upper Egyptian town closest to the archaeological site of ancient Ombos, the "citadel of Seth". Today most of the surviving archaeological site has been built upon and we mostly have to make do with the records of Petrie's early excavation of the necropolis. The modern highway from Aswan to Cairo cuts straight through the necropolis. I've superimposed Petrie's map over a view from Google earth.

Their myth could be read as saying that there was once a time, a long time ago, when Horus and Seth were the totems or local gods of two completely distinct pre-dynastic (late Neolithic) tribes. In this view they would have had their own distinctive genealogy, mythology and cult.

There is a way of looking at myth, which has the rather impressive name "euhemerism", which is the idea that when one culture supplants another there is a tendency to demonise the defeated gods. Thus the gods of one generation could function as the demons of another. In the conflict just mentioned, the followers of Horus appear to have triumphed, and their enormous city at Hierakonpolis is, according to the modern sampling techniques, the oldest in Egypt. It is an obvious and reasonable assumption to suppose that the malign nature ascribed to Seth could be due purely to the triumphalism of the victors in some ancient conflict, who earn the privilege to write the story to justify their own moral superiority.

If we assume for a moment this were true then it implies the deposed gods such as Seth, were not really bad at all, or perhaps not as far as his own people were concerned. It could be entirely the old cliché of beauty being in the eye of the beholder. This could also account for the fracture between the face a god shows to outsiders and that he or she has for those who are devotees. In the words of Liber AL " My colour is black to the blind, but the blue and gold are seen of the seeing. Also I have a secret glory for them that love me."[119]

TeVelde, accepts some of this, and he writes "In mythology and for many Egyptians, Seth was only a god of confusion, [but] for the faithful[120] he was also unrestrictedly god"; i.e great, gracious, kind, content, saviour, constant etc."[121] We contine to think this way, hence Michael Aquino, talking about Seth in modern reconstruction calls him "The Old Devil" and as such a very good god to his new disciples."[122]

Even so, Te Velde and others reject what I call "The Nagada Hypothesis" as being too simplistic. He agrees that other ways of seeing Seth may well have existed. "A religious phenomenon is not purely religious" it must also have social and historical aspects. Even so, he feels one cannot argue that myths *originate* in some historical-political incident. Myths, and indeed gods, so Te Velde opines, have already to be there, to be pre-existent before they start to function as details in the interplay of politics and propaganda. He quotes the views of other distinguished scholars

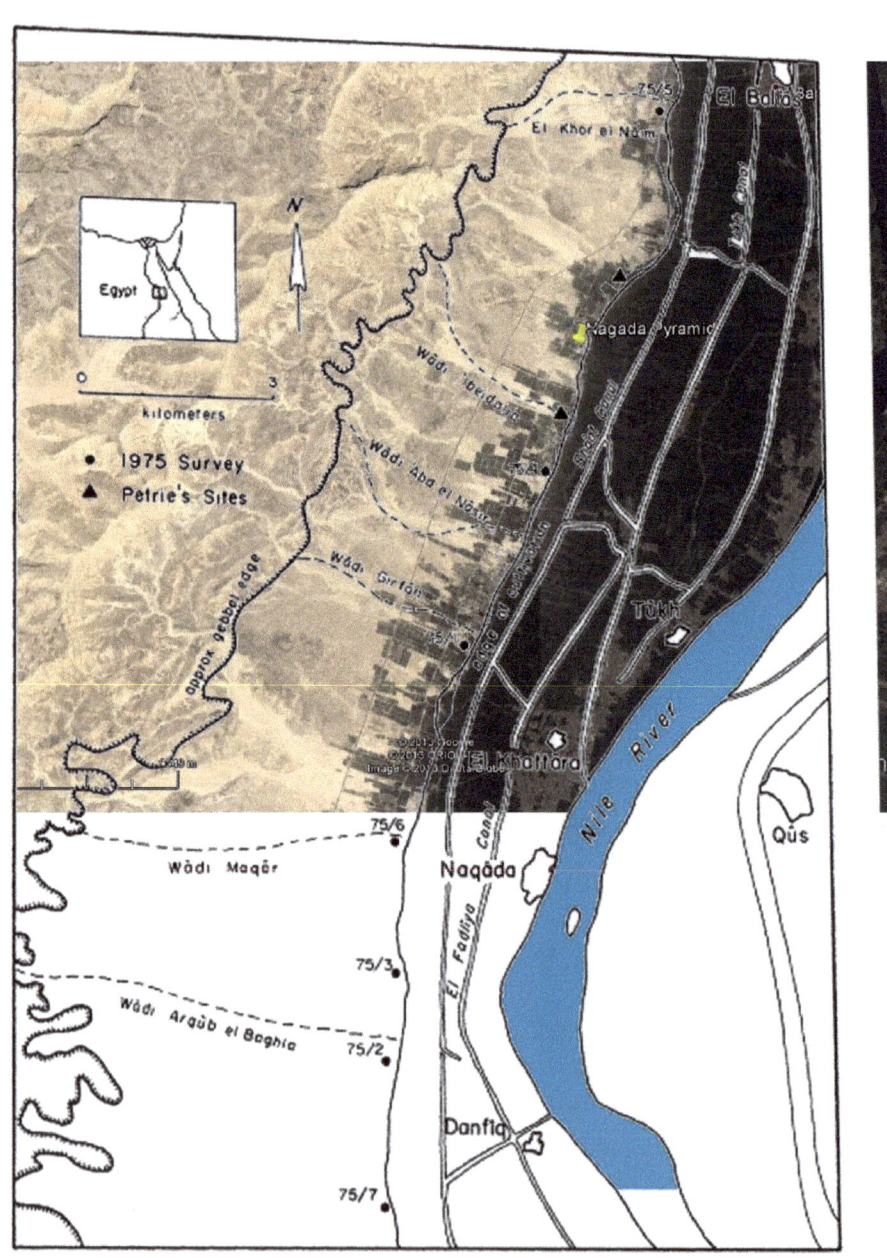

Petrie's map of Naqada cemetary overlaid Google earth

such as Helck that "from events conceptions do not arise" and Van Baaren "political events do not construct religion, but makes use of it".[123]

If you accept the above line of reasoning then in order for a myth to be true or have some validity it cannot be based on intellectual speculation or come out of political manipulation by an elite. But to be honest, I'm really not so sure about that. Yes the earliest gods were just there, they were natural forces that ruled our lives, left us awestruck, powerless and overcome by fear. But then again Egypt provides several examples of political myth becoming religion, notably the famous myth of Osiris and Isis. It has a political dimension very much connected with the establishment of the world's first organised state, and the institution of kingship. All the evidence shows this to be the case. Even so, it *becomes* a true myth given time, as people forget its origins, assuming they were ever party to them.

Judaism is another obvious example of a religion where the nature of the god is actually *revealed* by historical events. And indeed it does look like this happened for the devotees of Seth, who continued to worship him long after his supposed downgrading by the followers of Horus. As underdogs, one cannot help but wonder why they kept going and didn't just switch sides? Every society must have its downtrodden masses and Seth was in many ways the god of such people; so perhaps they had no choice but to accept their status?

I'd remind of what I wrote earlier of Seth's strangely inappropriate title as "guardian from the sea" and how some say this is just the borrowing of myth from Mesopotamia, and therefore a "corruption" of the cult. But then Seth's new name could after all have an entirely Egyptian provenance.

Plutarch also talks of Seth's oceanic connection, although it has to be said that his directions are at variance with native tradition where west is right and east is left (see *imnt* = right/west and Iabt = left/east)[124] However, Plutarch is likely recording genuine native views concerning the sea: "...among the Egyptians Osiris as the Nile united with Isis as the earth, while Typhon is the sea into which the Nile falls and so disappears and is dispersed, save for that part which the earth takes up and receives, becoming fertile through it. A sacred lament has arisen about the Nile, and it bewails him who is created in the regions of the left, and who is destroyed in those of the right. For the Egyptians believe that the east is the face of the world, that the north is the right, and the south the left; and so the Nile, flowing from the south and being devoured by the sea in the north, is said with reason to have its origin on the left and its end on the right. For this reason the priests hold the sea in abomination and call salt 'The spit of Typhon' and among other things forbidden to them is to put salt on the table."[125]

Also "The wiser of the priests not only call the Nile Osiris and the sea Typhon, but apply the name Osiris simply to the general principle and power of moisture, regarding it as the cause of generation and essence of seed, while the name Typhon is applied to the whole dry and fiery and generally scorching element which is hostile to moisture."[126]

Osiris is indeed associated with water: the Nile, libations for the cult of the dead, and the post mortem bodily efflux. Even so the terminology here is from Greek philosophy rather than the more concrete Egyptian view. Egyptians saw creation of the world in the watery Nun, from which Osiris also lies dreaming.

Professor Barry Kemp, director of the Amarna Project in Egypt, has written at length of the Egyptian capacity to rewrite their own story as myth.[127] 6000 years ago the Nile valley was settled by Neolithic tribes, relocated from an ancient oasis in what is now the hyper arid western desert. It is these people that some say were the original followers of Horus and Confederates [or Companions] of Seth. I also think so.

They settled into two ancient "cities"–Nekhen, the Greek Hierakonpolis, "Citadel of the Hawk" and Nwbt, and the Greek Ombos, "Citadel of the Golden One" - Seth. This is the source material for the Nagada hypothesis. Te Velde does not like this argument. He writes that it is speculative and that the archaeology is uncertain and the written accounts virtually non-existent. It is true that these "memories" are inferred from material at the very beginning of the Egyptian written language, where the best sources are individual or small groups of hieroglyphs found on ceremonial objects such as the world famous Scorpion Mace head.[128] In other words the meaning of these very early hieroglyphs is indeed a little speculative.

Even so, traces of Ombos are definitely there in the archaeological record though it is of course always possible to doubt that it really was the celebrated cult centre of Seth. Kings of later times such as Tutmoses I (circa 1493BCE) seem to believe it so, as what other motive is there for the construction of a temple, dedicated to Seth on the site? Are we justified in reading this association back in time to an earlier period? Assuming this wasn't just based on kingly conceit, what does tell us about the original, archaic character of the cult?

What is certain is that pre-dynastic Seth was a complex god. "Seth" writes Te Velde, quoting WB Emery, "is not assimilated and throughout Egyptian history he remains a deity apart … obviously on grounds of political expediency. Seth was considered to be the

Scorpion King Macehead, c. 3100 - 3000 BCE, Ashmolean Museum, Oxford.

personification of evil; so much so that in Classical times he was identified with Typhon".

These kinds of arguments also divide modern neo-pagans trying to revive the cult of Seth: it might be that the post-modern Temple of Set *favours* myths where Seth is a predatory, malign personification of evil, rather like their view of Satan. But there is also a smattering of other "Sethians" who lean toward the idea of an archaic Seth, who can represent the passionate, sexual, shadow side of our personalities without being in any way bad. Some form of the "Nagada hypothesis" is favoured by more liberal devotees of Seth.[129]

The ideas of Te Velde are a continuation of those expressed by the late Henry Frankfort (1897-1954) who wrote: "Horus and Seth were the archetypal antagonists – the mythological symbols for all conflict. Strife is an element in the universe, which cannot be ignored; Seth is perennially subdued by Horus but never destroyed. Both Horus and Seth are wounded in the struggle but in the end there is a reconciliation: the static equilibrium of the cosmos is established."[130]

It is not that Te Velde really denies the possibility of an archaic Seth, merely that the evidence[131] is insufficient to create any sort of complete picture. Thus he says "The origin of the myth is lost in the mists of religious traditions of prehistory".[132] All we know is the historical dualism of Horus (good) versus Seth (bad).

"Robber, Lord of lies; king of deceit, gang leader of criminals; who is satisfied with desertion and hates friendship; braggard among the gods, who causes enmity and occasions murder; Typhon, who creates rebellion; lord of looting, who rejoices at greed; master thief, who suscitates theft; who gives offence."[133] Well that's one view, this time from a magical papyrus written in the 17th year of King Nectanebo. It has been called a "Hymn to the devil". It originates from the House of Life at Abydos, one of the most sacred places of the ancient world, the cult centre of Osiris. Nectanebo belongs to the 30th and final native Egyptian dynasty. The above lines are just part of a long magical rite written when the storm clouds of the Persian invasion were gathering, presaging the end of native Egyptian rule. Nectanebo and his eponymous grandson Nectanebo II were bold in their attempts to take the war to Egypt's Persian enemies, using all means at their disposal including magick.

The priests of Abydos reusued an ancient daily rite intended to overcome Apep (Greek: Apophis) for whom they substituted Seth's name. The foreign aggressors were framed as the god Seth and his companions. It shows how in this period priests of Osiris felt completely validity in linking Seth with foreign rulers. From this point on his cult is largely a cypher, Seth is a god whose true nature is really only understood by a handful of devotees. Nectanebo was at the time co-regent with his son and successor Teos who in his short two year reign attempted to enlist the help of the Spartans in a military campaign against the Persians.

But the picture is uneven, Seth continued to be honoured with temples and cult right up until the end of the Egyptian empire and the loss of its territories to the rising Persian power. Whilst

Seth's cult was in decline, Te Velde's acknowledges that things were not always thus although contends that the seeds of Seth's ruin were *always* present.

Not uncontroversially,[134] Te Velde follows Plutarch's lead, where he says Seth's name means "confuser, oppressor, to overmaster, dismembered, one who dismembers, one who separates, is separate, who will desert."[135]

But these are false etymologies with no real basis in Egyptian language where the meaning of Seth's name is mysterious and uncertain. But there again Te Velde says these etymologies are "as valid as modern theories because they are in line with Egyptian sensibility". It is from this period that the most well known views of Seth originate, the basis of many modern reconstructions. This is the origin of the "satanic" Seth.

Margaret Murray, who still has much credibility as an Egyptologist, propounds yet another etymology of Seth's name as "one who intoxicates". And that the Egyptians are said to have attached three meanings to the name of this god: "Instigator of Confusion, Deserter, and Drunkard."[136] Some of these *negatives* could, to us post-moderns, be quite appealing, perhaps even "counter-cultural". However if we follow Te Velde's line of reasoning, we ought to feel there are *no* positive aspects of Seth; this deity, from a *normal* person's point of view, is wholly bad and always has been so. But as we know, some moderns despise the *normal* person, and identify more with the Nietzchean anti-hero, the superman, even the madman.

Seth is also known from ancient inscriptions as the "beast of fate or destiny"[137] which is in an ambivalent sense, signifying bad rather than good luck, or a change of fortune for the worse. The sphinx-like god Tutu, a late Egyptian deity who incorporates many characteristics of Seth, can also be controller of the demons who decide a person's fate.[138]

This might be what's called the luck of the hunter that by definition is bad for others, i.e. the prey? Even so, the literal meaning of Agathon is good, as in good daemon—which implies it actually has two forms. Very many ancient cultures believed that at the moment of a person's birth, a second spiritual entity came into existence and attached itself to the new personality, where it remains as a latent or hidden aspect of a person's psyche.[139] This is the antique equivalent of something known variously as the conscience, genius, personality, higher consciousness, the soul, or the self.

Ptolemaic, stele with Egyptian gods Bes & Tutu, 332-30 BCE, Brooklyn Museum.

I have written elsewhere at length on the nature of the daemons associated with one's birth. but there is always more to be said. The Sethian *agathon daemon*, is almost always shown as a snake, like many other of the god's companions and avatars. We met "the seven" earlier in connection with the vulture goddess Nekhbet.

The Demonic Calendar

Egypt seems to have invented this concept, and passed it over to the Greeks who developed it further. From Egypt the schema was transferred to India where it acquired a Shaivite gloss. With the arrival of Islam in India the concept was popularised throughout the Muslim world, thus returning to the Middle East, and from there to Byzantium and then the West. It continues to play a huge part in the magical world.

The individual is joined with the decans from the moment of their birth. This is naturally enough tied up with the observation of natal stars visible on the horizon. This is the celebrated ancient Egyptian observation of the decanal stars, and for all intents and purposes synonymous with one's birth daemon. Modern astrology is an obvious continuation of this same tradition.

One's fate as written in the stars is often very ambiguous and the magician must learn to de-activate, decondition and transcend what is written in the book of fate. Hence Seth's connection with transformation or protection from daemons, he is the serpent which surrounds our heart and it protects.

Because this information is based on a complicated series of interlocking astrological events, it is not possible to give more than a general idea of the complete schema. One day I will bring on the various traditions together in a definitive everlasting demonic calendar. In Appendix you will find an Indian version of the decanal system which was common to Egypt, India and the West.

MORE ON BIRTH DEMONS

The ancient Egyptian daemons are something to know about and be wary of. Recent research shows that there is a cycle hidden within them, that of the star Algol, rather appropriately "The Ghoul"in Arabic, whose existence must have been known to the Ancient Egyptians, because the good and bad days in some almanacs seems to take account of its eccentric movements. There may also be traces of an astrological observation otherwise moribund in standard astrology outside of the South—this would be the navamshas or ninth part of a sign, 3.33 recurring days.

In ancient birth oracles, words that include the Seth animal as a grammatical determinative, are almost always related to illness, crisis, storm, rage, to suffer, squalls of rain, to confound, to be violent, to roar, to be strong, battle-cries, snow, illness, and nightmare.[140]

Find me on Twitter and you will see my regular updates which helps me and fellow initiates, to follow the ongoing possibilities of attunement, de-conditioning and time-breath science.

This might give some comfort to those who seek to interpret Seth as a *predator*, a view that strikes a chord amongst some in the modern world, especially the theologians of the modern Temple of Set. To them, the mythology reveals a quintessentially human trait, we are predators now as were our early ancestors, hence the advocacy of Seth and indeed Satan is merely to acknowledge the truth of the human situation, and the way things really are.[141]

But here I part company with them, following instead the alternative "Nagada hypothesis". Despite its rejection by Te Velde it has not been completely vanquished as an academic argument and still has important advocates, and indeed new archaeological finds continue to add to the controversy.

So for example our reading of Seth might focus more on examples of *cooperation* among the early Sethians, perhaps even the presence of "kingship" being shared between two "brothers" or partners, even men and women sharing chieftainship. Or consider the prospect that many thought long invalid, of a matrifocal society.[142]

Prehistorian Elise Baumgartel, a refugee scholar from Nazi Germany, worked on the largely uncatalogued Nagada collection of Flinders Petrie. In her eventual publication she thought there was some evidence for a matrifocal society. These days, such claims of ancient matriarchy are not popular, largely due to the loaded manner in which these theories were first advanced.

The story of the discovery of ancient Ombos by Flinders Petrie is told in my book *The Bull of Ombos*. Speculations and arguments about early hominid development present us with another dilemma, a choice to make. The evidence of archaeology seems to mount up on both sides of the argument, were we savage predators, where the strongest dominated the weak, "might is right" or were early hunter-gatherer groups the ultimate co-operators? Underlying this is an important and perennial argument about human *nature*: pessimism versus liberal optiism. Perhaps we should remember the remark of the philosopher Goethe: "Treat people as if they were what they ought to be and you help them become what they are capable of being".

Seth, can disrupt the cosmic order–be rowdy, unpleasant, and a disturber of the peace. Te Velde actually compares Seth to Voodoo god Ghede but only in that he is also a divine joker and god of death. Even so, I doubt that Te Velde is actually saying that Seth is outside of the order in the way some moderns would like. Te Velde's point of view is more like a "Jungian" balance of light and shadow.

The ancient Egyptian Pyramid Texts refer to an idyllic "primeval period" when "no conflict had yet arisen", (Pyr 1463). Te Velde argues from this that it is Seth who first brings conflict into the world. So for example Seth is born on the third of five intercalary days that occur in the liminal space between the Old and New Year. For various reasons this day is viewed as the birthday of disorder, of storms, disturbing the neat and orderly sequence of a previous generations of gods.[143]

He's got a point, but actually, Seth is not alone, the birth of all five gods is disorderly and the Cairo Almanac or Calendar has special prayers to be said on all five days, the full text is given in my earlier book *The Ritual Year in Ancient Egypt*. So for example for Isis, who is born on the forth day, and after Seth, the name of the day is "He who makes terror" . In fact this whole generation of gods, and their mother, are ill omened or cursed from their conception. One myth astronomical myth even describes how Thoth played chess with the moon and won five extra days on the year, during which Nwt, banned by Ra from giving birth, could at last deliver the five gods; a cursed family from the beginning. Her crime, was taking too much time making love to earth god Geb, although this curse fell on her not him.[144]

Seth's mythology provides ammunition for a whole range of political speculations of the left and right. For examples some feminist historians see in this mythological overthrow of Seth a record or memory of the emergence of patriarchy. Others see further indication of Seth's "revolutionary" nature. Famously Seth murders his brother Osiris, born in the same intercalary period and enters into an extended episode of conflict with his nephew Horus, disputing any claim of his to the throne of his murdered father Osiris. The conflict is conducted before a mythical tribunal of the other gods but also by direct and violent combat involving violent incest, homosexual rape,[145] the temporary blinding of Horus and emasculation of Seth.[146] Eventually an uneasy peace is established in which Horus dominates Seth, or as Te Velde sees it, the rational dominates the instinctual.

Oxford Professor Richard Parkinson draws our attention to a lesser known version of the famous homosexual incident in which their union of the two gods seems more about mutual desire than sexual violence. He calls it the oldest gay chat up line in history which, as has been discussed many times, encodes an important magical secret, the sexual magick long used by the Magi:

> "And the Person of Seth said to the Person of Horus: How lovely your backside is! Broad are your thighs ..And the Person of Horus said: Watch out: I shall tell this!" [147]

ISOLATED CONSCIOUSNESS

This is a good point to discuss the Temple of Set's interpretation of Seth as representing "isolated consciousness". Seth as a deity is not really isolated from the other gods, he is very much part of the action. But he does have special qualities, his ability to see things the way they truly are. The neo-Sethian understanding of isolation seems to owe something the philosophy of Nietzsche, or at least as he is commonly, understood or perhaps misunderstood, where he talks of a "superman", which "... elevated the self to the 'all encompassing' prospective of 'higher man'".[148]

But it might also be an extrapolation from the position Seth occupies in Egyptian starmaps, reflections of the ancient sky religion. This and his already mentioned role as one who can look Apophis in the eyes without blinking as it were. Seth is routinely shown as the constellation *Ursa major* but shackled to the celestial pole and held there by his consort, the Hippo goddess Ipet. Due to the well known phenomenon of the precession of the Equinoxes, the actual Pole star changes overtime, on a long cycle of 26,000 years. In fact the northern Pole star can over time belong to any one of six constellations—Ursa minor (the current pole star), Cepheus (King), Cygnus (Swan), Lyra (Harp), Hercules (Hero), and Draco (Dragon).

Draco is often associated with the entity Apophis. The Pole star is also very like an eye in the heavens, around which everything revolves, which is interesting when you consider how the power of Apophis lies in his or her eye, said to be evil.

One possible problem for this interpretation is the fact that the constellations used by the Egyptians in their starmaps are actually different to those mentioned above, which only really applied from a late period after the Persian and Greek conquest. The way Egyptians parceled up the constellations, which as I've said before is an exercise in virtual reality, actually results in different clusters of stars being grouped together. Thus in the map from the Tomb of Sety I (KV17, Valley of Kings), *Ursa Major* is recognizable, as the bull, who in starmaps always faces away from Hippo (Damet)

Hippo takes the place of what would become known as Draco. She is a composite entity with the tail of a crocodile, which also rests on her back. Ipet means "nurse" or "midwife". Her other names are "Great One" (Waret); or "The Great One" (Ta-waret). Crocodiles are like dragons, and in later times they definitely morph into them: the earliest version of dragon-slayer St George from Coptic Egypt show him spearing a crocodile. Now Hippo, is a goddess, whose name in hieroglyphs is similar to that of Apep, it begins with the same Aa phonem but is otherwise a different word, meaning "great one of heaven" whereas Apep means "great evil".

Hippo, in her name Tawaret, is the consort or sometimes the called concubine of the god Seth. The thing one has to note is that the Egyptians did not envisage any great serpent here, which is the ubiquitous avatar of Apophis. But then again one strange thing that recurs in all representations of Hippo, is the serpentine ridge down Hippo's back, which is an obvious representation of the linear constellation we now called Draco!

Seth's constellation *Ursa major* never actually contains the Pole star although it often points to or reflects it. In Hindu philosophy we learn that human consciousness has within it an isolated seed or monad, which if you practice yoga, is the focus of the stripping away of layers (Kaivalya) isolating it until it is known in itself, in a one-pointed trance. Buddhism has a slightly different but related approach in which when one strips everything away, nothing is left but the Void, this is Nirvana, the emptiness of being blown away.

So my alternative take would be rather than viewing Seth as "isolated consciousness", which is obviously an important idea, perhaps we might say he is like Hindu *Buddhi*, meaning "discriminating intelligence" – that part of our nature that can contemplate the void or the monad – it never being absolutely certain which it is. In terms of the sky religion, sometimes the eye of the universe is in the constellation Draco but sometimes it is in empty space. All of which suggests a very revealing magical meditation.

SEXUALITY AND POLITICS

Sexuality and sexual politics are also very much tied up with this mythology. Thus Gwyn-Griffiths wrote that the "testicles" of Seth, which are wrenched from him in the fight with his brother Horus, represent political power. Thus sex is really a political metaphor for a struggle for dominance of one group over another.

Te Velde treats the sexual aspects of the myth differently, arguing persuasively that these elements reveal Seth as a god for *sexuality not canalised into reproduction*.[149] The privileging of fertility and reproduction supposedly characterises ancient patriarchal societies. The idea of a "Tantrik" Seth, who avoids reproductive sex, or focuses more on its transcendental potential, is actually quite an attractive aspect of the god, especially to neo-pagans.

"Tantrik" Seth is common ground for post-modern, Satanisms – it is the "Left Hand Path" perspective. It harks back to the 19th century anti-Catholic ideals where the Devil is sexual liberator. Control of fertility and the ability to separate sex and reproduction has a lot going for it. Some styles of religion, such as Catholicism, seemed obsessed with making sure this connection remains unbroken no matter how much misery it heaps on an overpopulated world – its almost as if this is a necessary part of their vision for humanity. Non-reproductive sex is much more attractive – in the words of the Church of Satan manifesto – "Indulgence rather than abstinence".[150]

Following on from the above is Seth's "role" as the cause of abortion, which patriarchal societies invariably oppose or tolerate in a semi-legal oppressive way, thus preserving the sense of shame or a necessary "evil" of modern life.[151] Opposition to abortion and reproductive rights, seem for some, to be one of the pillars of conventional social mores.

Further underlining Seth's position as sexual outlaw, Te Velde's contends that Seth suffers from an Oedipal complex. In a nutshell he is fixated on his mother, who happens to be the star goddess Nwt![152] Thus "Son of Nwt" is one of Seth most common epithets, occurring in very many surviving texts. Te Velde cites this is yet further evidence of the god's bad character. But first he must finesse other examples of a perhaps unnatural relationship between mother and son: "It is not to be concluded that between Nut and Seth there exists a link such as that between Isis and Horus (Harsiesis). Seth is not a child god and there is no trace of love on the part of or for his mother ... It suggests the idea of mother fixation in the sense of immaturity, in seeming contrast with the other epithet "great of strength." (Ah Pehti)'[153]

Against this view I draw the reader's attention to the presence of an image at the entrance to one of Egypt's most important monuments, the mortuary temple of Ramses III at Medinet Habu. It shows Seth and Nut together, holding hands along with several other auspicious, divine couples.

Although Seth is never a child god he does have a longstanding, and for many surprisingly, benign connection with childbirth as its protector. Nut is the mother of the gods and I suggest that Seth's epithet plays on this connection. Seth is the powerful emanation of Ra whose task is to protect Nut's solar foetus from Apep during a moment of danger.

We could also consider "Son of Nuit" because she is the star goddess and Seth is the leader of the stars in the decanal belt, a stellar parade of mostly demonic entities, which follow Seth in a celestial transit through her body, the night sky.

Northern Constellations from Ancient Egyptian Star maps - Hippo-Crocodile would correspond to Draco, the Bull is Seth. Astrological ceiling, tomb of Sety I, ValleyofKings. Detail from Giovanni Belzoni, who first discovered the tomb. Some Egyptian names or epithets, varies by monument but: Hippo-Crocodile (djamt-Ipet/Tawaret/hb-pet); Bull (Meshtyu); Crocodile (Hotep-redy ie Sobek); Horus (Anu - Falcon God "uplifter of wings or claws"); Scorpion Goddess (Selket); Man (no name); Bird (no name); Lion-god (ntr-rw); Sak, another crocodile, when shown is vertical with bent tale captioned "the plunderer".

Seth's sexuality is said to represent "the savage, elementary, yet undifferentiated urges that require to be shaped and integrated before they can be truly fruitful." Te Velde quotes cultural anthropologist K Kerenyi, who wrote about the trickster archetype, which is another way Te Velde suggests we characterise Seth:

> "Disorder belongs to the totality of life, and the spirit of this disorder is the trickster. His function in an archaic society, or rather the function of his mythology, of the tales told about him, is to add disorder to order and so make a whole, to

Representation of Tawaret or Ipet from astrological ceiling, tomb of Senmut. Note she is shown here with a crocodile tale or other piece of reptilian anatomy between her back and the crocodile!

render possible within the fixed bounds of what is permitted, an experience of what is not permitted." [154]

True, but the role of the trickster is also to reveal hypocrisy, which is especially common feature of official, "orthodox" sexuality, where the establishment may say one thing but do another. And as we have learnt, one of the things about Seth that makes him bad in the eyes of the establishment are his threats to reveal the secrets of the gods, which might be to puncture the fiction of divine kingship that is sold to the populace via the new myth of Osiris and the supposed miraculous birth of his son and heir Horus?

Again from the post modern "satanic perspective" it is the "savage, elementary" Seth that we believe may have been prematurely abandoned in favour of a piece of propaganda. Hence there must have been something like the "shock of recognition" when reading Te Velde's Jungian interpretations of the ancient myth. But there was less interest in the theme of integration and shaping of sexuality. If anything occultists believe that the forced suppression of primal, natural urges is what has led us astray. Thus one might accept the analysis of the meaning of the Horus and Seth conflict but still prefer Seth's "left hand path" over the conformity of Horus.[155]

A further question would be whether Seth represents "absolute evil". The papyrus illustration above shows a particular mythological episode. The Egyptian cosmos is threatened each day by a colossal serpent called Apep or Apophis. Apep has no cult or temple, at least not one that has survived. Seth is here an emanation of the Sun God, armed with his heavy iron spear with which he derides Apep each day and thus plays an important and continuing role *preserving* the cosmic order. If this interpretation of the myth is correct, then Seth also helps preserve the soul of the recently dead and this conflicts with the image of him as cosmic outsider; for here he is very much in the tent or rather the boat of Ra, the "all father"![156]

As you might expect, Te Velde works hard on his agenda, and thus says that even the myth of Seth repelling Apophis, does not imply he was ever a *good* god of another time, it is merely part of the same dialectic, where Seth does what any other creation of Ra must do—i.e. defend him from the *Urgod* Apophis, who is chaos. You can perhaps tell I'm not convinced, and think it does show Seth, at least in his older dynastic form, as part of the cosmic plan, upholding Ma'at (justice) and remaining within the principle of cosmic balance.

Te Velde says that most of these accounts of Seth deriding Apep are from Egypt's New Kingdom, when his star was at its zenith.[157] But there is clear evidence that they are part of a much older tradition, most likely Seth has always been there for the sungod his father. I wold say that the evidence of some decline in Seth's cult comes from after Egypt's new Kingdom and this fits with the "Nagada hypothesis". The cult of Seth plainly experienced numerous ups and downs, distinct moments of reframing, including a significant revival during the period of the Ramesside kings such as Sety I and Ramses II.

As if to make things even more confusing, in Egypt's third intermediate period, (the 1st millennium BCE) when the cult was supposedly in one of its periods of decline, the mythology of Seth and of Apophis, ("The demon of chaos and *non-being*") becomes less distinct. In other words, Seth is *identified* with Apophis. It is this late version of Seth that fits with the post-modern perspective of for example the Temple of Set. In other words their version of Satan/Seth is really more like Apophis.

Thus Michael Aquino, the founder of the modern Temple of Set writes "The Egyptians conceived the universe as actively controlled by conscious, natural principles (neteru). [neteru usually translated as god(s)] "[158] "Set is the 'neter' who is different from all the others. ... he is the 'neter' (god) who is against the neteru (gods), the entity who symbolises that which is not of nature".[159]

It seems to me that Apophis, the demon of non-being, is the neter who is most obviously against the Gods *per se*. Seth has a dispute with particular gods but not the entire cosmos. It is only when Seth's cult is in decline that the two mythologies coalesce.

There is something quite glamorous about Seth as anti-cosmic; it has what has been called "the lure of the sinister."[160] It is the apocalyptic mindset so familiar from the Abrahamic tradition but here transposed to neo-paganism.

Ironically, some modern practitioners have *chosen* to reify the most negative aspect of the historical cult, not necessarily as it was practiced by the devotees but as constructed of its ancient detractors. Post-modernism supposedly validates this approach.[161]

Post-modernism is defined by Stephen Flowers, and I believe endorsed by Michael Aquino *et al,* thus: "Postmodernism is … freedom from the pervasive modern idea of progress.–the idea that as time goes on, by applying increasingly rationality and scientific methodology, the problems of the world will be universally evaporated in the light of pure reason. The postmodernist realizes, as did the ancients, that such progress is only possible for *individuals*. Furthermore, the postmodernist is free of the constraints of modern progressivism: To the modern if it's not new, if its not the *latest* thing, then it is 'retrograde' or 'reactionary' and hence unacceptable. Post-modernists are free to

Seth has been erased but still recognizable from outline & text. together with mother Nut from gateway of mortuary temple of Ramses III, Medinet Habu.

synthesise elements from all phases of human history – in any shape or form that suits their purpose."[162]

True, even if we accept the post-modern view, it does not absolve us of rational choices. Depending on our temperament, equally authentic choices are available from the same material! After all why should one revive a cult from the end of a long decline, when it is at its most attenuated? It should be said that other post-modern followers of Seth, pick up the cult at its high point, yet others favour the "Nagada hypothesis" and relate to the cult at its most ancient, as they'll see most positive phase.[163]

Chapter Three
The Outsider

HUMAN GEOGRAPHY

I mentioned earlier how over the course of its long history Egypt acquired one of largest empires in the ancient world, stretching the length of the Nile valley from the Delta to the first cataract, but also eastwards into what are now Israel, Palestine, Jordan, and even parts of Syria. During the time of the Egyptian empire Seth acquired a special role, along with his female counterpart the goddess Hathor, as divine ambassador to the "foreigner". Thus the gods of foreign lands were often "cloaked" or perhaps we should say, "inter-translated"[164] into Seth. Thus a major god of the Hittites was represented in iconography in the form of Seth. This is perhaps comparable to the Roman inter-translation of Celtic gods such as Sulis as Sulis/Minerva.

It has become a cliché to say the Egyptians were xenophobic, but this is far from obvious. "Throughout Egyptian history foreigners occupied almost all social strata and occupations"[165] Some Egyptologists were once mislead by an over reliance on the records of a very small elite, rich enough to leave monuments. Professor John Baines says it may be inaccurate to equate the presence of ethnic foreigners with disorder and decline[166] or uncritically reflect the bias of ancient propagandists, blandly repeating talk of an Egypt "infested" by foreigners. Perhaps Egypt was always in actuality a multiracial, ethnically mixed culture!

In fact they had two views of the foreigner, an ideological or official view (topos) and an everyday more pragmatic attitude (mimesis). They tended to view the world with themselves at the centre and others arranged at the cardinal points. Thus they divided the other into:

1. those living to the south (Nubians and others);
2. those living to the west (western nomads)
3. 'Libyans' in the sense of anyone living west of the Nile and south of the Mediterranean)
4. those living to the east (Asiatics).

They supplemented this understanding with other people, i.e. from the Mediterranean, as they came into contact with them.

Surely this is nothing extraordinary, it is natural and not evidence of some special sense of xenophobia. When Egyptian monuments representing their neighbours either as subjugated (smited) or as bringing tribute, it was surely a natural consequence of living in a much coveted yet easily defended territory. It's important to contrast this with in the famous Jewish narrative in which the Egyptian king was blessed by Jacob for taking his people in during the distressed famine years.

Sketch based on Mythological Papyri Heruben B shows Seth defending sun-god Ra from Apep.

A Late Egyptian Story called "The Quarrel of Apophis" written in the Ramesside period is often viewed as key evidence of the growth of Egyptian xenophobia. But on closer inspection it is far from clear that this is so. This fragmentary narrative tells how northern King Apophis, ("Commanding voice", like the Hippo?) who was a worshipper of Seth, picks a quarrel with southern Theban King Seneqenra, complaining that the baying of the hippos, an emblem of Seth, in the nearby lagoon is disturbing his sleep. The punch line of the story is lost.[167] At the time of its writing, the god Seth was experiencing a revival, which makes it slightly mysterious as to why he should be identified with Egyptian's famous "usurpers", the Northern Asiatic rulers, also known as the Hiksos "rulers of foreign lands". Experts say the story may not even be about the Hiksos, but a coded way of criticising the Ramessides, who came from the same region of Avaris, which was a cult centre of Seth long before the coming of the Hiksos and long after their expulsion. King Apophis comes out of the story quite well compared with his dithering southern rival. It was therefore "perfectly reasonable, for the Rammeside authors to associate the Hyksos ruler with the Egyptian god Seth". There is no need to evoke xenophobia or some special relationship between Seth and the foreigner as explanation. It might just be that Seth is man of the people because the ordinary people are a mixed bunch. [168]

Care should therefore be taken with the term "foreigner". In modern parlance it can have pejorative even xenophobic connotations. In the Egyptian context it was not always so. Te Velde makes a similar point when he informs us that Seth "did not become lord of foreign countries because in history he happened originally to be worshipped in the border of the desert,[169] but ordering by locality required him, the mythical disturber of the peace, to be venerated on the verge of the cosmos."[170] Seth's status is perhaps more about centre justaposed with the periphery– as in the ruling elite versus the chaotic masses. [171]

Of course, Te Velde thinks the above serves to further underline Seth's "bad" character, as a consequence of which he gets the worst job, exiled to the provinces. Sethian people, so he says, are treated just like foreigners but this does not mean they are anymore alien than any one else, it's all mere propaganda. Thus "On a mythological level Seth is disturber of the peace, on a cosmic level a thunder god, and on a geographical level a foreigner."[172]

THE COMMON DEMON

One aspect of this designation that I find particularly attractive concerns demons, who like the common people and foreigners are all said to have strange esoteric practices, similar to those of Asiatics and barbarians.

There is an alternative view, and we've seen some of that from Professor John Baines. Perhaps before we stop using this language we should try seeing ourselves as the real foreigner, just another part of society talking about another. It reminds me of recent European Alt-Right attacks on new immigrants and how this ends up making everyone feel insecure, which is maybe their intention.

This could be the reason Seth is called "rekhyt", usually translated as "common", or of the lower classes, the vast and silent majority of Egypt's population, who may have been less worried about these things. As Professor Baines again reminds us "Dynastic Egypt is not a single culture belonging to a single ethnic group, speaking a single language and having a single set of shared values" [173]

Demons, the companions of Seth are also habitually envisioned as lower class and foreign. Even so such things fascinated the Egyptians, and so, it must be said are we. Unfortunately this is not an aspect or interpretation of Seth's cult that many modern followers choose to revive or focus on. One can see how it might cause problems to a "right-wing" reading. It also counts against the idea of Seth as elitist. "I seek the elect and none other" says Michael Aquino, supposedly channelling the voice of Seth in his *Book of Coming Forth By Night*, "for mankind hastens toward an annihilation, none but the elect may hope to avoid".[174] Inspired messages of the gods have often sounded thus but one is tempted to surmise that it's really the human channel that is speaking not the god. It all has a damaging psychology, by definition the majority cannot be elite and are therefore left is to feel very insecure or engage in serious status anxiety.

After the reign of Ramses III, (c1194-1163BCE) Egypt's empire was increasingly threatened by rising military powers of the Mesopotamian world, cultures such as the Assyrian, who would eventually conquer Egypt.[175] This was the beginning of the long process of decline or perhaps we should say transformation of Egyptian culture and indeed the cult of Seth, whose name became less popular as a personal name.[176]

Interestingly, no such decline in popularity affected Hathor, a goddess equivalent to Seth in many ways; although in her case many of her functions were taken over by Isis, whose cult eventually became an international phenomenon.

Some historians trace the origins of anti-Semitism to this decline in the cult of Seth but in truth this has very little connection. There is a line of reasoning that traces anti-Semitism to the writings of native priestly historian Manetho who in about 270BCE popularised a number of vicious stories about the Jews and their banishment from Egypt as bearers of plague. He wrote that their supposed sojourne in Egypt was worse than that of the Hiksos i.e. "Rulers of Foreign lands" who lorded it over much of Egypt during the 2nd intermediate period.[177] But there is no real connection with Seth and if anything Manetho says they, the Jews, were worshippers of Osiris (Osarseph).[178]

It is true that in extant apocalyptic writing of the time, the Egyptians dreamed of a saviour who would restore a legitimate native born king. Known as the *Oracle of the Potter*, it casts the hope of a restored king as the age old conflict of Horus and Seth, but this time Seth represents Egypt's conquerors, either Persians or Greeks. It is Horus who is the last best hope for a new age:

Apology of the Potter[179]

... and lawless. The river will flow without enough water, with insufficient, so that the land ... will be inflamed, but against nature. For in the time of the Typhonians they will say: "Wretched Egypt, you are wronged by terrible iniquities wrought against you."

The sun will be darkened, not wishing to look upon the evil things in Egypt. The land will not welcome the sowing of the seed. These ... will be blasted by the wind. And the farmer did not sow on account of this, but tribute will not welcome the sowing of the seed. These ... will be blasted by the wind. And the farmer did not sow on account of this, but tribute will be required of him. They are fighting in Egypt because of the lack of nourishment. What they till, another reaps and takes away

Image of donkeys from Tomb of Mehu, Saqqara

In this generation there will be war and murder which will destroy brothers, and husbands and wives. For these things will come to pass when the great god Hephaistos wishes to return to the city, and the Girdle-wearers, being Typhonians, will destroy themselves ... evil will be wrought. He will go on foot to the sea in wrath, and will trample on many of them because of their impiety. And out of Syria will come he who will be hateful to all men, and being ... he will come from Ethiopia ... and from the realms of the impious into Egypt and he will be established in the city which will later be laid waste.

And for two years our ... well ... The month of Amon and he said well. Their children will be defeated. And the land will

be unsettled and not a few of those dwelling in Egypt will abandon their own land and go to a foreign place. Friends will murder friends. There will be weeping and their ills will be worse than those of the others. And men will perish at each other's hands. Two of their number will pass on to the same place(?) because of the one help. Much death will fall upon pregnant women.

The Girdle-wearers being Typhonians are destroying ... And then Agathos Daemon will abandon the city being established and will enter Memphis, and the foreign city which will be built will be emptied. And these things will take place at the conclusion of the evils when the falling of the leaves occurs in the Egypt of the foreigners. The city of the Girdle-wearers will be laid waste as in my furnace, because of the unlawful deeds which they executed in Egypt.

The statues transferred there will return to Egypt. The city by the sea will become a drying place for fishermen because Agathos Daimon and Knephis will have gone to Memphis, so that some who pass through will say: "This city, in which every race of men dwelt, was all-nourishing."

And then Egypt will increase, when for fifty-five years he who is well disposed, the king the dispenser of good, born of the Sun, established by the great goddess *Isis*, is at hand, so that those surviving will pray for the resurrection of those who died before, in order that they might share in the good things. At the end of these things trees will bear leaves and the forsaken Nile will be filled with water, and the winter having been stripped of its natural dress, will run its own cycle. And then the summer will take its own course, and the winds shall be well-ordered and gently diminished.

For in the time of the Typhonians the sun was darkened, having shone forth on evil customs and having exhibited the poverty of the Girdle wearer. And Egypt ... [rest missing]

This is all rather reminscent of Aquino's inspired text *The Book of Coming Forth by Night* where he refers to Seth as the "Lord of Darkness", the counterpoint to Horus as Lord of Day.[180] The *Potter's Oracle* is part political propaganda, hence *"The sun will be darkened, not wishing to look upon the evil things in Egypt."*

It is well to remind ourselves that ancient Seth was still essentially a sky-god, and as such is associated with the constellation Ursa Major, which the ancient Egyptians thought to be among the imperishable constellations. Nevertheless he was tethered to the celestial pole by rings of meteoric iron, as a bull might be tethered to a sacrificial post. Thus tethered, Seth was required to lead all of the other constellations in the annual circumambulation of the celestial pole, and from this has come the idea that he rules the decanal stars, a special group of connected with the daemons of a person's fate. The decanal belt is not a complete circle in the way the zodiac girdles the earth.

Seth's mother Nwt, is also a sky deity,[181] the personification of the entire sky, including the Milky Way but also the other visible stars and indeed the day as well as the night sky. This last point makes it difficult to say that Seth's stellar affiliations make him by definition a creature of the night.

In the discussion of Te Velde's work, it would be easy to forget that Gwyn Griffiths also wrote of Seth's archaic cosmological role.[182] He thought the Contendings of Horus and Seth demonstrated the Egyptian's earlier interest in the moon. We must remind ourselves that Horus and Seth are also lunar deities – Horus most likely representing the new and Seth the full moon.

We could jump to the conclusion that this correspondence seems wrong., surely Horus is the full moon and Seth the dark moon. I couldn't swear, hand on heart that they never swapped roles, Egyptian symbols are not quite that settled. Mostly though, in the ancient world, it was the full moon that was viewed as malign or at least as anathema to the sun, who is at his/her most powerful in the moon's absence.[183] The gods Osiris and indeed Horus were born on the new moon. A great deal of Seth's character is light. Several stories relate how Seth's semen often appears where it shouldn't, having the attributes of *matter out of place* and as a consequence causing much havoc. All these stories describe it as a light substance, visible because it is so shiny and bright.[184]

Chapter Four
Gods of Sex and Death

One is on stronger ground to make Seth a god of death. One who according to Te Velde seeks to abolish death by killing his brother Osiris, also a god of death and of the underworld.[185] "Seth ... is a romantic figure who tries to vanquish death" and ends up cutting the ground from under his own feet.[186] Seth is[187] the "destructive demon of death" who gives a coffin (good) to Osiris but also then tries to dismember the body (bad). Thus the Book of the Dead, a composition written after the Pyramid Texts, and therefore when the theological balance had swung against archaic gods like Seth, one reads: "deliver me from this god, who seizes souls and licks that which is rotten, who lives on offal and is in darkness and obscurity, who terrifies the weary – it is Seth"[188]

In the new dualism of Seth and Osiris – Seth kills the god of death (Osiris), from which life arises; Seth is life who causes death.[189] "This would mean that he is the demonic initiator, who leads his brother to life through death by violence."[190]

BRIDE OF THE NILE

Which is a good opportunity to discuss the broader issue of sex & religion in Egypt. But first we must deal with some of possible misinformation about Egyptian culture, ancient and Coptic. The accounts of Bride of the Nile panders to the western taste for exoticism and the "barbaric" but fascinating East. In a nutshell, a beautiful maiden is supposedly married to the river god, her wedding day attended by many thousands of "well wishers"

A young woman, scantily clad except for a long diaphanous wedding veil, stands on a stone platform. She is barefoot, and chained by her ankles to a heavy rock; her hands are tied at her sides. She is to be thrown into the river as a sacrifice.
Bride of the Nile

The famous image above W. Gentz, taken from Eber's
(Aegypten in Bild und Wort (Picturesque Egypt) (1878) vol 1226.

concludes with her death by drowning. The practice was supposedly revived by Coptic Christians to indulge their Roman masters' taste for sex and death. Then again banned by the Muslim Omar within living memory but still celebrated in effigy in annual Nile regattas. It has inspired at least two modern Egyptomaniacal novels, one by the celebrated Georg Ebers, Egyptologist and novelist, whose main claim to fame is the discovering of the important medical papyri that bears his name. Hopefully you'll be pleased to learn that it never actually happened.

Sacred Prostitution

Herodotus wrote that Kheop's pyramid was built by proceeds of him prostituting his daughter Hetepheres, one stone per trick – a tall story, I think.

The Greek author Strabo wrote a voluminous *Geography* during the reign of emperor Augustus when a *pax romana* made it relatively safe to travel throughout the extensive empire. He visited Thebes (Luxor) in Upper Egypt and records how the once great capital had, since Homer's time, declined to a collection of villages on either side of the river. Although not mentioned by name one can assume that on the west bank of the Nile these are Qurna and Bayrat. Strabo's account is marred by what some say is a "remarkable example of the perverted meaning of a religious custom, by the ignorance of the Greeks and Roman writers".[191]

These remarks are from early 19th century explorer and pioneer Egyptologist Gardner Wilkinson. His work, still remarkably current and readable, is perhaps one reason why Egyptologists, unlike other historians of ancient history, have never really accepted the existence of sacred prostitution in Egypt.

For Strabo wrote that for "Zeus (Amon) whom is held in the highest honour, they dedicate a maiden of greatest beauty and most illustrious family (such maidens are called "pallades" (virgin-priestesses) or pallacide (harlots) by the Greeks); and she prostitutes herself, and cohabits with whatever men she wishes until the natural cleansing of her body takes place; (menstruation) and after her cleansing she is given in marriage to a man; but before she is married, after the time of her prostitution, a rite of mourning is celebrated for her." [192]

This and other passages are largely responsible for the myth of sacred prostitution in antiquity. Strabo visited Thebes (Luxor), travelling to its west bank, "The Libyan Suburb" (Contemporary land sales refer to it as such). Strabo viewed the so-called Colossus of Memnon, actually colossal statues of Amenhotep III that fronted his enormous mortuary temple, now largely destroyed. He may also have visited the remains of Medinet Habu before passing on to the Theban necropolis. [193]

A careful reading of Strabo's much abused account of life on the west bank of the Nile at Thebes does yield some useful information. His account of a special class of ancient priestesses is borne out by archaeology evidence from Medinet Habu. The fortunes of the village that grew around the sacred precinct has ebbed and flowed over the centuries, sometime seemingly completely abandoned then repopulated by others. Even today the sanctity of the site continues as evidenced by local "folk practices" many of which appear to be survivals or archaeological memories of these ancient times.

Stephanie Budin, in her recent study of the topic opines that previous scholars have misunderstood Strabo, what he is is really only recording the existence of local virgin priestesses, female temple functionaries, perhaps prophetesses. There is apparently nothing in his language to imply they were also "sacred prostitutes". Stephanie Budin's more neutral retranslation of the passage reads:

> "But for Zeus, whom they [the Thebans] honour most, a beautiful girl maiden of most illustrious family serves as priestess, [girls] whom the Greek called pallades; she serves as a functionary (prophetess) and accompanies whomever/attends whatever [rites] she wishes until the natural cleansing of her body; after her cleansing she is given to a man/husband but before she is given, a rite of morning is celebrated for her after the time of her religious service." [194]

I suspect this is a garbled account of the existence of the Tombs of the Divine Votaresses that can still be visited within the walls of the sacred precinct of Medinet Habu. The entrances to these tomb-chapels are conspicuous and face the Small Temple of Amun, the god whom these women all served. In my opinion, what one reads in Strabo is a memory of the existence of these high-ranking priestesses in Egyptian religion. Their cult was obviously still a living memory when Strabo visited and one can speculate that their tombs-chapels continued to receive cult offerings of some sort. Did their spirits continue to inspire those who served the god Amun in an Egypt under Roman rule? Priestesses of one kind or another had an active role in temple life although, as with their male counterparts, the end was nigh. Perhaps in difficult times they felt an affinity with their ancient forebears?

A votary is an uncommon word in English meaning someone who is devoted to the service of the deity, usually a monk or a nun. In ancient Egyptian the term used is "Duat Neter"- meaning divine adoratrice. Approximately thirty such tombs have been discovered in the temple precinct. None of them is intact. They cluster in three groups – the most significant are a dozen or so buried in crypts associated with the tomb-chapels of the divine votaresses. A second group of less elegant tombs are near the enclosure wall of the small temple of Amun and the third group lie beneath the

Colossus of Memnon (photo by the author)

floors of rooms in the main temple. Where names are known they are all women.

There are three Egyptian terms used to designate these special priestesses. The earliest, "divine consort" (Hemet Neter) is first encountered and is perhaps an innovation of 18th dynasty. The word *hemet* means womb (see N40 in the standard sign list). To us the most famous bearer of this title is Queen Hatshepsut (circa 1479-1458BCE), who was married to Amun and at the same time was favourite wife of king Thutmose II. She also bore the title "hand of the god" (djedet neter) and "divine votaress" (duat-neter). She was not celibate or if so perhaps only so on sacerdotal days. Her role was something to do with the fertility of the god Amun-Min. Was this, as some speculate, some sort of gross sexual stimulation of the ithyphallic god? Gay Robins doubts the necessity of manual stimulation for a god almost permanently aroused. She prefers to focus on the other possible connotations of "hand of god" as someone who holds executive power on behalf of the king[195] – like the "hand of the king" in *Game of Thrones* perhaps?

Over time the lifestyle of the divine adoratrice evolved and changed. By the time of what Egyptologists designate Egypt's Third Intermediate period (1000-700BCE) no single dynasty ruled the whole of the land. What we call dynasties overlapped. In 25th and 26th dynasties the institution of Divine Adoratrice was revived at Thebes (Luxor). Amun's divine consort were now royal princesses who never married. Their husband was Amun. They were treated like queens and had royal titulary. The succession passed from adoptive "mother" to "daughter" – coronation followed the mother's death.

She exercised some executive power as representative of the king in the Theban state. She also had great priestly power on a par with the high priest at Karnak, until that post was itself abolished around the time of Soror Niticris.

Above ground the stone structures of the chapels of the Votaresses have interconnecting doorways. This suggests some interaction between the different priestesses both during and after life. One can imagine the newly adopted priestess served firstly as understudy to the older woman during the latter's final years of life. The new priestess was responsible for continuing the cult of her predecessor in the corresponding tomb chapel and this no doubt included consulting the Ka of the deceased. Her function was complex, serving the cult of Amun but also that of her departed predecessor, making daily food offerings and channelling the messages of her ghostly ka spirit, perhaps also making prophesy. Each priestess had her own chapel-tomb, some of the oldest were of mud brick, although these were swept away in the 19th century clearance (déblaiement). The easternmost of these would have been the most ancient.

From the above arrangement, we gain insight into how a group of priestesses interacted and one can deduce quite a lot concerning the mechanics of ancient religious practice. One thing that seems obvious is the need for the living priestess to interact with her dead ancestor, presumably for on-going inspiration. This mirrors the way every Egyptian interacted with their own ancestors and how most tombs was designed to facilitate such a dialogue.

In both instances the living offer food and other supplies to the dead. Every important Egyptian temple was linked to a priestly scriptorium or "house of life" – perhaps this too enabled interaction between living and dead priests, a relationship they may have been initiated into between living mentor and student? It's a "technique" that one can envisage would still work in a contemporary religious setting such as one finds in neo-paganism.

Both accounts, then are wrong or garbled but they lead us into some useful and interesting aspects of Egyptian magic and how it regards sex and death. One that we can make use of in the modern revival Sex & Death. It helps with what I called the *Tankhem* project – a reconstruction or understanding of Egyptian magick that looks more like Hindu Tantra, the other great tradition that exerts an influence over western occultism.

Egypt actually takes quite an earthy approach to the mysteries. Thoth played chess with the moon and won five extra days on the year, during which Nwt, banned by Ra from giving birth, could at last deliver the five gods; a cursed family from the beginning. Her crime, taking too much time making love to earth god Geb, although the curse fell on her not him.[196]

I discussed in my book *Phi-Neter* the discovery of what might be considered as a new kind of erotic literature or sexual-magical literature in Egypt. Exploring this a little more, one of these is an ancient Egyptian "spell kit" written on a Ptolelaic ostraca that reads:

"For our good fortune:

The singers will come, the priests of *Tayy* who renders joyful the countenance of all who come to worshipped Nehemanit within the temple,

Nehemanit who dwells in the marsh.

When they are drunk, they will see the mer.et goddess by means of the vessel, Drink, truly, eat truly, Drink, eat, sing, get drunk. Those who proclaim Ai, those who proclaim Tay. She will not let drunkenness be far away for them on the day. (As for) the critics, his rejoinder (is) Ai has said "evil Indeed! Easting in the fullness of bounty is (to) their backs"

continues

"They say "may she be radiant" in a state of ecstasy. Ai will put them in a place of seeking – since they take care of them – in the hands of her corporation on a festive day. May it be granted, the emergence of Ai. Let him drink, let him eat, let him make love before *Tay.* "Tay, Tay" he says, namely the one who desires a companion, he who multiplies divine offerings, as he invoke Tay. "Let your voice come to me in accordance with the state of my heart. I do not neglect your vessel, Tayy, I will drink. I will feast, I will sing, I will become drunk. I will see the face of Ai daily."

Who are the Two goddess named in these invocations - Nehemanit and Ai ?

They are best seen as one goddess with a double nature – sex and death if you will. One side benevolent the other violent, ferocious, leonine, who cuts Apep in pieces. These dualities are more commonly represented by Sekhmet and Hathor or Sekhmet and Bastet.

The epithet Tayy – the image or figure is one that connects all these goddess – meaning they are all, one way or another an eye goddess, principally "The eye of Ra".

The Goddess Nehemanit.
Goddess of music and singing. *Meret* also means singing and dancing. So she is the goddess who brings joy whose name means "she who saves the one who is robbed" or "she who removes the claw/Talon" from the oppressor or "The beautiful saviour". Note that in Egypt, female musicians are often portrayed as wearing hardly any clothes. They sometimes also have a tattoo of Bez as patron. We could imagine this might have something to do with these objects found in a tomb of a priestess of Goddess Hathor, which may indicate the deceased's continued sex life in afterlife, also found in male tombs – called the "Bride of the Dead"

As an aside – these images also seem to have tattoos – which is probably also significant:

> "There are several examples of actual tattooed women, [and men] including the mummy of Amunet, a priestess of the goddess Hathor, which was discovered in 1891. However, ceramic figurines and vessels depicting tattooed women offer much more evidence. In the Middle Kingdom, footless faience figurines sometimes known as "Brides of the Dead" were created with patterns of lines and diamonds, primarily

on their abdomens, but sometimes on their thighs as well. Although likely not a portrait of any individual, this example (left top) is of a type of figurine often found in homes, temples, and tombs, functioning as household items, offerings to the gods, or accompaniments for the dead. In addition to the tattoos, which are seen as sexually suggestive, the figurines often wear belts made of cowry shells, a symbol of femininity, and would have had copious amounts of hair—which was considered especially erotic—attached through holes in the head. Thus, it's likely that the tattoos were considered one element of a woman's sexuality, and that they may have been included in the tombs to continue the deceased's sex life. Because some figurines have been found in female tombs, it's also possible that they functioned as images of ideal femininity, of which tattoos were an important part. In the New Kingdom a novel kind of tattoo was added to the Egyptians' repertoire. Women, especially musicians and dancers (left bottom), were sometimes depicted with images of the dwarf god Bes on their thighs, in addition to the more traditional geometric patterns. The Egyptians worshipped Bes as a protector of women in labor, children, and the home."

(Wednesday, October 09, 2013 Archaeology Magazine Anon)

Bes is connected with female sexuality – some ostraca show prostitutes with Bes tattoo, under his protection perhaps. Monkeys are are associated with sexuality

[Faience Figurine and Bowl Middle Kingdom, ca. 2033-1710 B.C. (figurine); New Kingdom, 1400-1300 B.C. ©Rijksmuseum van Oudheden, Leiden, The Netherlands)]

The Goddess Ai

This ferocious aspect of this goddess is rarely attested under the name but she was worshipped at Herakleopolis in Middle Egypt. Ai – aios – eye as in hand or actor of the god. Ai and Nehemanit both known as the eye of Ra which is why it is best to think of one goddess in two aspects here. Like the uraeus energy that can either blast with its heat or arouse the recipient.

Herakleopolitan Ai is the more ferocious, violent, lionine energy who threatens to burn miscreants in her ovens. Nehemanit is more benign, patroness of music and dance. In some versions of the dance, a dancer may even imitate the monkey as Bes or perhaps the Ape of Thoth.

Trance

One of the words used in this spell, *syhyh*, means ecstasy but in a sense that reverberates through the ages – including the Coptic *cizi* (deranged) – enchantment, possession, to be deranged, to shine.

Timing

The evidence shows this kind of ecstatic ritual was a regular occurence, although the one under discussion coinicided with what's called the Emergence, an annual barque festival on the river. This could be the well attested "feast of drunkenness" on 20th Thoth – performed in honour of Hathor of Denderah. The occasion for this feast was the "return of eye" after its winter sojourn in Nubia. Nubia is again interesting as it was thought by the Egyptians to be an exotic place full of magicians, and no doubt this attitude persists today in respect of Sudanese practitioners. There is also the famous Bubasteia mentioned in classical sources.

The festivities began in twilight, and climaxed deep in the night, with the arrival of goddess in a supernatural vision at sunrise.

Hathor Returns to Medamud - the venue [198]

It very much looks as if every temple had a special chamber set aside for this kind of ritual activity. Musicians are described in hymn to mother goddess Mut at Northern Ptolemaic gate to her temple at Karnak – the carving shows the king himself playing the tambourine (see Sauneron). The open courtyard at Philae was also such a venue. A particularly informative text shows dancers at the temple of Medamud where a special Hymn for the "return of far wandering eye of the sun" is written in vertical text next to dancing figure of Bez. The musicians accompanying the procession are labelled "Those who placate the malevolent one" The special room in the temple is set aside for the return of the distant goddess Hathor who is both the Sun and Sothis star.

This ritual chamber is referred to as the *marsh*, which, as it happens, is also a euphemism for sexual activity of all kinds. The tomb inscriptions refer to "wandering in the marsh" with this obviously in mind.

Because the Egyptian temple in Egypt is a microcosm, where the marsh is also a liminal space between the land and the outside world, this is the place where one first encounters the goddess upon her return (Smith).

But the rite could also occur in private houses where Hathor is known to appear in personal dreams, thus in the bedroom, no doubt incubated by these practices. I'm mindful that there is no impermeable barrier between private and temple spaces, both realms are related.

ACTIVITIES

Bear in mind that drunkenness, music, and eroticism were closely connected in ancient Egypt. Their common expression of a "a happy day" involved all of the above. Herodotus wrote in his history (II.64) "The Egyptians were first to make matter of religious observation not to have intercourse with women in temples not enter a temple without washing after being with a woman. And indeed a text from Edfu reads "do not sing in his domain or inside the gods house! Do not enter the women's quarters!". But this rule doesn't seem to have been universal and indeed the existence of the rule suggests is was often broken (see Lisa Manniche, *Sexual Life in Ancient Egypt*).

Naturally those who love the goddess are pleased to see her when she returns. They fall into an ecstatic trance and see her face. This practice has a tranquillising, narcotic and also stimulating hallucinogenic effect on her followers. The goddess is placated by pleasing her physical and sensual needs; the latter worshippers do vicariously by having sex. The following example is from one of many fragmentary accounts that exist, spread across various scholarly articles and books:

"Yes let us drink, and let us eat from the banquet!
Let us rejoice, rejoice and rejoice again!
May Bastet come to our feast!
Let is become drunk for her at her feast of drunkenness"
Then he [the priest] was silent, he paid homage to the crowd,
did obeisance and blessed them before Bastet.
As the people heard his words (groans?),
Their faces exulted, their bodies rejoiced
Bliss reached them as
Joy rose in their hearts,
They called out and screamed.

Fig. 10. — Le dieu Bès dansant.

They clapped their hands "complete the joy""
and Bastet has come, mollified.
We have reached … in drunkenness.
She has brought joy to us in the world.
She who love truth is her with truth."

"On the day when I saw her beauty
and my heart passed the day in her festival,
I saw the mistress of the two lands in my sleep
and she gave joy to my heart.
Then I was happy through her offerings
without any wish being unfulfilled"[199]

From this account we might suppose that a priest and priestess performed a sexual act, nearby, perhaps even publicly or symbolically?

It has to be said that this kind of milieu would be a good hunting ground for the sexual predator. One of the reasons for the obscurity of some of these sources was contemporary critics such as Clement of Alexandria who condemned this licentious excesses he saw connected with the Egyptian religion. He might also have noted, as many classical writers did, the number of prostitutes working at religious festivals, not as priestesses but taking advantage of the hightened atmosphere.[200]

SEX AND RELIGION AFTER THE PHARAOHS

This is the time when the religious ideas captured in the magical papyri including in the collection know as the Greek Magical

Papyri & Demotic Spells (PGM). The PGM abounds in sexual magick but mostly of an abusive nature, compelling others to have sex or exploiting their vulnerability in that regard.

There is however one example that seems similar to the above older tradition we discussed earlier this is PGM XXXIV. Some say this is a lost fragment of an ancient novel. Professor Richard Parkinson, there was a time when it was otherway round, scholars doubting the existence of narrative myth in Egypt, saying that fragments were all parts of magical spells. He says that surviving tales show both styles of literature exist. We have learnt, there is no impermeable line between story-telling and sorcery.[201]

" … [the sun] will stand still; and should I order the moon, it will come down; and should I wish to delay the day, the night will remain for me; and should / we in turn ask for day, the light will not depart; and should I wish to sail the see, I do not need a ship; and should I wish to go through the air, / I will be lifted up. It is only an erotic drug that I do not find, not one that can case, not one that can stop love,. For the earth in fear of/god, does not produce one. But if anyone has it and gives it, I beg, I beseech him: "Give! I wish to drink, I wish to anoint myself.""

"You say that a handsome phantom keeps appearing to your daughter, / and this seems unreasonable to you. Yet how many others have fallen in love with "unreasonable bodies". (PGM XXXIV 1-24)

Plutarch, as always, had something to say about it:

"That an immortal god shall take sexual pleasure in a physical body is surely hard to credit. Yet the Egyptians make a distinction here that is reckoned plausible: while a woman can be approached by a divine spirit and impregnated, there is no such thing as sexual intercourse between a man and a divinity." [202]

Dream books, some for men and some for women gives additional insights into inner lives and sexuality. Dreams were and still are the primary theatre of magick. Consider this ancient women's dreams: "If a woman dreams she has intercourse with a mouse, her husband will give her a [lacuna]" (the reader might like to insert their own appropriate response here). [203]

In the Coptic milieu the same dynamics continue as evidenced in a story from 10th century CE: The narrative relates how a monk, respected and reverence by all, after violating the virgin daughter of a king, is incited by the devil to murder her. This he does, giving out that she had died a natural death. But the queen, her mother is warned by the devil (*epiboulos*, "The Plotter") in a dream of the real manner of her death. She requires the monk to swear upon the holy vessels (*kumiliou*) that he is innocent of both crimes. He takes "the office and consolation of the priesthood", lays hold of the vessels and swears to her … "And in all this the wicked enemy left him not at peace, till he had estranged him from the hope of salvation of Our Lord Jesus Christi. And after that he had reduced him to desperation, he brought him forth from his monastery to a worldly life and to devilish joys and pleasures." But the merciful God, who desireth not the death of a sinner …[204]

So to complete the circle – as I said, my magick exists in some sort of imaginal sphere of the ancient world, a "region" that encompasses an Egypt and late classical India and the roots of what's known as Tantra. My contention would be that there is an ecstatic magical religion that unites both places, the precise mechanics of this I'll leave for another time and place.

Conclusions

In this book I have concentrated on the seminal works of two Egyptologists and scholars, Herman Te Velde and John Gwyn Griffiths. Their interpretations are of ancient history but nevertheless also strangely reflective of current philosophical and political issues. Ultimately, these gods are all about the origin of human nature. Te Velde's views were taken up by The Temple of Set, a contemporary neo-pagan group and also, according to some, a "political religion". Some say the relationships between the gods is the the ultimate source of politics. Although as more members of that group work with the Sethian mythos I suspect that they are also changed by the experience. I was recently asked to write a comment for a new book on Seth written by the current head of the temple. After reading through, I was immediately struck by the presentation of "an antinomian stance on a polluted and troubled world", a book for the hopeful, with a life-affirming Seth working behind the scenes.

The theology of the Temple of Set was first formed long before Te Velde's book was published. In it they may initially have thought they had found validation or confirmation of their views, that would not require any real change of heart. This vision of Seth were already formed in an earlier Nietzscheian manifesto of the Church of Satan.

Te Velde's erudite and persuasive arguments against Gwyn Griffith et al, made it easier to reject a more liberal view of human origins. Since the 1960s, new archaeological finds continue to fuel the argument from all parts of the socio-political spectrum.

For the purposes of this essay I avoided discussion of other significant influences on Pagan "political religion", principally those of R.A. Schwaller de Lubicz[205] and his successors. De Lubicz' main focus was on the cult of Amun-Min and he did not write anything substantial on the mythology of Seth. His views would be more a sanctification of a traditional and highly stratified society, which he perceived in the remains of Ancient Egypt. My guess is he was already predisposed towards the socially conservative and naturally enough this is what he found in the material. If one is not careful one does tend to find the things one is looking for.

From the summaries of the Egyptian material it is hopefully clear that Seth's mythology raises issues that are still very current. It should come as no real surprise that "political religions" of modern times have taken an interest in his cult.

Michael Aquino *et al*, rightly point out that Seth was conspicuous by his absence from the earlier occult theorising of for example Aleister Crowley. This lapse was corrected in the 1970s when Kenneth Grant re-interpreted Crowley's "religion of the will" (Thelema). Even so, the way these groups view the archetype is still very much through the older Crowleyian lens. Crowley had a vision of some sort of "satanic" geist. He believed he had found this when he channelled an ancient Egyptian entity called "Aiwass" ("I was"?).

It would be wrong to deny some resonance between his view of Satan and the ancient mythology of Seth, especially if one reads Te Velde. For Michael Aquino *et al* there was also a "shock of recognition" in the above book's apparent confirmation of their version of "Satan" as the Egyptian Seth. This revelation helped shaped their supposed rebranding of Church of Satan as a Temple of Set.

Aleister Crowley's own characterisation of Satan in his Thelemic "political religion" has itself be critiqued or reframed, most notable by his magical "son" Charles Stansfield Jones (Frater Achad). The differences between Crowley and Achad's interpretations of Thelema (Will) again mirror disagreements over the ancient Egyptian material by scholars and postmodern revivalists. Always there are two opposing ways of viewing the same material, a demand for one to make a choice as Crowley wrote all those years ago:

> I was in the death struggle with self: God and Satan fought for my soul those three long hours. God conquered — now I have only one doubt left — which of the twain was God?
> *Aceldama : A Place To Bury Strangers In* (1898) Preface.

It may surprise you to learn that even Aleister Crowley was prey to self-doubt. He came eventually to regard his own capacity as inadequate; he knew he was just too close to the material.

In a very perceptive moment, Michael Aquino characterised Crowleyianity as " 'The Law of the Jungle' raised to its most complex expression in the writings of Frederick Nietzsche".[206] Michael Aquino who also wrote "All ethics is verbal camouflage to conceal the reality of all actions as merely in the interests of the stronger (who by that same strength dictates all definitions of justice etc."[207] By now I hope you wouldn't expect me to agree.

Crowley advocated a "middle way" thought even this is a little twisted, one "enables the weak or injured to survive but only in order that they may prove their worth under other circumstances".[208] Well thank you very much for that, assuming that really is a middle way.

For some, resistance to the "Nietzschean" war-wagon is futile, so so hypnotic, articulate and infused with truisms as it is. As the poet Yeats, ironically also a dabbler in the black arts of fascism put it, "The best lack all conviction, while the worst. Are full of passionate intensity." ("The Second Coming")

It may never be possible to see Seth completely in his own right. He is just too complex, there are two many contradictions in the historical evidence, bound up as it is with human history, both good and evil.

Seth's connection with foreigners is a good example of something that can be seen as good or bad depending on one's presuppositions. Which is also very topical as Europe struggles with its own rise of xeonophobia. If you feel an affinity with the the oppressed, the common people, and the foreigner, then Seth, as "man of the people" is up there with the best – and like all Egyptian neters can say "never did I do any bad thing against the people."

The Two Ways

So there you have it – two ways. Time to make a choice – as in the rather dramatic Crowley poem quoted a few lines back: "God and Satan fought for my soul those three long hours. — which of the twain was God?" Now you know more if the ambigious character of the indigenous god one could also consider, as all do at some point, whether you will answer the call of the god, should you hear it?

I have here and elsewhere presented a wealth of liturgy and ritual material that could be used to answer such a call. But here follows the suggested steps.

Liturgy, Ritual, and Appendices

1. DRAWING DOWN THE PLOUGH

Many years have passed since on a starry night on a meadow just outside Oxford, two of us decided on impulse to use the same ritual usually directed at the moon but this time to the constellation Ursa major. The whole is nearly captured in this invocation-cum-prayer:

> Whenever I have need of you
> I draw down the Plough
> Standing under the night stars,
> The canopy clear above me
> Searching the heavens for your sign,
> An ox moving withershins,
> Tethered to a mast of flint
> In the northern part of the sky
> First I rouse your mate
> Who lies sleeping in the earth beneath
> Stamping the ground,
> So Bat for Bata will awake
> Tremors below rising through me
> A conduit for the seething cauldron
> As the power rises to my belly
> My arms upwards piercing the barrier
> Separating I and thou
>
> And down it flows
> that thing

into me,

or my cup

or via me to my companion

Dizzy now with the elixir

I follow your movements backwards

to the nameless aeon

when none ruled but I

AN ANCIENT SETHIAN RITE

In my book of the *Ritual Year in Ancient Egypt* I used the Bornless or Headless one ritual as liturgy for Seth, principally because of scholarly opinion and contemporary tradition that associates Seth as part of the hybrid or ambiguous entity invoked in the rite. I find this still a valid approach and indeed an important ritual. It has a complex hybrid of entities which we might consider as typhonian aspects of Osiris. There are indeed key magical secrets encoded in the Bornless rite. However, I've recently added the following more thoroughly Sethian spell from the same library of an ancient magician.

2. PGM IV 154-285 - *Nephotes (Nefer Hotep ie Khonsu) to Psammetichos*

First comes a frame story also known by scholars of this material as a *Historiola* (qv). Work with this long complex ritual is in an early stage - but I found that just reading the prologue is enough to set the process in motion, with gnosis intruding into dreams, with help of some special, discrete techniques, which I won't elaborate too much here.

Prologue Nephotes (Nefer Hotep ie Khonsu) to Psammetichos, immortal king of Egypt. Greetings. Since the great god has appointed you immortal king and nature has made you the best wise man, I too, with a desire to show you the industry in me, have sent you this magical procedure which, with complete ease, produces a holy power. And after you have tested it, you too will be amazed at the miraculous nature of this magical operation. You will observe through bowl divination on whatever day or night you want, in whatever place you want, beholding the god in the water and hearing a voice from the god which speaks in verses in answers to whatever you want. You will attain both the ruler of the universe and whatever you command, and he will speak on other matters which you ask about.

You will succeed by inquiring in this way: First, attach yourself to Helios in this manner: At whatever sunrise you want (provided it is the third day of the month), go up to the highest part of the house and spread a pure linen garment on the floor. Do this with a mystagogue. But as for you, crown yourself with dark ivy while the sun is in mid-heaven, at the fifth hour, and while looking upward lie down naked on the linen and order your eyes to be completely covered with a black band. And wrap yourself like a corpse, close your eyes and, keeping your direction toward the sun begin these words.

Prayer:
"O mighty Typhon, ruler of the realm
Above and master, god of gods, O lord
ABERAMEN [ThÔOU]* (formula),
O dark's disturber, thunder's bringer, whirlwind,
Night-flasher, breather-forth of hot and cold,
Shaker of rocks, wall trembler, boiler of
The waves, disturber of the sea's great depth,
IÔ / ERBÊT AU TAUI MÊNI,

I'm He who searched with you the whole world and

Found great Osiris, whom I brought you chained.
I'm he who joined you in war with the gods
(and some say against them)
I'm he who closed heaven's double gates and put to sleep the serpent which must not be seen,
Who stopped the seas, the streams, the river currents
Were'er you rule this realm. And as your soldier
I have been conquered by the gods, I have
Been thrown face down because of empty wrath.
Raise up your friend, I beg you, I implore:
Thrown me not on the ground, O lord of gods,

AEMINA EBARÔThER REThÔRABE ANIMEA*

O grant me power, I beg, and give to me
This favor, so that, whensoe'r I tell
One of the gods to come, he is seen coming
Swiftly to me in answer to my chants,
NAINE BASANAPTATOU EAPTOU MÊNÔPhAESMÊ PAPTOU MÊNÔPh AESIMÊ TRAUAPTI PEUChRÊ TRAUARA PTOUMÊPh MOURAI ANChOUChAPhAPTA MOURSA ARAMEI IAÔ AThThARAUI MÊNOKER BORO PTOUMÊTh AT TAUI MÊNI ChARChARA PTOUMAU LALAPSA TRAUI TRAUEPSE MAMÔ PhORTOUChA AEÊIO IOY OÊÔA EAI AEÊI ÔI IAÔ AÊI AI IAÔ."

After you have said this three times, there will be this sign of divine encounter, but you, armed by having this magical soul, be not alarmed. For a sea falcon flies down and strikes you on the body with its wings, signifying this: that you should arise. But as for you, rise up and clothe yourself with white garments and burn on an earthen censer uncut incense in grains while saying this:

"I have been attached to your holy form.
I have been given power by your holy name.
I have acquired your emanation of the gods,
Lord, god of gods, master, daimon.
ANThThOUIN ThOUThOUI TAUANTI LAÔ APTATÔ."

Having done this, return as lord of a godlike nature which is accomplished through this divine encounter.

Inquiry of bowl divination and necromancy. Whenever you want to inquire about matters, take a bronze vessel, either a bowl or a saucer, whatever kind you wish. Pour water: rainwater if you are calling upon heavenly gods, seawater if gods of the earth, river water if Osiris or Sarapis, spring water if the dead. Holding the vessel on your knees, pour out green olive oil, bend over the vessel and speak the prescribed spell. And address whatever god you want ask about whatever you wish, and he will reply to you and tell you about anything. And if he has spoken dismiss him with the spell of dismissal, and you have used this spell will be amazed. The spell spoken over the vessel is:
"AMOUN AUANTAU LAIMOUTAU RIPTOU MANTAUI IMANTOU LANTOU LAPTOUMI ANChÔMACh ARAPTOUMI, hither to me, O NN god; appear to me this very hour and do not frighten my eyes. Hither to me, O NN god, be attentive to me because he wishes and commands this

AChChÔR AChChÔR AChAChACh PTOUMI ChAChChÔ ChARAChÔCh ChAPTOUMÊ ChÔRAChARAChÔCh APTOUMI MÊChÔChAPTOU ChARAChPTOU ChAChChÔ ChARAChÔ PTENAChÔChEU" (a hundred letters)."

But you are not unaware, mighty king and leader of magicians, that this is the chief name of Typhon, at whom the ground, the depths of the sea, Hades, heaven, the sun, the moon, the visible chorus of stars, the whole universe all tremble, the name which, when it is uttered, forcibly brings gods and daimons to it. This is the name that consists of 100 letters. Finally, when you have called, whomever you called will appear, god or dead man, and he will give an answer about anything you ask. And when you have learned to your satisfaction, dismiss the god merely with the powerful name of the hundred letters as you say, "Depart, master, for the great god, NN, wishes and commands this of you." Speak the name, and he will depart. Let this spell, mighty king, be transmitted to you alone, guarded by you unshared.

There is also the protective charm itself which you wear while performing, even while standing: onto a silver leaf inscribe this name of 100 letters with a bronze stylus, and wear it strung on a thong from the hide of an ass.
Divine encounter of the divine procedure:
Toward the rising sun say:

"I call you who did first control gods' wrath,
You who hold royal scepter o'er the heavens,

*   ABERAMEN is the more common abbreviation for this long magical formula - as in this kind of magick, the abreviation is thought to be sufficient I omit in brackets.

SETH: THE TWO WAYS

You who are midpoint of the stars above,
You, master Typhon, you I call who are
the dreaded sovereign over the firmament.
You who are fearful, awesome, threatening,
You who're obscure and irresistible and hater of the wicked,
you I call,
Typhon, in hours unlawful and unmeasured,
You who've walked on unquenched, clear-crackling fire,
You who are over snows, below dark ice,
You who hold sovereignty over the Moirai,
I invoked you in prayer, I call, almighty one,
that you perform for me whatever I ask
of you, and that you nod assent at once
to me and grant that what I ask be mine

(add the usual) because I adjure you GAR ThAIA BAUZAU ThÓRThÓR KAThAUKATh IAThIN NA BORKAKAR BORBA KARBORBOCh MO ZAU OUZÓNZ ÓN YABITH, mighty Typhon, hear me, NN, and perform for me the NN task. For I speak your true names,
IÓ ERBÉTh IÓ PAKERBÉTh IÓ BOLChOSÉTh OEN TYPhON ASBARABÓ BIEAISÉ ME NERÓ MARAMÓ TAUÉR ChThENThÓNIE ALAM BÉTÓR MENKEChRA SAUEIÓR RÉSEIODÓTA ABRÉSIOA PhÓThÉR ThERThÓNAX NERDÓMEU AMÓRÉS MEEME ÓIÉS SYSChIE ANThÓNIE PhRA;
Listen to me and perform the NN deed."

*   Knowing this is a common magical palindrome of the time helps when trying to parse the words.

Appendix I
The Forms of the Decans

Taken from an Indian rendering of a Greek version. They are solar decans, based on the ecliptic and the zodiac. For sometime now I've been living an east-west version of magick, one that assumes there is a multinational pool of ideas, common to Egypt, India and the West; this text seems to be an obvious example of such a tradition:

1. Thirty-six are the thirds of the zodiacal signs, which are called Drekinas by the Greeks. They have various clothes, forms, and colours; I will describe them with all their qualities beginning with their characteristic signs.

2. The first Decan in Aries is a man garbed in red and having a red complexion, a fierce man whose limbs and hands are wounded and who attacks in anger. He bears golden mail and bright arrows, and his hand is upraised with an axe.

3. The second Decan in Aries is a pale-hued warrior whose eyes are pitiless to his enemies. He is clothed in white. His head is like an elephant's. He has arrows for weapons, and he knows the purposes of minerals and mercury. His limbs are heavy and hairy.

4. The third Decan in Aries wears dark blue garments and has a dark blue body. Armed with a club, he is fierce. He has a garland of blue diadems. He is strong with leaps (?), and his eyeballs are like a bull's. He is like Death in battle.

5. The first Decan in Taurus is a black woman, happy as her mind is agitated by sidelong glances (?). Round her neck she wears a

garland full of kadamba-flowers. She shines forth holding an axe in her hand. Her body is bowed down to by cow-herds.

6. The second Decan in Taurus is a red-faced woman whose arms and lower lip are also red. She is pre-eminent as she stands on one foot holding a jar. She is always intent on eating and drinking, and delights in gard woods.

7. The last Decan in Taurus is a woman ... with a tender body. She has a bull's hump, and wears a garland bright with campaka-flowers. Her eye- brows are fair, and her girdle hangs to the end of her buttocks.

8. The first Decan in the third sign carries a bow, and his hand is bright with arrows. He is adorned with a garland of many colours, and his necklace is pendant. The instruments of his craft are prepared. He knows how to use swords and missiles, and he wears a diadem and armour.

9. The second Decan in Gemini is a black woman whose girdle is beautiful and whose garments are brightly coloured. She delights in the arts, in singing, and in story-telling. Holding a lyre, she is pleased and delighted. Her brows are lovely, and she is graceful.

10. The third Decan in Gemini wears red clothes and a red, pendant necklace. He is pale with red limbs, violent and fierce. The tip of his staff is red (with blood). He is the chief of a multitude of men. He bears a sword and missiles.

I I. The first Decan in the fourth sign is a woman whose words are beautiful and full of grace. Holding a lotus in her hand, she stands in the water. Pining with love, she is as pale and fair as a campaka-flower. She wears a single white garment.

12. The second Decan in Cancer is a girl seated on a snake-throne, having a medium form (?) and beauty. Her nature abounds in politeness and affection. Her body, adorned with jewels, is beautiful, and her garments are of a pale hue.

13. The third Decan in the fourth sign is set down as a woman who is the colour of a dark blue lotus and is pleasing to the eyes. Her upper-garment is of silk and (adorned with) bright jewellery. She is barren, but puffed up with pride in her beauty.

14. The first Decan in Leo has a belly and a body like a lion's. He is fierce, armed with a sword, and arrogant with his mighty strength. His deeds are terrible and cruel, and he desires spicy foods. His fingers are many.

15. The second Decan in Leo is bold and has loosened hair. She is on a mountain peak, proud in taking away the wealth of others. Terrible she causes . . . ; her actions are like those of a monkey.

16. The third Decan in Leo is a woman whose actions are marvellous and who is cunning in respect to machines and to undertakings involving the arts, business, or jewels. Seated on an ivory throne, she considers (?) the murder of her enemies.

17. The first portion of Virgo is a black man who possesses a subtle knowledge of crafts and who knows the rules of calculating, cleverness, and story telling. He is attached to beauty and skill, and is determined in his purpose.

18. The second Decan in the sixth sign is a beautiful woman whose limbs are polluted by her menstruation. She loves a man in secret for the sake a child. She is learned; striving on behalf of the people, she journeys to a foreign country.

19. The third Decan in Virgo is a woman who is naturally coquettish and graceful. Her face is smiling, her countenance moon-like. Her one braid of hair is adorned with adoka-flowers, and her steps seem to stumble with intoxication.

20. The first Decan in Libra is a man in the market place with the implements of his trade prepared. His limbs are covered with silk and bright ornaments; his body is black and his eyes beautiful. His places are where there are gold, merchandise, mines, and treasure.

21. The second Decan in Libra is a fair-waisted woman who has learned a little of the crafts. She wears bright garments and a bright, pendant necklace. She is clever in the office of an intermediary (between lovers) for the sake the bridegroom. Her actions are like those of rogues and cheats.

22. The third Decan in Libra is a man about to attack. The tops of his teeth are far apart, and the hair on his body is long. . . . He carries a bow and wears armour and a turban. He engages in the tricks of rogues.

23. The first Decan in the eighth sign is a blazing man whose staff is fierce to his enemies. His sword is drawn, his armour is of gold; his flames are fanned by anger. He sports with serpents whose poison is sharp.

24. The second Decan in Scorpio is a woman with loose hair who is bound with snakes. She is robbed by thieves in the forest. With black body and completely naked she runs swiftly from a bandit, calling out terribly and shrilly.

25. The last Decan in the eighth sign is a cruel man wearing a golden suit of armour. Standing in a hole, he is clever (in obtaining) treasure and what he desires (?). He wishes to follow a vow that is broken. He knows how to use weapons, but is tormented, having been robbed by his companions.

26. The first Decan in Sagittarius is a man whose bow is drawn and whose speed is as violent as a horse's. He has knowledge of chariots and weapons, and bears the instruments for the sacrifice. His body is protected by gold, and his earrings flash with gold.

27. The second Decan in Sagittarius is a woman who is charming, graceful, and beautiful. She is seated on an auspicious throne, and is pale with a golden-hued body. Opening a golden casket in a heap of jewels, she takes pleasure in distributing (its contents).

28. The third Decan in Sagittarius is a bearded man with a black body. Clothed in silk and pining with love, he is graceful. On his breast hangs a string of pearls, and a bracelet is on his upper arm. He desires music and perfume.

29. The first Decan in Capricorn is the colour of collyrium. His teeth are as terrible as a crocodile's. He is armed with a staff, and his actions are like those of Time and Death. He stands in the middle of a cemetery with an armour of heavy hair and a strong body.

30. The second Decan in Capricorn is a man of blazing splendour whose teeth are dark blue and like a Pisaca's. He is handsome, having bound on his armour, sword, and turban (sirastrina). He wanders about constructing river-embankments, tanks, and aqueducts.

31. The third Decan in Capricorn is a woman with loose hair, a gaping mouth, and a hanging belly. Her red body is tall and thin. She holds a noose in her hand, and wears a winding-sheet. She delights in injury.

32. The first Decan in Aquarius is a man who has dreadful teeth. He knows how to practise magic. His is the colour of a dark cloud, and half of his hair is filthy. His actions are pitiless. Garbed in an antelope-skin, he has the nature of one who is not insignificant.

33. The second Decan in Aquarius is a man with a shining sword. Half of his hair is tawny. Covered with garlands of skulls, he wears armour. His is the colour of sunset-clouds, and his protruding teeth are fierce. He is covered with the strings of nooses and so forth.

34. The third Decan in Aquarius is a man with various weapons wearing a garland of golden Moons. His shape is boar-like, his form frightful. Producing red (sandalwood?) in his garden (or Mount Malaya), he is an ascetic whose hair is reddish-brown like a monkey's.

35. The first Decan in Pisces is a woman with a beautiful body whose eyes are expansive and long. Her body is adorned with silk and gold. She stands by the Great Sea, which she has crossed in a boat for the sake of a heap of jewels.

36. The second Decan in Pisces is a woman dreadful in strife, the foremost one. She is fierce, and has no clothes; her colour is white, red, and black. Her garments and ornaments are destroyed; desiring clothes, she shouts out.

37. The third Decan in Pisces is a woman whose hair has been loosened and who wears ornaments bearing the emblem of the aabhiiras. She shrieks, as she is frightened. She stands in the water adorned by troops of spirits having the shapes of jackals, cats, and boars.

38. By the great and authoritative Greeks who know the science of horoscopy these thirds of the signs which are called Drekkaas are described together with their thoughts and origins, which are connected with their natures (?).

39. Because of its doubtfulness, this perception of the organs of sense is combined with the (effects of) the lords of the Navaamshas (9th part of a sign or 3.333 recurring). The navaamsha themselves and the aspects of the planets, together with the various shapes, portions and characteristic mark in this world, it is real from the illustrations and forms.

41.What was said previously the distinguishing mark of a (each) planet and sign is to be determined by a wise man as the form, which arises from the changes due to their mutual combinations in order. As the form which arises from it in order.

Appendix II
Book(s) Of Overthrowing Apep

The inclusion here is more as a source of background myth and memory. I don't really expect the reader will want to use such a draconian execration, certainly not in full, although it existed and like much Sethian material we can learn a great deal from it.

Book I.

Part I
The Book Of Overthrowing Apep

Here Begins The Book Of Over-Throwing Apep, The Enemy Of Ra, The Enemy Of (Un-Nefer), Life, Strength, [And] Health [Be To Him] ! Which Is Recited In The Temple Of Amen-Ra, The Lord Of The Throne Of The Two Lands, The President Of The Apts,"[209] Throughout The Day Daily.

The Chapter Of Spitting Upon Apep.

Say the [following] words:
"Be You spat upon, Apep.
Be You spat upon, Apep."
Be You spat upon, Apep.
Be You spit upon, Apep."

Ra rests with his Ka (i.e., double), Per-Aa (i.e., the Pharaoh) rests with his Ka (i.e., double). Ra comes, the mighty one! Ra comes, (3). the victorious one! Ra comes, the exalted one! Ra comes, the one equipped [for battle]. Ra comes with rejoicing, Ra comes in beauty, Ra comes as King of the South, Ra comes as King of the

North, Ra comes with divine (4) offerings, Ra comes with triumph, and Per-Aa (i.e., the Pharaoh) shall come. Life, Strength [and] Health [be to him]. You have destroyed for him all his enemies even as he has over-thrown Apep for you. He has slain for you the fiend Qettu. He ascribeth praise to your might. (5). You are adored by him in all your risings wherein You shinest upon him, even as he overthrows for you all your enemies throughout each and every day."

PART 2. The Spell Of Stamping Upon Apep With The Left Foot

Say the [following] words:

"You are exalted then, Ra, and (6) your enemies are destroyed; therefore shine, O Ra, for your enemies have fallen. Verily Per-Aa (Pharaoh), Life, Strength [and] Health [be to him] ! Has destroyed for you all your enemies, O Ra. All your enemies have been destroyed for you, both those who are alive and those who are dead.[210] Verily Ra has gained the mastery over you, O Apep. (7) His shooting fire stabs you, and it has the mastery over you; the flames thereof are ready to attack you, and the blazings thereof rush out upon the enemies of Ra."

To be said four times:

"and the flame attacks all the enemies of Per-Aa (Pharaoh), Life, Strength [and] Health [be to him]. Ra has then (8) gained the mastery, and your Enemy has been trampled upon by you, O Ra, in your horizon. Those who are in the Sekti Boat"[211] give praise unto you, and the Ahiti gods circle round you and your Boat with rejoicings, and You renewest your rising upon those who possess the hearts of the gods within the Maati Boat."[212]

To be said four times:

(9). "Praise be unto you, Ra-Heru-Khuti (Ra-Har-machis)."

Part 3. The Spell Of Taking A Spear Wherewith To Smite Apep

Say the [following] words :

"Horus grasped his lance of iron and broke in pieces (10) the heads of the enemies of Ra. Horus has grasped his lance of iron and has broken in pieces the heads of the enemies of Per-Aa (Pharaoh), Life, Strength [and] Health [be to him]! Verily, Horus has grasped his lance of iron and smitten (11) the heads of the Sebau fiends which were in front of his boat.

Exalted are you, O Ra, for the Sebau fiends have been stabbed, and the slaughter of Apep has been performed, and the Smaiu fiends of the enemy Qettu have fallen headlong. And You too, O Per-Aa (Pharaoh), are exalted, (12) for the Sebau fiends your enemies are stabbed, your enemies have been slaughtered, and his Smaiu fiends have fallen headlong.

Come You, O Ra, in your splendours. The divine beings who are in their shrines (or, abodes) [in the Otherworld] accompany you, and they ascribe praises to your (13) beneficent acts. You rollest up into the sky and you sendest forth your light; your enemies are not. Your words of power (hekau) are the protectors of your members (or, body). And Per-Aa (Pharaoh) ascribeth praise unto

Ra. He makes his lance to pierce Apep, he seizeth fire and he hurleth it upon him; (14) he stabs the accursed bodies of your enemies. Fire be upon you [O Apep], flame be upon you [O Apep], and fire be upon you, O you enemies of Per-da (Pharaoh), Life, Strength [and] Health " [be to him]1 and it shall consume you."

"Exalted then be You, Ra, for your enemies the Sebau fiends are stabbed, and fire [has been hurled] (15) upon Apep, and it has eaten into the whole length of his backbone.

Hail! [There is] fire upon Apep.

Ra [sails] in a breeze of the wind, and his mariners receive him, and the beings with divine hearts who dwell in the horizon (16) exult at the sight of him. He has overthrown the Sebau fiends, the flame had gained the mastery over Apep, and over the roaring fiend Qettu; they are not in peace, they are not in peace.

"O Ra-Heru-Khuti, turn you your beautiful face to Per-Aa (Pharaoh), Life, Strength [and] Health [be to him]! and destroy (17) you for him all his enemies, for he ascribs praise to Ra in very truth.

Ra triumphs over Apep." [To be said] four times.

Pharoah triumphs over his enemies. [To be said] four times.

Part 4. The Spell Of Putting Fetters On Apep

Say the [following] words "(18) O you fetterers who fetter, put you fetters on Apep, that accursed enemy of Ra. You know not, Apep, what shall be done unto you when justice shall come upon you. O you who goes backwards at your season, (19) You shall Yourself, your throat shall be slit open, and the fetters shall hold you fast. Horus cries, "Be you fettered!

Ra cries, " Be you fast bound.'

There shall be neither love-making nor sexual pleasure to you, and (20). you shall not escape from under his fingers. Ra cried, Destruction to you ! And Heru-khent-an-Merti "cries, 'Be you fast bound.' "

Part 5. The Spell Of Seizing A Flint Knife Wherewith To Smite, Apep

Say the [following] words:

" Smite, smite, O divine slaughterer, (21) and overthrow the enemy of Ra with your flint knife. Smite, smite, O divine slaughterer, and overthrow the enemy of Per-Aa (Pharaoh) with your flint knife. Your heads, O you Sebau fiends, and that head of yours, O Apep, shall be hacked off (22) and battered to pieces with his flint knife.

"O You goddess Septet, who are ever ready with flames, O You serpent goddess Asbit, who presidest over the fire, overthrow you the fiend Qettu with your knife, slice up the fiend Unti (23) with your flint knife. Hack you them in pieces because of the evil [which they have done] to you, and cut them in pieces because of what has been done unto you by them. Let justice be with you, and deal you justly with them because of the evil which has been done unto you [by them].

"Ra has triumph over you [you fiends], and Horus hacks you in pieces."

Part 6. The Spell Of Placing Fire Upon Apep.

Say the [following] words:

"Fire be upon you, O Apep, enemy of Ra. The Eye of Horus has gained the mastery over the accursed soul and shadow of Apep, the burning radiance of the Eye of Horus ate into the enemy (1) of Ra, the burning radiance of the Eye of Horus shall eat into all the enemies of Per-Aa (Pharaoh), Life, Strength, [and] Health [be to him]! both living and dead."

And you shall recite the [following] words of power when [the figure of] Apep is put in the fire, and shall say:

"Taste You [the fire], perish, O Apep. (2) Get you backwards and retreat, O enemy of Ra, fall headlong, get backwards, retreat, begone. I have driven you back and have cut you in pieces. Ra triumphs over you, Apep." [Repeat] four times.

"Taste You [the fire] [repeat] four times.

(3) Back, Sebau Fiend, destruction be to you. I have heaped fire upon you and I have made you to perish, and I have doomed you to evil. An end and destruction be to you, taste you the fire], an end to you, you shall have no further being. (4). An end and destruction to you, an end to you, taste you [the fire] and come to an end. I have caused Apep, the enemy of Ra, to be destroyed. RA triumphs over you, O Apep." [Repeat] four times.

"Per-Aa (Pharaoh) triumphs over his enemies." [Repeat] four times.

Rubric : (5). NOW after [the figure of] Apep has been defiled by you with your left foot four times, You shall say as You standest before RA with your two arms bent [in homage] as soon as he has risen,

"Ra has triumphed over you, Apep." [Repeat] four times.

"Ra has made himself to triumph over you, Apep, in very truth."

To effect the destruction of Apep this (i.e., the above) Chapter must be recited. It shall be written upon a strip of new papyrus in ink of a green colour, and [recited over] a figure of Apep made of wax (7) whereon his name has been written in ink of a green colour.

The figure shall be laid upon the fire that it may consume the enemy of Ra.

And one shall place a figure of Apep in the fire at daybreak (or, sunrise),

at noon also,

at eventide when Ra sets (8). in the Land of Life (i.e., the West),

at the sixth hour of the night (i.e., midnight),

at the eighth hour of the day, when evening is about to come

and afterwards at every hour of the day and of the night

on the day of the festival, (9).

by day,

by month,

on the sixth day festival each month,

on the fifteenth day festival each month,

and likewise every day.

[Thereby] shall Apep, the enemy of Ra, be overthrown in the thunder-storm, and RA shall shine brightly, and Apep shall be overthrown in very truth. (10)

And when the figure of Apep has been burnt in a fire made of khesau[213] herbs, the remains (i.e., ashes) thereof shall be soaked in wine[214] and then thrust firmly into a fire.

And You shall make a repetition of this ceremony at the sixth hour of the night (i.e., midnight), (11). and at daybreak on the fifteenth day of the month (?).

And when the figure of Apep is placed in the fire, one shall spit upon it a very great many times at the beginning of each hour of the day until the shadow comes round. And as for what shall be done after these things, on the sixth day festival (12). each month, at daybreak, You shall place a figure of Apep in the fire, and shall spit upon it, and shall trample it into the dirt with your left foot; thereby shall be driven away the roarings[215] of the fiend "Stinking Face," and You shall make a repetition of this act (13), at daybreak on the fifteenth day of each month ; thereby shall Apep be repulsed and hacked in pieces at your Sekti Boat [O Ra]. And You shall make a repetition of this ceremony when lightnings blaze in the eastern parts of the sky, when Ra sets (14) in the Land of Life (i.e., the West), in order that the red ones (i.e., fire-fiends) may not be allowed to come into being in the eastern pares of the sky. And You shall repeat this ceremony many, many times to prevent a rainstorm coming on in the sky, and also to prevent (15) the occurrence of a thunder-storm in the sky. And You shall repeat this ceremony many, many times to [prevent] rain and to make the disk of the sun to shine, [for thereby] shall Apep be overthrown indeed. The doing of these things is a protection to a man on eareh and in the (16). Other World (Khertet-Neter), for thereby will power be given unto him to [attain to] dignities which are above him, and he shall be delivered from every evil thing in very truth. May I see [this] happen to me!

Say the [following] words:

"Fall down upon your face, Apep, enemy of Ra. Get you backwards, Enemy, Sebau Fiend, armless and (18) legless. Your fore pare is hacked in pieces, and things[216] are upon you; you have fallen down, and you are over-thrown. Ra-Heru-Khuti (Ra-Harmachis) has overthrown you, he has destroyed you and wounded you, and his Eye has (19) pierced your body. You have fallen down into the burning, out from which proceedeth the flame which proceedeth from its fire, and the fire therefrom comes forth at its opportunity against you. Your crocodile is repulsed.

The goddess Isis curseth you with her words of magical power. Your soul shall be cut in pieces, (20) the joints of your back shall be severed, Horus shall shower blows upon you, the Sons of

Horus[217] shall keep you in fetters, and you shall be destroyed at their opportunity.

Back, get you back; withdraw, withdraw Yourself, fallen one, retreating one, be turned back, Apep. (21) The Great Company of the gods who dwell in Anu (On, or Heliopolis) make you to retreat quickly. Horus makes your accursed crocodile to go backwards, and Set has paralysed you at the moment of your power. The goddess Isis has repulsed you, the goddess Nephthys has made gashes in you, and the Great Company of the gods (22) who dwell in the fore pare of the Boat of Ra makes you to go back. The staff[218] of Set is upon your neck, the [Four] Sons of Horus drive their spears into you, and the gods who keep ward over the secret doors of the Other World drive you back [from them], (23) and flames rush out against you from their fire.

Ho, You who goes back and retreats before the fire of the flames, which proceed from their mouths! Ho, You who falls, groveller, Apep! Ho, You who goes back (1) and retreats, You enemy of Ra, You are fallen at the moment of his power Those who dwell in his Boat have overthrown you, and You have been driven backwards. Words of exorcism have been recited over you, you are destroyed, and you have been repulsed (2) at your moment of power. Ho, be there fallings down to you! You have been turned back and your Ba-soul [has been carried away], You have been turned back and your flesh has been removed, blows have been rained upon you, the bruising of you and the hacking of you have been performed, your crocodile has been (3) destroyed, your ear has been removed, the flesh has been struck off from your body, your Ba-soul has been driven away from your shadow, your name has been blotted out, your words of power have been made of no effect,(4) You are destroyed, fallen, overthrown, and You shall never, never come forth from your den, and blows shall be rained upon you again and again.

You are fettered and chained by (5) the cruel warders, you are repulsed at the moment of your strength, your crocodile is driven back, Ra has seized your ear, and has made you to retreat to your place. You are fallen and driven backwards quickly, (6) you are condemned to an evil doom, you shall be kept under strict ward, and the period of your restraint shall never end (?). Your Ba-soul shall perish and your shadow be destroyed. The Eye of Horus has condemned you, (7) it has gained the mastery over you, and it eats into you to the limit of your face. Ho, an end to you, Apep The eye of Horus stabs you, it turns you back, it destroys you, it makes an end of you!" (8) Say the [following] words with firm [utterance]:

Down upon your face, Apep, Enemy of Ra!

The fire comes forth against you, proceeding from the Eye of Horus; the Great Flame comes forth (9) against you, proceeding from the Eye of Horus. You are pressed down into the flaming fire, the blaze of which rusheth at you; the flame of fire is deadly to your Ba-soul, and to your Akh-soul, (10) and to your words of power, and to your body, and to your shadow. The Lady of Fire (Nebt-Amm) has gained the mastery over you, her flame stabs your Ba-soul, she makes an end of your form, and she drives her dares (11) into your members.

You have fallen before the Eye of Horus which rageth against its enemy, and it gnaws you; the Great Fire penetrates you. The Eye of Ra has gained the mastery (12) over you, the flame consumes you, and there shall remain nothing of you to fall away from it. Get you back! You are cut asunder, your accursed Ba-soul is shrivelled by the heat, your accursed name is under restraint, (13) there shall be silence [concerning] your accursed name, your accursed name shall fall, You shall be unknown, thrust away, and threefold oblivion shall [cover] you. Retreat, get you back, You are hacked asunder; (14) begone You and be remote from those [gods] who dwell in the divine shrine of Ra.

Ho, a crushing to pieces, an end and destruction to you, Apep, Enemy of Ra! There is no existence to you, and no existence to your accursed Ba-soul. The Eye of Horus has gained the mastery over you, (15) and it shall gnaw into you every day according to that which Ra decreed should be done unto you, Apep. You host fallen into the flame of the fire, and the fire consumes you. You are doomed to the (16) fire of the Eye of Horus, the burning Eye which consumes you, and consumes your accursed Ba-soul, and your accursed Akhw-soul, and your accursed body, and your accursed shadow; never more, never more shall You enjoy the happiness of love.

(17) [Say] four times:

Ra triumphs over you, Apep.

[Say] four times: Horus triumphs over the Enemy.

[Say] four times: Per-Aa (Pharaoh) triumphs over his enemies.

Get you back and retreat before (18) this word of power which comes forth from my mouth on behalf of Per-Aa for ever. This word of power shall destroy you, and the opportunity [to escape] shall never come to you, Apep, enemy of Ra. Taste You [death], (19) O Enemy, Sebau.

[Say] four times.

The [above] shall be said by a man who is ceremonially clean and pure.

Rubric: And You shall prepare piece[s] of new papyrus and write upon them the name of Apep, (20) and You shall put [one] into the fire when Ra makes himself to appear [at dawn], and [another] at noon, and [another] when Ra sets in the Land of Life (Ankhtet), on the seventh day (quarter moon day denit), on each day, at every hour of every day, in the months, on the festival of the sixth day of each month, on the (21) festival of the fifteenth day of each month, and likewise every day, for overthrowing the enemies of Ra-Heru-Khuti.

Book II
Overcoming Apep (Another Version)

[Say the following words]: Fall you down upon your faces, O you enemies of Ra., all fiends (22) and enemies, children of helplessness, rebels, nameless Sebau fiends, fiends doomed to slaughter for whom blocks of slaughter have been prepared, according to the decree [of Ra], stubborn rebels, (23) accursed Katiu and Sebau fiends, however many you may be, who make rebellion, fall down, fall you down at the moment of the might of Ra, and perish I Ra casts you down. (1) He makes your heads to fall down, and lo, he destroys you and makes complete your slaughter. Ho, destruction and an end to you! He bringeth about your destruction, you are not, you have ceased to be, you shall never come into being again, and you shall never have existence. Your heads are crushed in, (2) your throats are slit, the joints of your backs are cut asunder, blows have been rained upon you, and the slaughtering of you has been effected. Fall you before the Eye of Horus, the flame whereof is ready to dare against you, and its fire shall have the mastery over you. The Eye of Ra rises upon you, (3) his power smiteth you, his Eye has the mastery over you, it devours you, it peirces you in its name of Ami, (the fiery one) and it gains the mastery over you in its name of Sekhet:[219] Its (4) cruel (or, deadly) fire, and the flames of burning come forth from its blaze. Ho, it burns you to ashes! Ho, the fire comes forth against you and burns you to ashes, O Enemy of Ra, O Rebels of Horus, and it consumes your accursed Ba-souls, your accursed bodies, and your accursed shadows.

(5). The fire comes forth! Roasting it roasteth you, frizzling it frizzleth you, shrivelling it shrivelleth you. The goddess Apt-s-ur breaks you, devours you, and consumes you, she destroys your accursed souls, and she drives her fiery (6) dares into your shadows. Ho, an end to you! You are destroyed, destroyed ! You are burned up and hacked in pieces, and the slaughter of you has been effected. You are doomed to the fire and the flame. The fire of the goddess Aat, the Lady of Flame, eats (7) into your accursed Ba-souls, and she drives her fiery dares into your accursed bodies. She presses you down into her great fire, and she slices you with her knives, she attacks you in her fury, she devours you (8) with her fire, her flame burns you up, she parcheth you with her scorching heat, she consumes you with her fire, she burns you with her burning. She crushes[220] you in her name of 'Set' (i.e., (9) Fire). She judges[221] you in her name of Apt-s-ur. Her fire which is filled with quickly-burning flames overthrows you, and the heat consumes your accursed souls.

Ho, fall down, fall (10) you down, you shall fall down headlong. You are fallen, yea overthrown, for Ra has overthrown you and you are fallen through the fierce attack of Ra in his moment of power. He has made an end of you, and you are come to an end. He has destroyed you, he has overthrown you, he has hacked you in pieces, he has brought you to naught (11) and he has annihilated you. He has blotted out your names, he has hacked in pieces your accursed souls, he has put you under the restraint of fetters, he has destroyed you, he has dragged you along with hooks, he has driven his dares into you, he has overthrown you. You have fallen down into the fire, and it has destroyed you, and there is no [further] existence to you. (12)

Ho! an end to you, destruction to you, destruction to you! Assuredly there is an end to you. An end to your accursed Ba-souls and an end to you. An end to your accursed bodies and an end to you. An end to your accursed shadows and an end to you. You shall have no existence, and your (13) accursed Ba-souls shall have no existence. You shall have no existence and your accursed bodies shall have no existence. You shall have no existence and your accursed shadows shall have no existence. You shall have no existence and your Eyes shall have no existence. You shall have no existence, and your progeny (?) shall have no existence. Your heads shall nevermore be attached to your bodies. (14) Assuredly you shall retreat [before] him (i.e., Ra). Assuredly you shall go backwards, O Sebau fiends. Assuredly the god Thoth shall never more give you existence][222] by means of his words of magical power. The great god is more powerful than you are, he drags you along by means of hooks, and he causeth to be done unto you that which you hate. (15) The fire which proceedeth from his mouth comes against you, and you shall therefore be consumed, O Sebau fiends, and assuredly the god Thoth shall nevermore give you existence by means of his words of magical power. He (i.e., the great god), has overthrown you and hacked you in pieces, and he has destroyed you. The flame of the Horus-fire which comes forth from the Eye of Horus consumes (16) you to the limit of its power,[223] and it destroys you with its mighty blaze, and it is not repulsed at the moment of its greatest strength, which is the desire[224] of its heart, in its divine name of Mert.

Therefore shall an end be to you through the Horus- fire. Get you back therefore from before it, retreat you therefore from before it, (17) withdraw you therefore from before it, O every enemy of Ra and every enemy of Horus. The Horus-fire shooteth into you, it drives you back, and it destroys you; therefore shall you come to an end before it, therefore shall you be crushed to powder before it, and you shall never enjoy the happiness (18) and fruits of love.

Justice has made Ra to triumph over Apep and the accursed children of impotent revolt, and over the chiefs of the accursed fiend Betesh. ['These words shall be said] four times.

Horus has triumphed over his enemies. [Say] four times.

Osiris, (19) Governor of those in Amentet, has triumphed over his enemies. [Say] four times.

Per-Aa (Pharaoh), Life, Strength [and] Health [be to him] I has triumphed over his enemies. [Say] four limes.

I have overthrown Apep, and Sebau. and Sheta[225] and Qettu, and the children of impotent revolt in every station wheresoever they are, and in every place wheresoever they are. (20)

I have overthrown all the enemies of Ra in every station wheresoever they are, and in every place where-soever they are.

I have overthrown all the enemies of Horus in every station wheresoever they are, and in every place where-soever they are.

I have overthrown all the enemies of Amen-Ra, (21) Lord of the Throne of the Two Lands, Governor of the Apts,[226] in every station wheresoever they are, and in every place wheresoever they are.

I have overthrown all the enemies of Ptah Shema aneb-f[227] Lord of the Two Lands, in every station where-soever they are, and in every place wheresoever they are. (22) Likewise every enemy of Atum[228]; likewise every enemy of Thoth, Lord of Khemenu;[229]

likewise every enemy of Iusasit,[230] Lady of Anu, and of Hasor, Lady of Hetep-hemt,[231] and of the Shadow of Atum; [likewise] every enemy of Heru-khent-khatti,[232] Lord of Ka-Kamt,[233] (23) [likewise] every enemy of the goddess Khauit.[234] . . .; [likewise] every enemy of Bast, the great goddess, Lady of Bubastis ; likewise every enemy of Osiris, Lord of Tettut (Busiris); likewise every enemy of the Ram, the Lord of Tetu (Mendes), the great god, the Life of Ra.

I have overthrown every enemy of An-her[235]Shu, the son of (24) Heru-Temam;[236] and every enemy of Amen-Ra, Lord of the city of Sma-Behutet;[237] and every enemy of Anpu (Anubis), Lord of Siut:[238] and every enemy of Horus, Lord of the men and beings of the East; and every enemy of Horus of the Two Eyes,[239] the Lord of the city of Shetenu;[240] and every enemy of Horus, dweller in …

(1). and every enemy of Hera Smai-taui,[241] the Lord of Khatet ; and every enemy of Horus in the town of Pe and of the goddess Wahjet in the town of Tep;[242] and every enemy of Heru-ur,[243] the Lord of the country of the South, in every station wherein they are, and in every place wherein they are.

I have overthrown all the enemies of Keb (2) in every station wherein they are, and in every place wherein they are.

Rubric The [following] words shall be recited by a man who is washed clean and is ceremonially pure:

Ho, every enemy of Ra, ho, every enemy of Per-Aa (Pharaoh), Life, Strength [and] Health [be to him] in life and in death! You are made an end of, and so are all the schemes which are in your heart. And the names of their fathers, and their mothers, (3) and their children, each and all, shall be written in green (or, fresh) ink upon a new piece of papyrus, and their names shall be cut upon their bodies, which shall be made of wax, and they shall be tied round with the hair of a black bull. Then spit upon them, (4) and defile them with the left foot, and drive a flint spear through them, and put them into the flames of the fire of the metal workers, after [uttering] the name of Apep.

And You shall make a fire of khesau grass [and shall burn these figures] when Ra appears [at dawn], and when Ra [appears] at noonday, (5) and when Ra sets in the Land of Life, and at the first hour of the day of the night, and at the second hour of the night, until the third hour of the night, and at daybreak; and likewise at every hour of the night and at every hour of the day of the festival of the new moon, and of the festivals of the sixth day and of the (6) fifteenth day of each month; and likewise every month, [for thereby] shall be overthrown the enemy of Ra, and Apep shall be overthrown in very truth, and the enemy of Ra shall be overthrown.

And a copy of this book shall be done into writing when the Boat [of Ra] goeth forth to overthrow the enemy (7) of Ra, and every enemy of Heru-Merti in Aat-Peka. And it shall be most beneficial to a loan if he recite this book before this holy god completely and regularly, millions of times.

Book III
The Book of Overcoing the Foe of Ra Daily

Fall down (8) upon your face. O Apep, enemy of Ra. Sink You into the waters, sink You into the waters, and come forth into unknown places. Turn back, turn back, get you gone, get you gone, as You go, entering in and coming forth. There is overthrow for you at the lake of Nu, (9) and it is Ra who has commanded the slaughter of the to be performed. The Great Flame blazes up against you being ready, and it proceeds from the god Heka; (or Apt-Heka) O You whose eyes are open, who beholds the Two Lands, the god Ur-Heka,[244] comes forth against you from the hall which is in his sanctuary. The Divine Hawk comes forth (10) against you, and the uraei, the guardians of the secret pylons, attack you in wrath, and fire comes against you from out of their mouths. An end to you, O Enemy. Sebau ! Be fettered, Apep.

Ra rests upon his standard within his sanctuary. (11) Homage to You, O Ra, who are within the folds of your serpent Mehen.

Your voice is triumphant over Apep. [Say] four times.

Your voice is triumphant over your enemies. [Say] four times.

The voice of Per-Aa, Life, Strength and Health [be to him]! is triumphant over his enemies. [Say] four times.

Be spat upon, Apep. [Say] four times.

Book IV. The Book Of Turning Back Apep The Great Enemy.

Recite this Book at the time of dawn and say the [following] words:

Be spat upon, Apep, enemy of Ra! [Say] four times.

Verily You are turned back from him that is in his sanctuary (i.e., Ra). An end to You, Sebau!

Fall You on Your face!

Let Your face be spat upon!

Get You back into Your place! (13) May Your roads be obstructed, may Your paths be blocked up, and may You be confined in the place wherein You were yesterday. Let there be no strength to You. Cowardice be in Your heart. May Your members be in a state of helplessness. You shall be annihilated and there shall never be escape to You. You have been ordered to be (14) among those who are in the chamber of the block of slaughter, the headsmen are ready with their knives, they shall cut off Your head, they shall chop Your neck, and they shall strike blows [on You] again and again, again and again. Then shall they cast [Your body] down into the fire, and their fierce attack upon You shall terrify You more than the flame at the time of its greatest strength. (15) The flame has the mastery over You, it eats into Your members, it devoureth Your bones, it stabs Your flesh, and the god Khnemi has carried off Your children to his chamber of the block of slaughter. Your members have passed into the flames, which penetrate Your Ba-soul, and it shall nevermore journey over the eareh, and your arms (16) shall nevermore have their being in this eareh, O Apep, enemy of Ra.

Heru-ur,[245] the son of Isis, has destroyed You. You shall nevermore be conceived and You shall nevermore be born. Your accursed Ba-soul shall never walk over that which Shu supports.[246] You shall not be able to see, and you shall have no sight. You are destroyed. (17) and Your shadow, O Apep, enemy of Ra., shall not exist.

Be You spat upon, O Sebau fiend! Let there be an end to your name! Let the remembrance of You cease to be I Be fast bound in fetters ! You shall be spat upon in the face each time remembrance is made of You! Ra has rained blows upon you. Isis has bound you in chains. (18). Nephthys has set fetters upon you. The magical powers of Thoth are employed in your destruction. Your accursed Ba-soul shall have no being among the accursed Baiu-souls, and your accursed body shall have no being among the bodies of the dead. The fire shall bite into you, the flame shall eat into You, and shall make a blazing fire of You, and it shall rest upon You, (19) O Apep, You enemy of Ra. Ra shouts for joy, the heart of Atum beats with great gladness, and the heart of Heru-ur is exceedingly happy, for Apep has been borne away to the fire, and his serpent fiend Nekau has been transferred to the flames. Nevermore shall Apep, the enemy of Ra, exist; nevermore shall his shadow have being either in heaven or upon the earth. (20) Be you spit upon, and an end be to you, O Apep.

[Say] four times.

Rubric : Say the [above] words over [a figure of] Apep made of wax, [with his name] cut upon it, [and write his name] upon a piece of new papyrus also, and put them upon the fire before Ra every day, and on the festivals of the first and sixth and fifteenth days of each month, and (21) then Apep shall be overthrown on the water, and on land, and among the stars.

Book V
The Book Of Knowing The Creations Of Ra And Of Overthrowing Apep

Say the [following] words:

The Lord of All spoke after he had come into being, saying : "I am he who came into being in the form of Khepra. I the Creator[247] of (22) created things, created myself, the Creator of all created things, after I had created multitudes of created things which came forth from my mouth. Heaven was not created. Earth was not created. Creatures which belong to the ground and reptiles had not been made in that place; I raised[248] up them from the (23) divine water[249] out of a state of helplessness (or, inertness). I did not find a place whereon I could stand. I made use of magical words of power in my heart. I laid a foundation in the form of Shu,[250] and I made forms [thereof] of all kinds. I was one by myself, [for] I had not [then] made Shu of the liquid of my body, and I had not created Tefnut from my spittle; there was none other (24) who worked with me. I laid a foundation in my own heart, and the creations of created things [which were] from the creations of [their] offspring [and] from the creations of their offspring became very many. I made my hand my consort, I had union (1) with my shadow,[251] I poured seed into my own mouth, I emitted Shu, and I vomited Tefnut.[252]

My father Nu says : They had injured my Eyes [placing it] behind them up to the Henti periods when they proceeded from me. From being one god (2) I created myself into three gods, and I came into being in this land. Shu and Tefnut therefore rejoiced in the mass of inert water wherein they lived, and they brought to me my Eye along with them. Then did I gather together my members, and I shed tears upon them, and men and women (3) came into being from the tears which came forth from my eye. [And my Eye] growled at me after it came and found that I had made another in its place. [Then] I arrayed a it in splendour, and I brought it forward to its position in my face, and from that time until now it has ruled (4) This earth to the limits thereof. Moments [of calamity] fall upon it through the clouds, (4) [but] I restore what they carry away from it. I came forth from the clouds (or, bushes), I created reptiles of all kinds, and everything came into being from them.

[And] Shu and Tefnut produced (5) Geb and Nut, and Nut gave birth to Osiris, Horus-Khentán-Merti, Set, Isis, and Nephyths from one conception, one after the other, and their offspring have become many in this earth.' [253] Urt-hekau, the divine KA of words of power, says (6). They are commanded to destroy mine enemies by the magical might of the utterance of their mouths, and they are commanded to hear what has happened to my members.' [254]

[Say the following words]:

That evil enemy is overthrown. Apep has fallen into the fire. A knife of flint has been [plunged] into his head, (7) his ear[s] have been cut off, and his name doth not exist upon this earth. I have been commanded to strike him with [many] blows. I have driven the spear into his bones, and I have destroyed his accursed Ba-soul in the course of each day. I have cut out the joints of the vertebrae of his neck, I have sliced away with a flint knife (8) the fat from, his flesh, and I have cut slits and holes in his skin. He has been given to the fire, and it has gained the mastery (sekhem) over him in its name of Sekhmet;[255] it has glorified (khut) itself over him in its name of Khut, the consumer of the enemy. His accursed Ba-soul has been stabbed, (9) his bones have been burned to ashes, and his flesh has passed into the fire. Horus, the mighty one of strength, has given the order for him to come to the front of the Boat of Ra, and he has tied him up thereto with the deadly fetter of iron. He has made his members to cease to be, and repulsed him at his moment of power, (10) and destroyed him, and made him to vomit what was inside him. He is under restraint, fettered, and fast bound. The god Aker has carried away his strength so that I may strip the flesh from his bones, and bind his feet in a snare, and cut off his two hands, and (11) seal his mouth and lips, and break his teeth, and cut out his tongue by its roots, and take possession of his words, and destroy the sight of his two eyes, and remove his ear, and dig out (12) his heart from its place, that is to say, its seat or support, and may make him to cease to be. His name shall not exist, and his offspring shall not exist. He shall not exist and his kinsfolk (?) shall not exist. He shall not exist and his house shall not exist. He shall not exist and his heir shall not exist. (13) His egg (i.e., germ) shall not flourish (or, be permanent), and his seed shall not be stablished, and his seed shall not be established and his egg shall not flourish. His accursed Ba-soul, and body, and Spirit-soul, and shadow shall not exist; and his words of power shall not exist. His bones shall not exist and his skin shall not exist. He has fallen down, he is overthrown, and he shall nevermore exist.

The flame of the (14) Horus-fire shall burn holes in him, the slaughtering god Henti and the Amenhiu gods who hold the knives shall perform the hacking of his body, and shall drive their knives into him, and he shall fall down under a shower of their deadly blows. Now have I decreed [these things to be done] throughout each (15) and every day upon his wicked form. The goddess Sekhet (or, Sekhmet) falls upon him with a knife, and she hacks at him and cuts off his head from his neck, and she digs out their hearts,[256] and (puts) them on the fire with her foot (?), and puts them into the flame. Her flame (nesert) (16) is in him in her name of Set-nesert-di. Her flame is in him, and she drives away his accursed Ba-soul from his accursed body. She has gained the mastery (sekhem) over him in her name of Sekhmet.[257] She boasts herself (khu) over him in her name of (17) Khut-Nebat (i.e., 'Flaming Eye'), she devours his heart, and the flame of the fire of her mouth consumes him.

The goddess Uatchit throws herself before his cavern, so that he may nevermore, nevermore, come forth therefrom. She constrains those who are (18) under her restraint, and they cut in pieces his accursed Ba-soul, and his body, and his shadow, and his Spirit-soul, and his words of power. They tear out his heart from its seat, - and they blot out his name. He has fallen down and he shall nevermore exist. I haves decreed his destruction and the destruction of (19) his accursed Ba-soul. His throne shall not exist, and his habitation shall not exist. She has seized the bows of the god Shu in the abode of Am-Uatchit,[258] and she giveth his tongue to the goddess Pekhat[259] (4) The goddess Set (Sati?) is ready to destroy him at the moment of her fiercest attack.

The goddess Sekhet (or, Sekhmet) giveth (20) his heart to the flame of her mouth. He falls through her slaughter. His eye is blinded [by her], he is scarified, yea, Apep is overthrown. Ra himself has overthrown Apep. Ra has triumphed over Apep in the presence of the Great Company of the gods, and a flint knife (21) is driven into his head in the presence of Ra every day. The gods of the South overthrow him, the gods of the North overthrow him, the gods of the West overthrow him, and the gods of the East overthrow him. The star-gods of Orion in the Southern heaven bind him fast in chains, the (22) Great Bear (Meskhet) in the Northern heaven drives him away, and those who dwell in the Decans heap fetters upon him. The fire eats him, the flame consumes him and pierces his bones and his skin, it burns up his (23) flesh, it makes to shrivel his skin, and he is overthrown by the hands of the gods. His name shall nevermore have existence in the mouths of men, and it shall nevermore be remembered in the hearts of the gods. Each time that his name is mentioned shall he be spat upon. (24)

Ra has showered blows upon him; there is an end to him, an end to him! Apep is slit open, slit open; the flame has torn him to shreds, torn him to shreds. The Serpent-god Henbu has pierced him. He shall not breathe, he shall not breathe. He shall nevermore snuff the breeze; he shall nevermore snuff the breeze. He is on the fire, which burns up his two eyes, (25) the flame thereof consumes him, and devours his skull. The gods who are in the Boat of Ra long to attack him and the tears which come forth from my Eye[260] are against him.[261] Shower your blows, O you [gods of the Boat of Ra], upon his accursed body. (26) O you gods, [grant not existence to him] O you gods, let neither his abode (or, station) nor his tomb have being, O you gods, let not his accursed name exist. O you gods, let not his Ba-soul, or his Spirit-soul, or his shadow, or his bones, or his hair (or, skin) have being. O you gods, let him not have the breadth of his two hands.[262]

(1). [O you gods], let him have neither children nor heirs. O you gods, let not his seed germinate, and let not his members be healthy. O you gods, let not his words of power have effect. O you gods, permit you not him to have being either in heaven or on the earth. O you gods, permit you not him (2) to have being among the Beings of the South, the Beings of the North, the Beings of the West, or the Beings of the East. O you gods, permit you not him to have existence among men and women. Let him be in the fire of the Blazing Eye of Horus, and let it have the mastery over him in the course of every day. Let it [burn] into him, and let it never, never be quenched in him. (3) Let it seize him at his moment of power, let it drive back his crocodile, let him burn, and let him perish and come to an end. Let it pierce you, and let the fire make you to fall. Ra has overthrown you, and Ra has triumphed over you. Verily I have hacked you in pieces. Verily I have made your name to perish. (4) You are given to the fire each day, and there is done to you each day what Ra has decreed. Look, O Ra, and see, and hear also, O Ra, verily I have destroyed your enemy, and I have crushed him into the dust with [my] two feet, and I have spit upon his face. Ra has been made to triumph over you, and over every enemy of his; they have fallen down (5) and have ceased to be. The name of Apep is burnt up, and I have destroyed his station and his throne and his sepulchre. I have destroyed his accursed Ba-soul, and his Akh-soul, and his body, and his shadow, and his words of power, and his seed, and his egg, and his bones, and his hair (or, skin), and I have placed him in the fire every day. These things has Ra commanded (6) to be done to him.

Destruction, a hacking to pieces, and burning in the fire shall therefore be to all the enemies of Per-Aa (Pharaoh), Life, Strength, and Health [be to him] ! In death and in life. Grant that their flesh may be hacked to pieces, that their skins (or, hides) may be slit into shreds, and may the Lords of Anu fight against them, and destroy (7) them before you, O Ra, every day. Fire be upon you.

And let not have being their accursed Ba-souls, and their Akh-souls, and their bodies, and their shadows, and their words of power, and their bones, and their hair (or, skins), and their spells, and their incantations, and their words! And let not have being their (8) graves, and their houses, and their caverns, and their sepulchres And let not have being their groves (or, orchards), and their sycamores, and their shrubs which bear flowers[263] And let not have being their cisterns of water, and their bread, and their lamps and their fires! And let not have being their children, (9) and their descendants, and their heirs, and their families! And let not have being their heads, and their hands, and their feet, and their ears, and their seed ! And let not have being their thrones upon their lands! And let not water be poured for them (10) either among the living in this land, or among the Akh-souls who are damned in Khert-Netert.

You have decreed them to the chamber of the block of slaughter of Sekhet in At-nebt-Asher, You have overthrown them at the moment of great strength of the Mighty Babe, and You have pronounced the doom (11) of those who are among the fettered ones who dwell in Amenti. The accursed Ba-souls shall never be permitted to come forth from the Tuat, and they shall never have being among the living who dwell upon the earth, and they shall not behold Ra with their eyes each day. They shall be fettered with chains and fast bound in a pit (12) in the nethermost pare of the Tuat, and , their accursed Ba-souls shall never, never come forth therefrom. Your decree of doom shall be fulfilled on them because they cursed Ra in his habitation, and the gods therein shall deal justly with Apep, and shall cut off (?) his hands. (13) The Eye of Horus shall have the mastery over them, and they shall burn on the fire altars of Sekhet [and] in the furnace chamber wherein green things (?) are consumed. They shall be slit in pieces in your presence, O Ra, each day, according to what you have ordained to be done unto them forever and ever. You are in your divine habitation [O Ra]. (14) You sail in the Sekti Boat, and You rest in the Anti Boat, and pass over your two heavens in peace. You are mighty. You have life. You have health. You endur, You have splendour. You destroy every enemy of your by means of your ordinance, [and every enemy] who would do evil to Per-Aa (Pharaoh), Life, Strength, Health [be to him] (15) with deadly dares, and every man, and every woman, and every person who is damned, and every spirit of whatsoever class and kind, and every being from the countries of the East, and every enemy of Per-Aa (Pharaoh), Life, Strength, and Health [be to him]! Both dead and alive. I have destroyed [you], I have made an end [of you]. Vomit you and fall down, Apep.

Ra triumphs over you, Apep. [Say] four times.

Per-Aa (Pharaoh), Life, Health, [and] Strength [be to him] ! triumphs (16) over his enemies. [Say] four times.

Rubric : This (i.e., the above) Chapter shall be recited over [a figure of] Apep drawn on a piece of new papyrus in green ink, and the papyrus shall be placed inside a covering (?) whereon his name has been written, and this shall be tied up and bound round and put in the fire each day, [and this figure] shall be stamped on with your left foot, and You shall spit upon it (17) four times in the course of each day. When You place the figure in the fire You shall say four times :

Ra triumphs over you, Apep. Horus triumphs over his enemies. Per-Aa (Pharaoh), Life, Strength, [and] Health [be to him]! And behold You shall write on the inside of the covering (?) the names of all the male Sekhti and of the female Sekhti (18) whereof your heart has fear, with [the names of] all the enemies of Per-Aa (Pharaoh), Life, Strength, [and] Health [be to him]! both the dead and the living, and the names of their fathers, and the names of their mothers, and the names of their children, and place the covering in a figure of wax whereon is cut the name of Apep. And You shall put the figure in a fire that is blazing when Ra (19) appears in the morning, and assuredly You shall do it again at noonday, and again when Ra sets in the Land of Life, whilst there is still light upon the pass (?) of the mountain. And You shall recite these words over every picture [of Apep] in very truth. The doing of this is most beneficial [for a man both] on earth and in (20). Khert-Neter (i.e., the Other World).

Book VI
The Book Of Knowing The Creations Of Ra And Of Overthrowing Apep

Say the [following] words of Neb-er-tcher, who says: I created the creation of creations. I came into being in the form of the creations of Khepera, coming into being in primeval time. I came into being in the form of the creations (21) of Khepera. I created the creation of creations, that is to say, I rose up from the primeval matter [which] I had made. I rose up in primeval matter. My name [is] Ausares (Osiris?), the primeval matter of primeval matter. I have done every-thing I wished (22) in this earth. I have spread widely in it. I lifted up my hand (?) I was quite alone; they (i.e., the gods) were not born, for I had not then made Shu from the solid matter of my body, and I had not created Tefnut from my spittle.

I brought [to] my own mouth my name, that is to say, a word of power, and (23) even I came into being in the form of created things. I came into being in the form of the creations of Khepera, and I came into being out of the primeval matter, multitudes of creations of created things taking place straightway. No created things of any kind whatsoever had come into being in this earth [before these]; I made everything which was made. I was quite alone, and there existed (24) no other [being] who worked with me in that place. I made all the things, which came into being at that time through (or, from) that Soul which I raised up there out of the Water-of-heaven god (Nu) out of a state of inactivity. I did not find a place whereon I could stand. I recited a spell in my heart. I laid a foundation (25) in (or, on) my face. I made everything which was made. I was quite alone. I laid a foundation in my heart, and I fashioned multitudes of created things, the created things of Khepera; and their children (or, offspring) came into being from the creations of their children.

(26) I sent forth matter from my body in the form of Shu, I spat in the form of Tefnut, and, from being one god, I made of myself the three gods who are the creative gods in this land. Then Shu and Tefnut rejoiced in Nu (i.e., the sky), and they lived there. As concerning my Eye[s],'[264] I brought (27) them after henti[265] periods, and they came to me. I gathered together my members which came forth from out of my own person after I had commerce with my hand ; my heart came to me from my shadow,' and the seed fell into my mouth. I sent forth (1) matter from my body in the form of Shu. I spat in the form of Tefnut, and, from being one god, I made myself the three gods who are the creative gods in this land. Then Shu and Tefnut rejoiced in Nu (i.e., the Sky), and they lived there. As concerning my Eye[s], I brought them after henti periods, (2) and they came to me. I gathered together my members which came forth from out of my own person after I had commerce with my hand; my heart came to me from my shadow,[266] and the seed fell into my mouth. I sent forth matter from my body in the form of Shu, I spat in the form of Tefnut.

My divine father (3) the Water-god of the sky says: Many, many bushes[267] (or, plants) in their following obscured my Eye for many henti periods, [both] bushes and serpents. My Eye cried out to[268] the divine Tear, which I shed on myself, and men and women came into being from it. (4) I bestowed upon my Eye the Uraeus of Light (Khut), and it raged at me. After it had come another grew up in the place, and its angry attack over-threw the bushes thereof [and fell] upon the bushes. I equipped it, I set it in order; (5) advancing then to its place before me it rules the whole earth. [Then] Shu and Tefnut gave birth to Nut, Osiris, Horus-Khenti-an-Merti, Seth, Isis, and Nephthys. Behold, they produced and fashioned multitudes of created things (6) in this earth, through the creations of offspring, through the creations of their children, and [these] invoke my name, and they overthrow their enemies, and they create words of power for overthrowing Apep, who is (7) held fast bound by the two hands of the god Aker. His hands shall not exist and his feet shall not exist, and he shall be fettered in one place, whilst Ra shall shower upon him the blows which have been decreed for him. He shall be cast down upon his wicked back, (8) and his face shall be slit open because of the evil which he has done, and he shall remain lying upon his wicked back. The children [of Shu and Tefnut] shall overthrow him, and shall turn away his accursed soul from his body and sh'adow, and the beings of knowledge who dwell in the Divine Boat, [and] the tears of my Eye desire (9) to enter into them. Disaster has been decreed for him, and he shall never perform his courses on this earth according to his will. He is ruined, and his accursed soul is ruined. Those who dwell in the South overthrow it. Those who dwell in the North overthrow it. Those who dwell in the West overthrow it. (10) Those who dwell in the East overthrow it. The beings of knowledge who dwell in this earth [overthrow it].

O Company of gods who came into being from my body, watch you to destroy Apep. Curse you and destroy his name, and let your arms overthrow him. (11) Cause [you] his name to be scattered abroad. His children shall have no existence, and his throne and his accursed Ba-soul, and body, and Akhu-soul shall have no being.

He shall be in the power of the Eye of Ra, it shall have the mastery over him, and it shall eat into him. I am deputed to overthrow him, to blot out his name, (12) and to cut in pieces his name and his words of power. I have decreed it to the fire, I have counted it for the flame, and I have given it to the Eye of Ra. The flaming uraeus Khut shall crush it with her teeth, and she shall devour his accursed Ba-soul, and his Akhw-soul, and his body, and his shadow, and (13) his words of power. Never, never shall he enjoy the delights of love.'

Rubric: Say the [above] words over a figure of Apep made of wax. His name shall be written upon it with green ink. And write it also upon a piece of new papyrus, together with the names of every enemy of Per-Aa (Pharaoh) (14) both alive and dead. [And make figures of them] in wax, and write their names upon them with green ink, and tie them up in cases. Then spit upon them, and stamp upon them with your left foot; make gashes in them with a stone knife and put them into a fire (15) made of khesau grass, which. You shall extinguish with the issue of an unclean woman. And You shall paint the names of Apep, and of every enemy of Per-Aa (Pharaoh), Life, Strength, [and] Health [be to him] both alive and dead, on a tile (?), set it on the ground, and stamp upon it with your left leg, as if it were actually the spirit of a person. (16). Ra, and the gods who have come into being from him, know this image, and he triumphs over his enemies.

This Book shall be kept hidden in the Seh-chamber; let no person whatsoever look upon the mysterious Book of the Overthrowing of Apep.

BOOK VII
The Words Of Power
& The Utterance Whereof

(17) Destroys Apep, And Hacks In Pieces His Fiends, And Makes Ra To Triumph Over His Enemies, And causes To Journey Onwards The Boat Of Ra In Peace, And Makes Apep To Retreat Into The Fire, And Makes Him To Depart To The Slaughter Chamber.

The Crocodile of the Horrid Face is destroyed (18) in very truth. His accursed Ba-soul, his body, his Akhu-soul, his shadow, his children, his kinsfolk, his family, his relatives, his heirs, his skin (or, hair), his form, his creations, his body, his egg, (19) his name, his sub- stance, his hands, his feet, his teeth, his words of power, his magical spells, his seat, his cavern, that is to say, his tomb, have been brought to ruin, that is to say, he has been overthrown, and his ear has been removed from him. Your Sekti Boat advances, O Ra, (20) and the flint knife which is driven into Apep each day in the presence of Ra has gained the mastery over him.

Rubric : Whosoever shall hear this Book read shall be made strong in heart. And the Boat of Ra shall be made to travel thereby, and Apep shall be destroyed in every name of his. Thanks be to the god who makes his strength to come into being. Tie up the (21) writing, the accursed fiends Nekau and Qettu are hacked in pieces, and the god rejoices in what has been done. Ra says unto Isis: Turn back the Sebau fiend. Blind his two eyes so that he may not hide the height of heaven in very truth. Tear with hooks his accursed soul and body. (22) Turn back his bones and put them into the fire, and make him to gnaw his own body. Consign him to the hands of the executioners of Ra, and drive him away.

Recite the [following words]:

Back, You Apep, You thing of flesh whereon Ra treads ! Back, You claw of strife, (23) You Enemy, You Sebau fiend, without arms and without legs; [your] progeny (?) is destroyed coming forth from within your cavern Ra turns [you] back. I know the evil which You have wrought. Your head shall be cut off, and your slaughter completed (24). You shall not lift up your face against the great god. Fire be upon your face, and flame be upon your accursed Ba-soul. The knife (?) of the Great Block shall be in your flesh, and You shall smell the slaughter of the great god. The goddess Serqit shall cast a spell over you, and she shall make you to turn backward. (25) Enter, enter ! You shall fall, You shall fall through the enchantment in my mouth. You shall be given to the fire and it shall make an end of you. The Eye of Horus shall cast fire upon the top of your head. Fall down on your face. Your accursed Ba-soul is overthrown. The eye of Ra obtains the mastery over you. You are fallen, (26) You are fallen, turned back, turned back. O serpent, without arms and without legs, fall down upon your face. Your tomb shall have no existence. Enter You into the cauldron of fire. The god who created himself has overthrown you, those who are in his Boat (27) have made an end of you through the spells uttered by their mouths, and through the words of power which are within their bodies. You are hurled upon your back, the windings of your body are cut in pieces, and the executioners of the goddess Sekhet are hacking at you with their knives.

(1) They [thrust] their mouths into your flesh, they spill your blood in the fire, they break open your head with knives of flint, and the great god remove from you your ears. Haste backwards, haste backwards; retreat, retreat. You are overthrown, You are destroyed. (2). Get you back then on your footsteps; the great god shall carry away your legs. Ra comes forth, Horus the Elder rises ; mighty are the words of power which [they direct] against you. Ra triumphs over you, Apep. Vomit You, O Enemy. Ra hacks you in pieces; vomit You. You are fallen (3) and Thoth has made an end to you. In your two eyes are his words of power so that he may seize you. Your form is made an end of for you, your attributes are destroyed, your body is made an end of, and your shadow and your words of power are destroyed. He (Thoth ?) snatches away your life, and your spittle (4) and your breath shall cease to be, cease to be. A falling down to you! Annihilation to you Gashes be to you, O Sebau fiend, from the god. You are counted for the great slaughter, and your are destroyed ... You are without arms, You are without legs, and there is no magical power to your heart on its throne.

(5) You are hacked asunder, hacked asunder. Retreat, retreat, get you back ! The spear of Horus comes forth against you, and the fetters of Set are placed on your head. Ra himself has destroyed you, and your voice is broken, and your words of petition do not exist. Hail, You are destroyed (6) and brought to an end, and your form no longer exists. You belongs to the Eye of Horus, which shall have the mastery over you throughout each and every day. O Apep, Enemy of Ra, Ra has destroyed you, and Atum has turned you back by means of the spells, which their mouths have uttered. Hearken You to my words of power, (7) [and I shall do] according to what Ra decreed should be done unto you. O Enemy of Ra, I

know what shall be done unto you. Come, turn you back in accordance with your evil luck. You shall fall down at your unlucky moment, and You shall remain still. Ra uttereth curses on you, and the Great Company of the gods bear testimony (8) against Apep, the Enemy of Ra. You are fallen and overthrown, and at the moment of your overthrow You shall be slit up, O Apep. You are given over to the flint knife, and Ra has the mastery over you by means of those knives, which are in his divine Boat. You are [given over] to the fire, and it gains the mastery over you (9) in the course of each day. You are [given over] to the block of slaughter, your face is [set] upon it, and Isis overthrows you by her words of power. You are [given over] to the Eye of Horus, and Usert, the Fire-goddess, burns up your accursed Ba-soul. You are [given over] to Horus, into the hands of the great god, and the spear, which is in his hand, leaps forth (10) against you. You are [given over] to Set, the son of Nut, who fetters your back, and rips open your neck, and ties you to the victorious neck-stake Y which is in his hands. You are [given over] to the Eye of Ra, and to the fiery heat of Horus, which eats a way into your accursed body. (11) You are [given over] to the mariners of Ra, and to those who paddle in his boat, and they set your head upon the earth. You are [given over] to tleru-khent-an-Merti, and he cuts you into strips with his knife (?) which is in Sekhem. You are [given over] to the Guardians of the Hidden Pylons, (12) and their fires shall leap out against you.

Great terror shall rest upon your accursed body, O Apep, enemy of Ra. You shall not move, You shall not come onwards, (13). You shall have no being, You shall not rise up, and your accursed soul shall not come forth to you from among those which are in Amenti.

You are [given over] to the fire [which comes] from the mouth [of Ra], and the Hawk of Horus comes forth against you from among those who are in the East. You are [given over] to the words of power which are in his body, and those who are in their divine shrines (14) make their arrows (?) to find places in you. They slay you again and again. You are given over to the fire of the god which is on the altar that consumes the Wadjet stone, and to the cavern of the mariners of Ra, and to the block of slaughter of Thoth. (15) All the gods seize their weapons [and drive them] into you. Their hearts are content [when] performing the slaughter of you, O Apep, enemy of Ra.

Get you back, retreat, and let your head [fall] on the earth. Your ears are made an end of (or, stopped up), your eyes are put out, you are annihilated. You shall not exist, images of you shall not exist, (16). your form shall not exist, You shall never more approach Ra in his two heavens, for Ra is in his two heavens, and he has made [himself] to triumph over you. Your tail shall be placed in your mouth, You shall gnaw into your own hide, and [then] You shall be hacked in pieces on the altar of the gods of (17) the Great Company who dwell in Heliopolis.

You have fallen and are overthrown; the gods have overthrown you. Their dares spring out, their flames leap forth upon you from the fire, they hiss at you from out of the fire, their faces threaten you from out of their flames, (18) they slay you with their sharp weapons of flint, they burn wounds into your winding body, and they destroy you with the slaughtering knives which they hold in their hands. The [Four] Sons of Horus destroy you, their words of power enter into you, (19) their spells take effect against you. You are cursed by their words of power on the water (?) and You are cursed by their words of power because of every evil thing which You have made at the evil moment of your power. You shall not [exist, You are] hacked to pieces.

The Sekti Boat of the gods (20). makes you to retreat, O Sebau fiend. Your accursed soul is destroyed, You are cut to pieces. You are driven away from the Divine Boat, and spells have been cast upon you. You are overthrown. The Eye of Ra eats into you. Get your back, Sebau; an end to you ! The arrows of Horus (21) are fastened in your nose. Hail, Apep is destroyed, and Ra has gained the mastery over his enemies. The Khut uraeus devours you in its name Ami ' (i.e., Flame), she eats into you, she consumes you by her words of power, (22). and by her spells. They slay you, they kill you, they cast you down, they repulse you, they have the mastery over you, they make you vomit. An end to you ! Get you back.

The Great Company of the gods who are in Anu (Heliopolis) hack you in pieces, and the great ones (23) who multiply the deadly flames of the fire tear you into shreds. You are [given over] to the flames of those who are in the mouth of the fire, and it makes an end of you, Apep, and it drives you back whensoever You wouldst come forth. The flame is against you, and it bites into your flesh, it makes a fire of you and burns up (24) your accursed soul, and fire is poured out on your bones and members. The blaze of Horus and the Eye of Ra work against you. Seth has driven his lance into your head, and You are [given over] to the Lion-god of the Fierce Eye (Maau-hes), who is the son of Bast, the Lady of Slaughter, and he is gratified with your blood. Therefore (25) is there fire upon all your paths. The goddess Pekhit wounds you, and she from whom great flames burst forth, the Lady of Slaughter, the Queen of Fire, snatches away your flesh, she destroys your accursed soul, and the flame burns you up, (26) O Apep, enemy of Ra. Those who dwell in the shrine of the Great Company of gods on the Divine Boat devour you, so that you may have no being, and may come to an end. You shall lie down in bitter sorrow, and you shall never wake up again, for Ra has overthrown you forever and forever.

You shall have no permanent abiding place in heaven.

(1) You shall not live on the earth, You shall be chopped in pieces by the Great Knife, You shall be slain again and again, and You shall fall down by the knife of the god. A net of chainwork shall be on your head, a spear shall be driven into your body, and the harpoons of Ra (2) shall fasten themselves in your person. You shall fall headlong at the time when You are doing evil with all your might, and Horus shall burn you up at the moment when his fires are hottest.

The god comes forth against the Sebau fiend, and Apep is overthrown. Your face [Apep] is laid upon the block of slaughter in the place where Ra spits, (3) and You shall be destroyed thereon for ever and ever. You shall not enjoy the pleasures of love, You shall have no male offspring, your egg shall not flourish, and the gods who came forth from the Eye of Horus shall cut you in pieces. You halt fallen, Ra-Hors-Khuti has overthrown you (4) the spear which is in his hands leaps forth against you, and his arrow[s] fly against you.

You shall cease to be, and You shall come to an end, O Apep, enemy of Ra. [Say] four times.

You shall ma se to be and your accursed Ba-soul shall cease to be.

You shall cease to be and (5) your body shall cease to be.
You shall cease to be and your children shall cease to be.
You shall cease to be and your hands shall cease to be.
You shall cease to be and your limbs shall cease to be.
You shall cease to be and your bones shall cease to be.
You shall cease to be and your words of power shall cease to be.
You shall cease to be and your mouth shall cease to be (6).
You shall cease to be and your form shall cease to be.
You shall cease to be and your attributes shall cease to be.
You shall cease to be and your creations shall cease to be.
You shall cease to be and your skin shall cease to be.
You shall cease to be and your possessions shall cease to be. (7)
You shall cease to be and your issue shall cease to be.
You shall cease to be and your substance shall cease to be.
You shall cease to be and your seat shall cease to be.
You shall cease to be and your abode shat cease to be.
You shall cease to be and your cavern shall cease to be.
You shall cease to be and your sepulchre shall I cease to be.
You shall cease to be (8) and your paths shall cease to be.
You shall cease to be and your seasons shall cease to be.
You shall cease to be and your spells shall cease to be
You shall cease to be and your entrance shall cease to be
You shall cease to be and your advance shat cease to be.
You shall cease to be (9) and your steps shall cease to be.
You shall cease to be and your motion shall cease to be.
You shall cease to be and your sitting down shall cease to be.
You shall cease to be and shall not flourish.
You shall cease to be and your body shall cease to be.
You shall cease to be, and every place wherein you wouldst be shall not exist. (10)

O Apep, enemy of Ra, perish you, perish you! Oblivion, oblivion be to your name! Your teeth shall become weak, and your spittle shall disappear. You are blinded and sightless. Fall upon your face. Be overthrown, be overthrown. (11) Be destroyed, be destroyed. An end to you, an end to you. By the knife, by the knife, cut up, cut up, dismembered, dismembered, hacked in pieces, hacked in pieces, sawn asunder, sawn asunder! Your head shall be cut off with a flint flint knife in the presence of Ra each day. The god Aker judges you, he turns back your bones. (12) Retreat You, Ra-Hero-Khuti has overthrown you.

You are given over to the god who bringeth destruction upon you, and he says: 'The spears of Horus are fixed in your skull. Your head is cut off from your neck. Your accursed soul has fallen, your accursed shadow doth not exist. You have been destroyed on the block of torture (13). Your head has been cut off and placed on your back. Get you back, Sebau fiend, You Enemy of Ra. You are hacked to pieces when You make your evil appearance. The uraeus of Horus eats you, she bites into you and is gratified in so doing, and her flame is against you, (14) her fire is against you. Get you back, Apep, with your evil foot.[269] The Company of the gods lift up their faces against them, they spit their flames into your eye. The fire is against you, the flame is deadly and it has the mastery over you. (15). It burns you up and consumes you. You are [given over] to the flame which is in its mouth, it hacks you to pieces ; turn away your eyes, says Ra. You are blinded by Horus from his divine Boat, which has the mastery over you and your face (?) and worketh your slaughter.

The knife is against you, and it destroys (16) your members. You shall not approach the Boat of the Great God, for Ra himself shall turn then back. You are [given] to the block of slaughter; your face is laid upon it. The gods who are in his shrine have overthrown you, You are overthrown and shut up, (17) and your ears are made deaf. Isis has overthrown you by her words of power; she has smashed your mouth, and carried off your ears and (10) shall never, never place her in your power. The spear of Ra goes deep into your limbs; silence is upon you. (18) Hooks tear you ; perish, live not. Isis and Nephthys overthrow you, and they join together and drive back your crocodile. Get you back, retreat; retreat, get you back. You are blinded, an end to you ; an end to you, You are blinded. Your accursed soul is destroyed ; nevermore, nevermore shall You live. (19)

The moment of your strength has departed, and the flame of the fire has snatched away power from your body. There is fire upon you, it tears your body, it burns your bones to dust. [When] the fire appears it burns up your Ba-soul, it gnaws (20) into your body. The goddess Apt-s-ur tears thm, her fire is upon your members, return to your block of slaughter. Ra has made Thoth to slay you with his words of power. You shall not approach the Boat (21) of Ra, for Ra himself shall turn you back ; he knows all the evil which You have done.

The goddess Sept (Sothis) and Anqet say: 'The flame of those who are in the south shall be against you, and it shall have the mastery over you; and they decree what shall be done unto you. The goddess Wadjet, (22) the Lady of Pe-Tep, says 'The flame of those who are in the north shall be against you, and it shall have the mastery over you' ; and she decrees what shall be done unto you. The god Aha, Lord of those who are in the west, says: 'The flame of those who are in the west shall be against you, [and it shall have the mastery over you]'; and he decrees what shall be done unto you. Sept, Lord of those who are in the east, says: 'The flame of those who are in the east shall be against you, and it shall have the mastery over you'; and he decrees what shall be done unto you. (23) You shall never have your being in any place where You [goes].

You are given over to the fire of the Eye of Ra, and behold, it has the mastery over you, and it drives forth its flame against you in its name of 'Wadget.' It eats into you in its name (24) of 'Ami'; it has the mastery over you in its name of 'Sekhet'; it sends forth flame against you in its name of 'Khut.' The flame of the fire makes an end of you, the Eye of Horus strikes you blind, it has the mastery over you, (25) it carries away your arms, and remove your legs, and showers blows upon you. Ra says : 'Evil shall be upon you!' Horus says : 'Let the slaughter of you be carried out. You are fettered, You are chained, You are overthrown. Your accursed Ba-soul shall be carried away from your shadow. (26). Your head shall be bound with chains,' or, as others say, 'your head shall be cut off. Your bones shall be crushed, your flesh shall be hacked off your limbs, your accursed Ba-soul shall be turned away from your shadow, your body is brought to nothing, You shall have no being. You are given over to the fire, You are made to lie down in death, You are cast out (27) and overthrown by the fierce attack of the two divine Uraei of Ra. The fire which comes forth from their mouths devours you.'

You have been given over to the flame of the fire which kindles in you, and burns up in you, and destroys [you].

(1) Your accursed Ba-soul is at the block of slaughter of the gods.

The great Company of the gods growl at you because of the evil things which You have done with your hands. Amen in his Apts crushes you, and he drives his horn through your body. Isis makes a decree, saying 'Your paths shall (2) be stopped,' and her son Horus shuts up your name. Tefnut says : 'The water shall raise up waves against you, and You shall be speared on the water when You appear on it. Shu shall drive his spear into you, and You shall sink to the bottom of the water, and shall never rise up again to the surface, O Apep, enemy of Ra.' (3)

Taste You [death], O Apep. [Say] four times.

Taste you [death], O all you enemies of Per-Aa (Pharaoh). Life, Strength, Health [be to him]! both from the dead and from the living.

Say the following words:
Hail, Ra. Hail, Atum. Hail, Khepera. Hail, Shu. Hail, Tefnut. Hail, Keb. (4) Hail, Nut. Hail, Osiris. Hail, Horus. Hail, Isis. Hail, Nephthys. Hail, Shu. Hail, Tefnut. Hail, Hu. Hail, Sau. Hail, Horus, Lord of Kakem (Kochome). Hail, Heka, the Ka of Ra, Per-Aa (Pharaoh) comes to you. He has set the flame against Apep. (5) He has removed the of the fiend Qettu, and has caused happiness to be in the divine Boat of Millions of Years. The hearts of the mariners of Ra. exult within his shrine, the Baiu-souls of the gods have taken up their places in his horizon, and the gods who are therein ascribe praises to him. (6) Ra is the President of Het-Mesq (the Other World), and Horus has made his appearance upon his standard.

Ra triumphs over Apep. [Say] four lines.

Per-Aa (Pharaoh) triumphs over his enemy. [Say] four times.

BOOK 8
Another Book Of Overthrowing Apep

Say the following words: O every man, O every woman, O every dead person, O every spirit whatsoever, (7). if it be that you accomplish any evil design against Per-ha (Pharaoh), the gods shall assuredly do evil to you on account thereof. Let him be regarded by you as a great god and lord of heaven. Let all his tongues (?) cry out to Nebau, when he sails over the two heavens and the earth in a full, strong breeze, (8) and Ra destroys his enemies. May he be a messenger to Anu (Heliopolis), who shall propitiate the heart of Atum and the hearts of his sovereign Chiefs, and shall make happiness to be in Anu of the South (Hermonthis), and Anu of the North (Heliopolis). Let him be regarded by you as the Abtu Fish (9) of gold which [swims] under the Boat of Ra. All the enemies of Ra shall fear him. He shall have given to him the power which is in the heart of Horus. He shall break the enemies of Ra. He shall set gladness in the heart of Horus. He shall place the steering-pole in the Divine Boat of the Mighty Heart; whilst Ra reposes (10) in his shrine he shall destroy all his enemies. The Maat Boat is strong-hearted, and the Sektet Boat is in peace, or, as others say, is in the winds of Maat (?). The goddess Heset unites herself to her Lord with cries of joy. Ra is safe-guarded, and he safe-guards the soul of (II) Per-Aa (Pharaoh), and safe-guards him, safe-guarding him against every man, and every woman, and every fiend, and every spirit whatsoever. Ra shuts every mouth which speaks any evil word whatsoever against Per-Aa; he will strike him blind [also]. He shall watch every person who would do unto him any (12) wicked or evil thing whatsoever. He shall open the mouth of Per-Aa, Life, Strength, Health [be to him] I against every man, and every woman, and every fiend, and every spirit.

Rubric: This Chapter shall be recited when Ra is on the ridge of the lake of Desdes, in order to make him prolong his life and become old. The name thereof is Book of the lord of all.

HERE ENDETH THE BOOK.

Book IX
The Names Of Apep
Which Shall Have No Existence

(14). Apep Kher em nesht. Apep the fallen, mangled

(15) Apep Kher Tui Apep the fallen, The most evil

(16) Apep Kher Hau-ber. Apep the fallen, The fierce-faced

(17) Apep Kher Hemhemti Apep the fallen, The roarer

(18). Apep Kher Qettu Apep the fallen, The Ill-disposed

(19). Apep Kher Qerner Apep the fallen, The KRNR

(20) Apep Kher Iubani Apep the fallen, TBNY

(21) Apep Kher Amam. Apep the fallen, The Devourer

(22). Apep Kher Aba-taiu. Apep the fallen, The Breaker open of Lands

(23) Apep Kher Saatet-ta. Apep the fallen, The Despoiler of Lands

(24) Apep Kher Khermuti. Apep the fallen, The Enemy

(25) Apep Kher Kenemmti. Apep the fallen, Dark One

(26). Apep Kher Sheta. Apep the fallen, Tortoise

(27). Apep Kher Serem-taui. Apep the fallen, The SRM

(28). Apep Kher Sekhem-her. Apep the fallen, Potent of Glance

(29) Apep Kher Unti.. Apep the fallen, The Wnty

(30) Apep Kher Kariu-memti(?). Apep the fallen, KRIW MNTY

(31) Apep Kher Khesef-her. Apep the fallen, Averted of Face

(32). Apep Kher Seba ent Seba. Apep the fallen, Sba of Aba

(33) Apep Kher Khak-ab.. Apep the fallen, Crooked of Heart

(34) Apep Kher Khanre . . . –. ua, or Kha Apep the fallen, KhNRI KSKHR

(35) Apep Kher Nai. Apep the fallen, the Na-Serpent

(36) Apep Kher Am. Apep the fallen, Devourer

(37) Apep Kher Turr (?). Apep the fallen, TWR

(38) Apep Kher Iubau. Apep the fallen, YB

(39). Apep Kher Uai. Apep the fallen, Evil-Minded

(40). Apep Kher Kharbutu. Apep the KhRBD,

(41). Apep Kher Sau. Apep the fallen, the broken

(42) Apep Kher Beteshu (?) Apep the fallen, the slain

(43) **Rubric** The cases for the writings shall be made of new papyrus, and [You] shall write upon them, and cast them down (44) on the fire. Than shall make [a model] of a serpent with his tail in his mouth, and a knife stuck (45) in his back, and You shall throw it down, saying Apep, Fiend, Bethet (46) And You shall do another hidden thing. Make images of the Four Enemies, having faces of [serpents] (47) bind them with ropes, and tie their hands behind them, saying Children of unsuccessful revolt! Make another [model of a (48) serpent] with the face of a lion (or, cat) and having a knife [stuck in his back saying: Hemhemti (i.e., Roarer) (49). Make another [model of a serpent] with the face of a duck and having a knife [stuck in his back], saying Aqr-wb. (50) Make another [model of a serpent], with the face of a crocodile, and having a knife [stuck in his back], saying: "Hau-na-her-her."[270] Make another (51) model of the Enemy with the face of a duck, and

having a knife [stuck in his back], saying: "Unti". Make another [model with the face of (52). a] white cat, tie [its hands] and bind a cord about it, and stick a knife [in its back], saying : Apep, Fiend. (53) Make other models of the Four Enemies, with the faces of ducks, tie their hands and their feet and bind them behind their (54) backs, and plunge knives into them, saying You are the Mesu beteshu (i.e., sons of impotent revolt).

(1) And after these things [have been performed] the words of the [following] Hymn of Praise to Ra shall be sung:

"Hail, Father, Lord of the Gods, You Chief of the Great Company of the Gods, You primeval matter (2) Whereof the gods were made, maker of men, creator of all the created things which were creased after Khepera had come into being! I am your son, your heart in truth, that strength of heart which (3) comes forth from your mysterious being. I glorify their creation before you, and words of power (4) which shall make your beneficent protection [to be with me] come forth from my mouth. I am perfect in [my] designs.

Come, Ra, look You upon me (5) with your two eyes, and be You pleased with what I have done. I have overthrown Apep for you at the moment of his greatest strength, and I have made an end to him (6). in his den. Heru-Merti[244] holds his weapon [ready] to out off the head of your Enemy, and Menhi (7) holds his great knife [ready] to cut off the heads of your Sebau fiends, and the fire devours him and flame tear open (8) his accursed Ba-soul at his block of slaughter. Your Ba-soul rejoices, your Ba-soul rejoices, and it sails over the heavens with fair winds [behind it].

Come, (9) I pray, [O Ra! and look You with your eye at what I have done to the body of Apep the enemy. He is shut up within walls, (10) his accursed body is destroyed, and it is made an end of in Aat-Peka and in your two heavens. Your cities are permanent, well- founded, and well-established, (11) and you yourself are strong (or, vigorous) and heal Your. You renew your youth; you renew your youth. You roll up into the sky, You roll up into the sky. You shine, you shine, each day. You rise up in the Divine Boat, (12) your heart is glad, that which You fashioned gives satisfaction to your heart. To Apep-Kheriu-Uamti- Nebau-her[272] (13) You cry "Away with you"! And You[273] make evil noises near the block where he is slaughtered, and he rushes round and round and breaks (14) his face.

Hail, You who come forth into the horizon and the Two Lands (i.e., Egypt) with divine strength, your heart, O Ra., rejoice each day. Apep has fallen into the fire, (15) and the flame has carried off Nekau. The heart of Amen-Ra, Lord of the Throne of the Two Lands, President of the (16) Apts,[274] rejoices, [for] his enemy has fallen beneath him.

[Say] four times

Ra has triumphed over Apep. Amen-Ra, Lord of the Throne of the Two Lands, (17) President of the Apts, has triumphed over his enemies.

Thoth, Lord of Anu (Heliopolis), has triumphed over his enemies.

Thoth, (18) who is skilled in words of power, Lord of hieroglyphic writing, has triumphed over his enemies.

HERE ENDETH THE BOOK.

Overcoming Apep
(A Personal View by Diti Morgan

Part of my day job is reading and editing books, recently I was preparing the ebook edition of Seth & The Two Ways (Morgan 2019). Reading Appendix 2 - Book(s) of Overthrowing Apep (Bremner Rhind Papyrus 3), a papyrus found in Thebes (in Upper Egypt), probably from the tomb of a priest from the Ptolemaic period, filled with the most powerful and hostile of curses. To get the editing job done, I had to read the nine books in one go. Working on these texts I noticed a strange feeling creeping over me. As I read the first two books, I felt upset, unsettled, as if the disturbing words of the text caught me off guard and were now literally directed towards me. By the time I got to book three, the heavy feeling of despair changed to something else, difficult to describe. By books three and four, I could feel a surge of energy shooting up and down my spine and I could sense a powerful circle forming around me. When I started book five, The Book of Knowing The Creation Of Ra And Of Overthrowing Apep, I could almost see the circle of power enclosing me, on all sides. I felt protected and at the same time strong and ready, but for what?

By the time I finished reading book six, I had an insight about the nature of cursing and the importance of the god Seth in the Egyptian Cosmology and its pantheons.

The ninth book vibrates the victorious rhythms of mission accomplished, the priest ferried through the most horrendous and atrocious curses, his spirit never failing, his heart never broken, his body fully charged with the primaeval power of the ancient serpent that vibrates with the secrets of creation. He is one with the Dark Lord, with the Red God, with the Black power of the North, he is ready to take on the ancient worm.

By the time I finished reading the ninth book, I felt powerful, strong, determined, and mighty. I was ready to slay a dragon.

Most of the curses and "grimoires" we are familiar with are working on a very specific psychological level – earthy and primal, to intimidate and bully a person, in the most extreme and influential ways, to make them believe they are cursed. As we know, this power is indisputable and when a person believes in something, it can be nearly impossible to argue with them or to change their minds.

This type of cursing is directed straight to the emotional centre, resonating with the lower and earthly vibrations to cause fear and upheaval in the lives of the 'victim'. On the other hand, the person who does the cursing is as much trapped in the emotional realm of aggression and intimidation as the target is.

In order to curse an awesome and primaeval power such as Apep, the priest who conducted the ritual, needed to be as strong and as powerful as Apep, probably stronger.

I have come to believe that the Book(s) of Overthrowing Apep was meant to be read and performed as one ritual without a break. Like many other Egyptian texts, the Bremner Rhind Papyrus 3 is a text that takes us on a journey of becoming. The priest or priests building up their mental and physical resilience by vibrating those hostile words, channelling the power and assimilating them into themselves, transforming those nine books of curses into a powerful and mighty weapon of protection and strength.

I mentioned above how these texts were probably found in the tomb of a priest. They were included as part of the funeral rites and preparation for the underworld or night journey. Whichever way one looks at it, one can't avoid the awareness that Apep is eternal, bornless and cannot be killed. This realisation could cause a psychological battle in the mind of the priest, leading to doubts, despair and resentment of his beliefs, and losing their ability to perform their roles properly in the temple. By turning the tables and learning the secrets powers of the curse, the priest acquires a tool of power, channelling the powers of the cursed one onto himself, freeing himself from the mundane state of existence, transforming and attuning his mind into the cosmic rhythm of the eternal.

Being equipped with such a papyrus, with such a powerful curse, in the tomb on your final journey, would be like the ultimate insurance policy against the immense forces of Apep the eternal, to protect his "soul" (Ba, Ka, Akh) on the final journey.

The Names Of Apep Which Shall Have No Existence

Book nine is like a repetitive mantra to be chanted and written on a papyrus and to be burned in the fire. In the mantra, the name of Apep is repeated twenty nine times! Each repetition is written with one of his terrible and horrific powerful characteristics, for instance - (21) Apep Kher Amam (Apep, The Fallen, The Devourer) (25) Apep Kher Kenemmti (Apep, The Fallen, The Dark One) (28) Apep Kher Sekhem-her (Apep, The Fallen, The Potent of Glance). Ostensibly it looks as if the priest is chanting and writing a very fierce curse. From my personal experience with mantra chantings, I can say that the more you repeat the same word, vowel or seed mantra, the more one can actually feel the energy gathering, charging and vibrating around and within you. You are becoming one with the rhythm, like the physical vessel of the mantra vibrations. The repetition of Apep's name is the way in which the priest channels and charges the power into himself.

According to the instructions on the Abydos Temple walls, the daily temple ritual was performed three times a day. Based on information from Temple Ritual at Abydos by Rosalie David (2016), before entering the temple, the priests had to purify themselves in the water basins, the sacred lake or any other convenient pure water source. Weapons must be left outside the temple and only then can they approach the shrine door.

They open that door while saying: "I remove the finger of Seth from the Eye of Horus" and step into the shrine and look at the God, saying whatever comes into their mind as a greeting. Perhaps something like this: "Be not unaware of me (Ra), If you know me, I will know you". They

move into the shrine and stand before the altar and clean away any debris, tidy the place, light the fire and anointed all the deities statues and figurines with the daily perfume and made an offering of food etc saying : "Hetep di nesew asir neb djedu neter Aa neb Abdu" Which was the standard offering formula in Egyptian rites and can be adapted to any deity. Once all this was done, the priest positioned himself in front of the offering table and started to reading the Book(s) of Overthrowing Apep, building up the energy to the triumphant crescendo of the chanting the words of book nine - The Names Of Apep Which Shall Have No Existence, finishing the rite by throwing the papyrus into the purifying flames of the temple fire.

One can almost see the rite taking place, almost feel the vibrations of the chants resonating within the temple. Now imagine how would it feels to visit that temple when the ritual of Overthrowing Apep has been performed a myriad times, since the Middle Kingdom when its existence was first recorded. For the uninitiated and the laymen, the temples in which this rite has been regularly performed must have been the most forbidding and eerie of places, haunted by wild eyed priests. For the cult and its initiates, this was a place of power, a place to immerse yourself and to be charged with the endless baraka of the eternal one.

The Sethian myth is established on the sacred triad: Ra, Seth & Apophis, none could exist without the others. It is the battle-dance of creation, one dies, another must kill and one must shine.

Notes

1. I've used two principal sources
   Michael Aquino (2009) *The Church of Satan*, ebook 6th edition http://www.xeper.org/maquino.
   Michael Aquino (2010) *The Temple of Set*, ebook http://www.xeper.org/maquino
2. Te Velde (1977 [1967]) : 3) *Seth, God of Confusion: A study of his role in Egyptian Mythology and Religion*, Brill, for summary of available forms of the god's name.
3. Kenneth Grant (1972) *The Magical Revival*, Muller, London : 47 & Glossary. American Edition Weisers (1973). Library of Congress also has a copy of UK edition.
4. Gerald Massey (1907), *Ancient Egypt The Light Of The World A Work Of Reclamation And Restitution* In Twelve Books, : 833
5. Michael Aquino, *op cit* (2010 : 188)
6. Kenneth Grant & John Symonds (1972) *The Magical Record of the Beast 666* (Duckworth, London) : x. John Symonds makes this connection although it's a fair assumption that it was Kenneth Grant's idea.
7. Kenneth Grant, (1973) *Aleister Crowley and the Hidden God* (Muller, London)
8. Michael Aquino (2010) loc cit
9. Michael Aquino (2010) loc cit. The page reference is to Aleister Crowley (1973) Magick, edited by John Symonds and Kenneth Grant, London, RKP.
10. Eg The Brotherhood of SeTh (TBOS) http://www.ashejournal.com/tbos/history.html (accessed 23/5/2012) circa 1984-1995. The Companions of Seth (ComSet) http://www.ombos.co.uk
11. Michael Aquino (2010) loc cit, his authority S G F Brandon (1969) *Religions in Ancient History* NY Charles Scribner : 102-132. Although one needs to know if the word was ever used
12. Plutarch's *de Iside et Osiride*, translated b J Gwyn Griffiths (Cardiff, University of Wales Press 1970) - Hereafter referred to as Plutarch IAO
13. J Dieleman (2005) *Priests, Tongues, and Rites: The London-Leiden Magical Manuscripts and Translation in Egyptian Ritual (100-300 CE)*, Brill

14 *The Theogony of Hesiod*, translated by Hugh G. Evelyn-White, [1914]
15 Gwyn Griffiths (1970 : 121/2f)
16 Plutarch IAO. 27d
17 Herodotus (2.144)
18 Gwyn Griffiths (1960) *Hermes* 88 374ff.
19 Plutarch IAO 26b p157
20 Plutarch IAO. 30e.
21 Gardiner, A.H. (1935) Hieratic Papyri in the British Museum (HPIBM) series III vol 1, text, discussed in Morgan, M (2011) *Supernatural Assault In Ancient Egypt*, Mandrake pp55sq
22 ibid
23 Rita Lucarelli "The Donkey in the Graeco-Egyptian Papyris" in Crippa, Sabina & Emanuele M Ciampini Langiages, *Objects and the Transmission of the Rituals : An Interdisciplinary Analysis on Ritual Practices in the Graeco-Egytian Papyri (PGM)* p 89-103 (p 91)
24 Plutarch IAO. 50d
25 H C Youtie "Heidelberg Festival Papyrus" in *Studies in honor of A C Johnson : Roman Economic & Social History* p178-208
26 A Lajtar, *Journal of Juristic Papyrology* 21 pp53-70 quoted in David Frankfurter *Religion in Roman Egypt* Princeton 1998 (p64)
27 Eugene Cruz-Uribe "Sth Aa Phty 'Seth: god of Power and Might" JARCE 45 (2009) pp201-226
28 Inscription 10 IV 8-10 = Vandier *Mo'alla* 220-224 quoted in P I Kousoulis PhD "Magic and Religion as a Performative Theological Unity: The Apotropaic 'Ritual of Overthrowing Apophis' ", University of Liverpool 1999 (19)
29 K Kousoulis "Magic and Religion as a Performative Theological Unity: The Apoptropaic 'Ritual of Overthrowning Apophis" PhD Thesis, Liverpool 1999 p41 see also Naii snake "Seed of Shu" (p41) and sA-tA "son of Earth"
30 Eugene Cruz-Uribe "Sth Aa Phty 'Seth: God of Power and Might' " *JARCE* 45 (2009) pp 201-226
31 J Dieleman *Priests, Tongues, and Rites: The London-Leiden Magical Manuscripts and Translation in Egyptian Ritual (100-300 CE)*, Brill 2005 (p 132).
    Source Yavn Koenig Magie et magiciens dans l'Egypt ancienne [Paris 1994) 147-149] This is from a 4th century mss, Urk VI S Schott Bucher und Spruche gegen den gott Seth 2 vols (Leipzig 1929-1939) translated by Posenen: "Liez, liez ? vous préposés

aux ordres. Empoignez, empoignez, vous préposés aux cordons: votre ligoté est ce vil ennemi, Seth, fils de Nout, et ses acolytes, qui a fait le mal, qui a caus la souffrance, qui a comploté la souffrance et l'injustice. L'aîné qui a été désigné pour régner avant de venir au monde, ne lui a pas échappé. I s'est moqué de l'order du maître universel, de ce qu'avant dit celui qui a créé ce qui existe. Il a créé le mal avant de venir au monde, ayant suscité le désordre avant que son non n'existe. Faites exister le mal pour celui qui l'a suscité."

32   J Dieleman *Priests, Tongues, and Rites: The London-Leiden Magical Manuscripts and Translation in Egyptian Ritual (100-300 CE)*, Brill 2005 (p 132)

33   Discussed in Morgan, M, *Supernatural Assault in Ancient Egypt*, Mandrake pp 149

34   CT 1 229 g 230 a,b (quoted on Te Velde *Seth God of Confusion* (1967 (Rev 1977))

35   PyrT 972a-c quoted in Gwyn Griffiths *The Origins of the Cult of Osiris* 1966

36   The Bremner-Rhind Pap "The Book of Overthrowing 'Apep" RD Faulkner, JEA Vol 23 No 2 (December 1937) pp 166-185) . Hieratic Papyri in the BM, series 3 edited by Gardiner (Bremner Rhind 10188)
Contains Book of Overcoming Apopis – long set of spells from beginning of Middle Kingdom? [383.2 Lon G [Text, La Fol] but seems to be bound as one volume.]
Verse 10

37   Peals of thunder (?).

38   Sister of Apep – sp111, 144-6 in L Borghouts *Ancient Egyptian Magical Texts* (Brill 1978).

39   BD (39) see J Borghouts *BOTD 39 From Shouting to Structure* Harrassowitz p40. 26.16

40   AKHET (INUNDATION) SECOND MONTH, DAY 25 "it is the day of finding the children of Apophis, wrapped in the archiac way on their sides."

41   There is another, extraordinary expression that occurs in a long cup divination from the PGM XIV 239-295 line 263-265, for moon god Khonsu: translation from F Li Griffith & H Thompson The Demotic Magical Papyrus of London and Leiden 3 vols (london Grevel 1904). Apophis appears in this spell under the name Wonte ie Pessiwonte "daughters of Wonte" & this is

identified as a name of Apophis in the great lexicon compiled by Erman & - where the name has the Apophis serpent as its determinative:

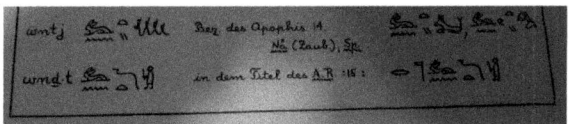

see also PGM XIII line 264: "Stay, for you are Aphyphis" (Apophis) - spell to kill a snake

42 ibid
43 I.e., Karnak, the Northern Apt, and Luxor, the Southern Apt
44 The written part of the spell is itself consider the epitome and referred to as "It is a secret book of the House of Life which none see, the secret book of overcoming Apep" trans Faulkner *JEA* 24 :page 42 (29, 17)
45 The khesau herb, (Bryony) of which there were several varieties, was much used in medicine.
46 Or perhaps, "mixed with filth."
47 Peals of thunder (?).
48 [Curse from Bremner-Rhind
"If any persons whatsoever, from any country whatsoever, whether they be Nubians Or Kushites or Syrian, shall remove this book, or carry it away, or steal it, offering shall never be made to their persons, they shall never bathe in cool water, they shall never sniff the breeze, neither son nor daughter shall rise from their seed, their memories shall never be preserved by means of children, and they shall never behold the light! On the other hand, if any person whatsoever shall see this book, and recite it for the stablishing of my Ka and my name among the favoured ones, the same shall be done for him after his death in recompense for what he hath done for me." Hieratic Pap in BM III p x)
[example of Ptolemaic ritual]
BM 10081 has a ritual in which one slays a bird and a fish while burning on a fire of bryony a wax image of Seth place in a fish skin" Ritner p210
49 Coffin Text II [160], 375 b ff. (= BD 108 Budge 218, 12) quoted and discussed in J F Borghouts "The Evil Eye of Apopis, JEA Vol 59 (Aug 1973) pp 114-150 p114 .
50 P I Kousoulis PhD "Magic and Religion as a Performative

Theological Unity: The Apotropaic 'Ritual of Overthrowing Apophis' ", University of Liverpool 1999 (19)
51 P ChesterBeatty VII, RT 5/2-5 Other versions of similar spell found in same Papyrus. They allude to the notorious incident described in PchesterBeatty XI (BM 10692) "The Story of Isis & Ra with other magical Spells . pp116-118. *Hieratic Papyri in the British Museum* 3rd series, Chester Beatty Gift 1935 edited by Alan Gardiner.
52 IAO 38b
53 IAO 14e
54 IAO 39e
55 Richard Parker *The Calendars of Ancient Egypt* Chicago 1950
56 IAO 40a-b
57 J F Borghouts *Ancient Egyptian Magical Texts*, Brill 1979 spell 23 & fn 59 & 61
58 PT Spell 247 J P Allen _The Ancient Egyptian Pyramid Texts_ 2nd edition sbl 2015 . 45. Possibly also sp 311 "I will blow away the deluge for you, drive away the clouds for you, and break up the hail for you."
59 Frank Goddio & Aurelia Masson-Berghoff *Sunken Cities: Egypt's Lost Worlds*, BM 2016
60 IAO 42d
61 One deben of solid measure is approx 91grammes
62 D H Aufrère, Encyclopéedie religieuse de l;universe véegétal – Croyances phytoreligieuses de l;Égypte ancinne ed Sidney Aufrere "Parfums et onguent liturgigues. Presentation des recettes d'Edfou" p213-263 (243-246) Montpellier 2005 vol 3 quoted in F Goddio Sunken Cities 2017
63 D Meeks *Masked God, Headless God* CNRS 1991 Unauthorised translation by Len Warner, NY on Scribd – See E Chassinat, Le mystere d'Osiris au Mois de Khoiak II Caire 1968 – p 596
64 IAO 44f
65 IAO 44a
66 Gardiner, Papyrus Chester Beatty I, pp 8-26 & pls 1-16
67 P Boylan *Thoth The Hermes of Egypt* OUP 1922 (p30sq)
68 See *Conflict* p124ff for native source. Seth as power of darkness]
69 *Book Of The Dead* 39.8, trans TG Allen, Chicago 1974. Stephen Quirke 2013 has it as "clears". Ink sA stS ad Xnnwt kri – Xnn (vb) mean disturb, interfere or command, kri = storm
70 pAmum 3,8 Guglielmi & Buroūh 1997 : 120,147. Discussed in

Rosalie David, *Temple Ritual at Abydos* 1973: See also PT Mercer 48a "Osiris, take to thy self the finger of Set, which causes the white eye of Horus to see."

71 IAO 45b
72 Randy Conner Personal Communication
73 *Sethian Gnosticism & the Platonic Tradition* John Douglas Turner
74 IAO 48c
75 IAO 49c
76 Gardiner, A H (1935), *Hieratic Papyri in the British Museum (HPIBM) series III* vol 1 text. Quoted in Chapter on Egyptian Psychology in (Morgan *Supernatural Assault in Ancient Egypt* pp55-81)
77 IAO 55e
78 W M Flinders Petrie, Koptos, London 1896 p 22
79 IAO 367d
80 IAO 62b.
81 IAO 63d.
82 IAO 64a
83 *Metamorphoses 5. 139 ff (trans. Melville) (Roman epic C1st B.C. to C1st A.D.)*
84 IAO 72e-f
85 IAO 73c-d
86 NKTK BN in Demotic. NKTK meaning sleep, which I would say was a synonym for the evil dreams discussed at length in Szpakowska, Kasia (2003) *Behind Closed Eyes: dreams and nightmares in Ancient Egypt*, Wales. The most commonly used word for dream was rsw.t, a noun with no verbal form - signifying that a dream was a concrete vision rather than an activity of the sleeper.
87 Dieleman, Jacco (2005) *Priests, Tongues and Rites - the London-Leiden Magical Manuscripts and Translation in Egyptian Ritual* (100-300CE), Brill. pp130-135
88 IAO 73d-3
89 See PGM XIII, The Unique or 8th Book of Moses, fn 43
90 Denderah -Osiris Chapel on north terrace (Marriette IV pls 78 & 79).
    Edfu, Chamber on west (south) stairs of main temple (Chassinat I pp 511-512). Philae, pronaos of Isis temple (Berlin Photos ie H Junker & H Schafer Berliner Photos des preussischen

Expeditdition 1908-10 Agyptologische Microfische Archive3 (Weisbaden 1975) photos 1358-1364)
91 J Capart (1940-) Fouilles D'el Kab executee par la fondation Egyptoloqoque Reine Elisabeth, Parc du Cinquantenaire a Bruxelles 2 vols
92 Jean Capart, "Les Sept Paroles de Nekhabit" *Chronique d'Egypt* N0 29, 1940
93 Plutarch IAO 73.
94 Southgate, Minoo (translator) (1978). *Iskandarnamah : a Persian medieval Alexander-romance*. New York: Columbia Univ. Press.
95 Aquino 2009 : 624 "A Grotto is an autocracy not a democracy"; also Michael Aquino "That Other Black Order" *The Cloven Hoof* IV-4 1972: 611sq "There is nothing in the Nazi philosophy that conflicts with the basic desires of the human personality."
96 Aquino (2009: 102) and need to reserve secrets from initiated. But also essay: L Dale Seago "The Implications of Elitism", Aquino 2010 appendix 38 " "I seek my elect and none other, .. and I think not of those who think not of me" BOCFBN. "In dealings with those outside the temple it may at times require the will to be coldly and utterly ruthless." "In the words of Set spoken at the first conclave, 'Ye are alien to mankind".
97 Michael A Aquino *The Temple Of Set* Draft 11 edition 2010 p298
98 Ibid p299
99 See Zeena La Vey preface to Anton LaVey, The Satanic Witch (formerly: The Compleate Witch) retitled, pii (Feral House 2002) "a guide to selective breeding, a manual of eugenics- the lost science of preserving the able-bodied and able-minded while controlling the surplus population
100 Michael A Aquino *The Church of Satan* 6th edition 2009: 41
101 MA COS : 28 "Indulgence instead of Abstinence" is from the opening manifesto of Anton La Vey (?) The Satanic Bible.
102 MA COS fn p 99. Admits that a large section of Anton LaVeys Satanic Bible is lifted from an earlier political track entitled "Might Is Right". The Loompanics reprint of this obscure text sported an new preface by Lavey and a controversial "Neo-Nazi" cover.
103 "The four Abremelin princes Satan, Lucifer, Belial and Leviathan – were accorded summer, spring, autumn and winter respectively. The magic year was begun in December with the Winter Solstice on the 22nd. The month was dedicated to Set as Lord

of the Wasteland." Aquino (2009 : 68)
104 Aquino (2009) : 68
105 Aquino (2009) : 111
106 Mogg Morgan *The Ritual Year in Ancient Egypt.* (2011) : 40
107 Te Velde, loc cit p 74
108 *JEA* 55 (1969) p 226-277
109 Authoring the entry on Seth, in prestigious reference work Lexikon
110 Aquino (2009 : 334)
111 Aquino (2010 : 387sq)
112 "Solar eclipse of 1207 BCE helps to date pharaohs" Colin Humphreys Graeme Waddington *Astronomy & Geophysics*, Volume 58, Issue 5, 1 October 2017, Pages 5.39–5.42, https://doi.org/10.1093/astrogeo/atx178 Published: 01 October 2017
113 Aquino (2009 : 389)
114 Te Velde himself is not immune to the "neo-pagan" sensibilities of the 1960s. His monograph exhibits a knowledge of Voodoo & Tantrism, he compares Seth to Ghede–divine joker but also god of death and it is not impossible he may read news reports of Satanism in America etc.
115 To further emphasise the importance of Te Velde to the neo-pagan movement, consider that a hard cover pirated edition was produced w/jacket but no publisher information. Rumours circulated back in the late 80s that this was secretly published by Skoob Books but no confirmation on that.
116 Mark Lehner (1997) *The Complete Pyramids*, Thames & Hudson.
117 Faulkner "The God Setekh in the Pyramid Texts" in *Ancient Egypt* March 1925, 5ff quoted in J G Griffiths, (1960 : 16-17)
118 Percy E Newberry "The Set Rebellion of the 2nd Dynasty" in *Ancient Egypt* 1922 211-225
119 Crowley *Liber Al* I.60
120 For possible devotees version of same ideology see :from the New Kingdom, The *Tale of Two Brothers* (Papyrus d'Orbiney / Papyrus BM 10183) which appears to be a version of same constellation of myths but told from the point of view of followers of Seth rather than Osiris.
121 Te Velde (1960 : 138) At Abydos the name of war god Monthu seems to have been substituted for Seth perhaps in the manner of an unspoken understanding. Other code words are also used. There is also some indication that in theology there is some

esential identity betwen Osiris and Seth indicated by enigmatic writing of name Set with hieropglyphs of Osiris (sh) and Isis (T). (p132fn).
122 Aquino (2009 : 28)
123 Te Velde (1960 : 74)
124 Gwyn Griffiths. IAO commentary p.421
125 IAO 32e
126 IAO 33a
127 Barry Kemp (2006) *Ancient Egypt: Anatomy of a Civilisation* NY p.61sq
128 Scorpion King Macehead, c. 3100-3000 BCE, Ashmolean Museum, Oxford
129 Te Velde (1967 : 11) quoting W B Emery (1961) *Archaic Egypt*, Harmondsworth
130 Henry Frankfort (1948 :22) *Kingship & the Gods* quoted in Griffiths (1960). "... the oldest political institution in Mesopotamia was the assembly of all free men, they left power to deal with current matters in the hands of a group of elders; and that in times of emergency they chose a 'king' to take charge for a limited period." p 215 on primitive democracy
131 Te Velde (1967 : 11) Such a theory is too simplistic, asks, how can you rule out Seth as already malign but also friendly (wohltuend) – ie even predynastic Seth might be quite a complex god. The first un-contentious Seth animal is found on the Scorpion Mace
132 Te Velde (1967 : 78)
133 Urkunden mythologische (mythological documents) , published and translated by S Schott and known from two papyrus copies in the Louvre and British Museum, the latter made during the rein of pharaoh Nechanebo I . Urk VI 7, 13-21 discussed by E Drioton, *Pages d'Egyptologie* , essay on Egyptian theatre p 322 and quoted in Te Velde p151
134 See Gwyn Griffith review in JEA
135 Te Velde (1967 : 7)
136 Te Velde (1967 : 7)
137 See Seth animal at Beni Hassan (Te Velde 1967 : 23)
138 Kaper, Olaf E. (2003) *The Egyptian god Tutu : a study of the sphinx-god and master of demons with a corpus of monuments* (Peeters)
139 Examples: Hindu : Gandhava; Egyptian Ka;
140 Te Velde (1967 : 24)

141 Aquino (2010 : 97) "contrast to the harmony of the cosmos ... strengthing human instinct etc"
142 E L Baumgartel (1947& 1960) *Cultures of Prehistoric Egypt* & (1970 : 124) *Naqada Excavation: A Supplement*
143 Op cit p33. Seth as Friend and Enemy of H Te Velde thesis of birth of Seth (on third intercalary day) as birth of disorder because disturbs the neat sequence of primary couples – [feminist might this whole myth as of the patriarchal age – hence there is room for another interpretation]
144 R Shumann Antelme & Stéphane Rossini *Secrets d'Hathor* Translated as *Sacred Sexuality in Ancient Egypt*, Inner Traditions
145 The grabbing of tentacles again may not be aggression as such but a remnant of the original unity. (p 39). Earlier research would have missed it because these section left in Latin. The idea of historical war does not fit with homosexual incident/primary as description of the primary unity. [?] p.39)
Downplays the military aspect of the myth – does not think the Egyptian saw it that way, despite iconography of Edfu (40). If really a war, why are not more of the gods involved and why "theft of testicles".
146 Te Velde (1967 : 25) For Seth as death god also consider Osiris myth.
147 PcairoCCG 58040 quoted in Richard Parkinson & Max Carocci & Kate Smith, (2003) A Little Gay History, Desire & Diversity, across the World BM Books 2003
148 Aquino (2010 : 577)
149 Te Velde (1967 : 55)
150 Anton Szandor LaVey (1969) *The Satanic Bible* "Satan represents indulgence, instead of abstinence", 1st of the 9 Satanic Statements
151 Seth and connection with abortion [seen as bad thing?] Te Velde 1967 : 30
152 "Son of Nuit" – never a child god (that we know) so is really about his mother "complex" rather than mother/son paring.
153 Te Velde (1967 : 28)
154 R Radin *The Trickster*, with commentaries by K Kerenyi & C G Jung London 1956 p 185 quoted in Te Velde (1967 : 56)
155 Worshipped as "spirit of disorder", as the lord of the unbridled forces innature and civilization. Te Velde (1967 : 56)
156 Te Velde (1967 : 123)

157 Te Velde (1967 : 123) A classic example of the scene is found on the 21st dynasty (ie 1113-949BCE) Papyus of Her-Uben B which is perhaps a counter example. . A Piankoff, *Egyptian texts and Representations*, Vol 3 *Mythological Papyri* (Bollingen 1957) Same goes for the New Kingdom, ie Ramesside innovation of naming one of the army battalions after the gods Amun, Re, Ptah & Seth (TV p126)
158 Aquino 2010 p 23.
159 Aquino 2010 p 26
160 Gareth Medway (2001) *Lure of the sinister : the unnatural history of Satanism*, New York University Press
161 *Stanford Encyclopaedia of Philosophy* (online) "Postmodernism", *First published Fri Sep 30, 2005*
162 Stephen Flowers (1995 : 14) *Hermetic magick*. Weiser
163 "Powers of order, the Gods are born (if they are not in the long run Ur of Gods and thus again categories of the chaos), and are mortal: Osiris will die and be reborn, the sun God and the stars daily are the new born, after Nut swallowed and/or. after those that richly the dead through-changed and tapered themselves there. Their " immortality" that of the cosmic cycle is by death and again birth. Nowhere however is whole of birth and death apophis talks, he is simply there, as God-dislike the elementary natures of the fairy tales, he and all this stand outside of this cycle." Hornung "Chaotische Bereiche in der geordneten welt" ZAS 81 1956 p 28-32)`
164 David Frankfurter (1998) *Religion in Roman Egypt : assimilation and resistance*
165 Donald B. Redford, (ed) (2001 : 599) *Oxford Encyclopedia of Ancient Egypt*.
166 John Baines (1996 : 360) "Conceptualising egyptian representations of society and ethnicity" *The study of the ancient Near East in 21st Century: William Foxwell Albright Centennial Conference* edited by Jerrold S. Cooper and Glenn M. Schwarez. p360
167 Alan Gardiner (1932) *Late Egyptian Stories*, Bruxelles
168 Camilla de Biase-Dyson (2013 : 193-230) *Foreigners and Egyptians in the Late Egyptian Stories* , Brill. Seth used to cloak foreign deities – the Hiksos probably did worship Baal, but this was a painful time for native Egyptians. Later as Asiatic influence increased – Seth-Baal of Cananites was depicted same way.
169 Te Velde (1967 : 117)

170 Te Velde (1967 : 118)
171 Assuming Nagada, just a few kilometres north but similar in geography to Luxor, really is a border town. It must be said some of this thesis about Seth the foreigner relies on I Te Velde typifying of Nagada as a "frontier" town also requires seeing Ombos/Nagada as a "frontier" town? (SGOC p 116): "Ombos or Nwbt means "gold town". From the name alone, without regard to its location, one might deduce that this town was in contact with the gold mines in the Eastern desert." Which would be across the river, via the enormous settlement of Quft (Koptos)? One might qestions whether Ombos much more "frontier" than the villages of the west bank at Luxor?
172 Te Velde (1967 : 118)
173 Baines (1996 : 360)
174 Aquino (2010 : 203)
175 Te Velde (1967 : 66) In last millenium bc contact with asiatics became increasingly unfavourable – and those with dealings with foreign lands – ie soldiers might feel the pinch along with the cultof Seth. The "verfemung" (outlawing) hornung used the amduat line – where confederates are repulsed – to 18th Dyn and Hyksos
Te Velde (1967 : 140fn) for Asiatic period sources – increasingly rare though he conveniently excludes PGM as outside the scope of the study.
176 Te Velde (1967 : 59) After New Kingdom reconciliation seem impossible and Seth demonic nature is the common view
177 Te Velde (1967 : 68) The origins of anti-Semitism in Egypt. hatred of semites, associated then with Seth.
Seth become scapegoat for the decline. Exceptions Antyweh, 10th nome where Horus-Seth was celebrated until late period p 89 (Kees, H. (n.d.). Seth : ägyptischer Gott. Stuttgart: J.B. Metzlersche)
Long section goes back to Peribsen and so-called Seth rebellion – which he does not accept but agrees there was a renewed interest in Seth reconciled with Horus .
178 Manetho, English translation by W G Waddell (1940 : 131)
179 The "Potter's Oracle" (Rainer Papyrus, c.220 B.C., and / or c.130 B.C.) accessed at http://www.anchist.mq.edu.au/222/222weekly.htm
180 Aquino (2010 : 180)

181 The relegation of Seth to the sky parallels fate of his mother, the earth left to Horus and man. Amun Ra does the dividing. The division of the lands is cosmological rather than political – this is proved by the crown of lower Egypt maybe also this may reflect the geo-politics of upper and lower Egypt

182 Griffiths (1960) *The Conflict of Horus & Seth: a study in an ancient mythology from Egyptian and Classical sources,*

183 Edmonds, Radcliffe (2003) 'At the Seizure of the Moon: the absence of the moon in the Mithras Liturgy' in *Prayer, Magick, and the Stars in the Ancient and Late Antique World*, Edited by Noegel, Walker & Wheeler, Pennsylvania State University Press. isure of the Moon"

184 Te Velde (1967 : 60) The separating of Horus & Seth is equalled to setting a boundary between the cosmos and the chaos surrounding it like a flood. The Egyptians link all sorts of other distinctions to this dichotomy.

185 Ph Derchain: mythes et dieux lunaires en Egypt. Te Velde (1967 : 43q) follows his theory as of Contendings as lunar story. Ritual of filling eye take place on 6th rather than 15 day. Light (eye) & sexuality (testicles) are elsewhere seen as antagonistic principle – as in inner illumination v sexuality etc. (although Egyptian would not see sexuality as degenerative). The reasons may be different but the connection between light and semen is there, perhaps "Gods and the world" although Horus emerges as leader. "We see neither necessity nor a decisive reason for tracing the religious symbolism of the eye and testicle to blinding and emasculation during acts of war between prehistoric Egyptians. Eye and testicles form a stock pair of symbol, an give the impression of stemming from a single, grandiose religious conception, This would also imply that the contrast between Horus and Seth might be primary, and not a secondary historical-political development or a commixture of a separate Horus religion and a separate Seth religion." p53

186 Te Velde (1967 : 112)

187 Te Velde (1967 : 94)

188 Book of the Dead 17 quoted in Te Velde

189 Te Velde (1967 : 111)

190 Te Velde (1967 : 114)

191 Wilkinson on pallacides see his Ancient Egyptians vol I p 203 – "The remarkable example of the perverted meaning of a

religious custom, by the ignorance of the Greeks and Roman writers."
192 Strabo, Geography 17.46 translated by Jones 1959 [1932] : 125
193 B Lesko "Women and Religion in Ancient Egypt" in Diotima http://www/stao.org
194 Stephanie Budin (2008) Myth of Sacred Prostitution in Antiquity, Cambridge jii 45 b
195 Gay Robins (1983) "God's Wife of Amun in the 18th Dynasty" in Images of Women in Antiquity edited by Averil Cameron & Amelie Kuhrt
196 Schumann-Antelme, R., & Rossini, S. (1999). Les secrets d'Hathor : Amour, érotisme et sexualité dans l'Égypte pharaonique (Champollion). Paris: Éditions du Rocher.

Schumann-Antelme, R., & Rossini, S. (2001 : 13). Sacred sexuality in ancient Egypt : The erotic secrets of the forbidden Papyrus : A look at the unique role of Hathor, the goddess of love. Rochester, Vt.: Inner Traditions.
197 Richard Jasnow & Mark Smith "As for those who have called me evil, Mut will Call them Evil" Origiastic Cultic behaviour and its Critics in Ancient Egypt" Encoria Zeitschrift fur Demotistik and Koptologue Band 32, 2001/2011 : 25
198 Darnell, J. (1995). Hathor Returns to Medamûd. Studien Zur Altägyptischen Kultur, 22, 47-94.
199 Ryholt, K. (1997). The Carlsberg Papyrus Collection. Copenhagen: Carsten Niebuhr Institute, University of Copehagen. (quoted in Mark Smith Encoria fn88)
200 Montserrat, D. (1996). Sex and society in Græco-Roman Egypt. London: Kegan Paul International. -p 163-179 & 126-128
201 Richard Parkinson Voices from *Ancient Egypt: An anthology of Middle Kingdom Writings*, Oaklahoma 1991 (p120 (42)
202 Plutarch, Tatum, W. Jeffrey, Pelling, C. B. R., & Scott-Kilvert, Ian. (2013). The rise of Rome : Twelve lives by Plutarch : Romulus, Numa, Publicola, Coriolanus, Camillus, Fabius Maximus, Marcellus, Aratus, Philopoemen, Titus Flamininus, Elder Cato, Aemilius Paullus (Revised ed.). London. Numa IV,4
203 pChester B III (BM10683) Pcarlsberg XIII A Voltern, Demotische Traumdeutung, Copenhagan 1942.
204 Crum (1905) 382-3 (Crum (1905) 382-3 BM mss 919 (Boharic Lower Egyptian dialect Add. 14,740A fol 19 – Parchment; a

complete leaf, torn across the middle,. The text, in one column divine into paragraphs, is written in 36 lines of an even, square hand (cf Hyvernat pl xxxiii, xl 1) Initials and letter Phi have red dots; stops in red)

205 French Alchemist, independent scholar of Egyptology and also founder of esoteric right-wing group called *Affranchis*, (the vigilantes)
206 Aquino (2010 : 216) – commenting on the notorious Liber Al II vers 21sq.
207 Aquino (2009 : 298)
208 Aquino (2009 : 243)
209 Karnak, the Northern Apt, and Luxor, the Southern Apt
210 Literally, "in life in death."
211 The boat in which Ra travelled from midnight till noon.
212 The boat in which Ra travelled from noon till midnight.
213 The khesau herb, (Bryony) of which there were several varieties, was much used in medicine.
214 Or perhaps, "mixed with filth."
215 3 Peals of thunder (?).
216 Portions of his body
217 Their names were: Kestha, Hapi, Tuamutef and Qeblasennuf
218 This staff was made of iron, and had at one end a fork, with a strap, in which the captive, or prisoner, was made to place his neck. The captor, taking the other end of the staff in his hand, drove his prisoner before him.
219 Or Sekhmet "Mighty one"
220 A play on the words set "to crush," and set " fire."
221 A play on the words apt,"to judge," and the first portion of the name of Apt-s ur
222 Raise you up from the dead
223 Literally " face."
224 There is a play on the word inert," desire," and the name Mert."
225 The Turtle-fiend
226 The Apt of the North, the modern Karnak, and the Apt of the South, the modern Luxor.
227 Ptah (to the] south of his wall a form of Ptah worshipped at Memphis.
228 Or Temu, a solar god of Heliopolis
229 The "city of the Eight Gods," who formed the Ogdoad of Thoth, the Hermopolis of the Greeks.

230 A consort of Temu, and mother of Shu and Tefnut
231 A district of the Heliopolitan nome
232 Horus in the womb.
233 The Kochome of the Greeks.
234 A form of Hathor.
235 A very ancient god of Upper Egypt
237 Temam = the piercer, a title of Horus as the piercer of Set.
238 A famous shrine of Amen in the seventeenth nome of Lower Egypt (Diospolites).
239 The modern Asyut.
240 Heru-Merti, or Horus as a solar and lunar god.
241 A city in the Eastern Delta
242 Horus, uniter of the Two Lands
243 Pe-Tep, a double city in the Delta, the Buto of the Greeks
244 Horus the Elder, the "Old Horus", the Haroeris of the Greeks.
245 Great One of worth of power, or spells.
246 Horus the Elder.
247 The sky. When Shu raised up Nut, the female counterpare of Reb, from Keb, the light of the sun was able to fall on the earth, and the first day dawned. '
248 Kpr – meaning shapes or forms, created things
249 Or, I woke them up from a state of inactivity.
250 The celestial ocean which formed the source of the Nile on earth.
251 Light, or air.
252 Faulkner says "fist"
253 The personification of moisture.
254 The sun...
255 Or, I restored its splendour
256 Literally bushes ; the light clouds were regarded as the, fleecy eyelashes of the sun
257 The hearts of the fiends.
258 The goddess Uatchit speaks.
259 A play on the name of the goddess Uatchit.
260 Or, she causeth his tongue to be slit.
261 I.e., men and women.
262 Literally you.
263 Room for his forefeet to stand in.
264 No Trees or bushes
265 I.e., the Sun and Moon.

266 The henti were two periods of time, each of which contained sixty years; here 'Jena means indefinite time.
267 Or, hand.
268 Bushes and serpents are names given to the light clouds and to the long, heavy clouds which hide or obscure the sun at sunrise and in the early morning.
269 Or perhaps, my Eye meditated upon.
270 Words of power
271 "Retreat, get back, [fall down] upon (your) face !"
272 Horus of the two eyes.
273 All names of Apep.
274 Or He
275 Luxor and Karnak.

Index

A

Aa pehti, "great of strength" 96, 104, 156
Abortion 120, 156
Abraham 84
Abramelin 123
Abrasax 12
Abtu 263
Abydos 26
African 70
Afterlife 185
Agathon Daemon 146, 147, 172
Ai 184, 188
Air
  Empty 79
Aker 240
Akh-soul 243
Akhenaten 61, 127
Akhet 44
Akhw 59
  Demon 58
Alexander
  IV of Macedon 40
  Romance 115
Algol 148
Alt-Right 167
Amarna 141
America 120
Animals 76
Anti-Semitism 169
Antinomian 196
Anu (Heliopolis) 256
Anubis 56
Apep
  38, 40, 46, 144, 157, 159, 216–264, 251
  Names Of 265
Aphrodite 17, 122
Apophis 71, 144, 152, 153, 166

Apophis (King) 130
  Quarrel of 166
Aquarius 214
Aquino, Michael 14, 117, 124, 161, 168
Arabic magick 92
Aries 209
Arrow 96
Asiatics 165
Assault 42
Astrology 147, 148
Astronomy 72
Atlantis 60
Atum 233
Avaris 60

B

Ba-soul 226
Ba'al 58, 60
Backbone 219
Backwards 221, 225
Badesh 44
Banned 151
Bast 31, 99
BAT 29
Bata 201
Battle 91
Bear 72
Beast 666 10
Bebon 76
Bedroom 190
Beer 32, 73
Bergs 88
Bes 43
Besant, Annie 116
Bez 185
Bird 73
  Goddess 29

Birth
  Demons 148
  Disorder 150
Bitumen 64
Black 137
  Magick 117
Blatvatsky, H P 117
Blind 151, 241
Blood 79, 81
  Impure 81
Boat 217, 264
Body
  Phallus 79
  Reversal 80
Bolt 70
Book of the Dead 69
Bride
  of the Dead 185
  of the Nile 175
Brothers 149
Bull 153
  Headed 105
  Of Ombos 149
Butchers 113

C

Cairo "Calendar" Almanac 150
Calendar 57, 147
Canaanite 58, 60
Cancer 211
Cannibalism 30
Capricorn 213
Carob 64
Cattle 30
Cause 70
Cavern 241
Celestial pole 173
Cepheus 153
Chaldeans 71
Chamber 189
Chaos 81, 161
Children 258
  of impotent revolt 232, 266
Chronicle of Egypt 113

Chronus 17
Church of Satan 10, 116
Citadel 91
Class 168
Clearance 182
Clement of Alexandria 192
Clouds 239
Companions 141
Company of the gods 225
Conflict 77, 90
  Horus and Seth 174
Coptic 188, 194
Coptos 74
Corn mummy 61
Correspondence 72
Cow 67
  Story of the Heavenly 84
Crime 151
Crowley, Aleister 11, 198, 200
  Liber ABA: Magick 15
Crypts 180
Culture 168
Cursed 151, 183
Cut 221
Cygnus 153

D

Daemon 26, 117, 146
Darkness 69
Dawn 228
Day
  Break 81
de Lubicz, Schwaller 197
Death 150, 175
Decan 147, 209
  belt 157
  Indian 209
Decapitation 80
Defensive magic 93
Deir El Gebrawi 106
Demon 167, 168
  Emissary 78
  167
  of death 175

of non-being 161. *See also*
   Daemon
Denderah 67, 188
Desire 151
Destiny 146
Devil 137, 194
   Hymn to the 144
Diabolè/diabolic 78
Diamonds 185
Dieleman, Jacco 41
Dionysus 74
Discriminating intelligence 154
Disease & medicine
   Phylactery 79
Dismember 66, 145, 175, 259
Disturber 150
Divorce 120
Dog 77
   days 84
Donkey 37, 55, 79, 80
Draco (Constellation) 153
Dragon 91, 114
Dreams 32, 82, 190
Drought 77
Drunkenness 184, 188, 190, 191
Dwarf 186

E

Ear 239
East 140
Eating 33
Edfu 34, 42, 63, 75, 190
Egg 277
Egyptian empire 164
Eileithouias-polis 84
Elite 164
Elkab 86–90, 113
Elysium 133
Emasculation 151
Eroticism 190
Etymologies 145
Euhemerism 136
Evil 81, 143, 153, 156, 159
   daemon 77

eye 52
Sleep 42, 78, 105
Execration 40, 216
Executioner 99
Existence 265
Exodus 127
Exorcism 225
Expediency 142
Eye 54, 69, 73, 152, 153, 251
   of Horus 226

F

Faience 185
Falcon 31
Famine 50
Fate 146, 147, 173
   Book of 147
Ferro, John A 126
Fetters 220
Fiend 217
Fifteenth day 228, 237
Finger 70
Fire 47, 217, 221, 226
Five
   Extra days 151, 183
   Gods 150
Flame 241, 259
   Lady of 230
Flint 201, 220
   Knife 239
Flood 56, 88
Flower 109
Foot 259
Foreigner 75, 164, 165
Form 70
Four 257
Fourteen parts 66
Frankincense 64

G

Gay 152
Gazelles 90
Geb 17
Geist 197
Gemini 210

Gender 44
Genitals 74
Geography 164
Germinating 62
Ghede 150
Ghost
   Handsome phantom 193
Ghoul 148
Gods 118
Goethe 150
Goetia 44
Golden 141
Grant, Kenneth 12, 197
   Magical Revival 12
Greeks 215
Green 222
Grimoire 93
Groveller 225
Gwyn Griffiths, J 23
   Conflict of Horus & Seth 124

H

Halloween 67
Hamlet 134
Hand 181
Hathor 29, 56, 164, 188
Hatshepsut 127, 181
Hawk 141
Headless 66, 68
Healing 59
Health 216
Heart 105, 231
Hekau 218
Heliopolis 263
Helios 17, 204
Herakleopolis 188
Hercules 153
Hermes 74
Hermonthis 37, 263
Herodotus 80, 190
Heroes 26
Hesiod 26
Hetepheres 177
Hierakonpolis (Nekhen) 28, 90, 126, 141
Hieroglyphs 90
Hiksos 59, 60, 126, 166, 169
Hippopotamus
   32, 73, 131, 152, 153, 166
Historiola 59
Hittites 164
Homosexuality 120
Honey 64
Horoscopy 215
Horus 34, 57, 129, 133
   Sons of 225
House of life 183
Howler 44
Hunter-gatherer 150

I

IAO 33
Ibises 77
Ilithyia 85
Imhotep 27
Incest 151
India 147, 148
Inflamed 108
Ink 222
Intercourse 190, 194
Intoxicates 145
Ipet 152
Iron 76, 103, 112
Isis 18, 68, 224, 225
Isolated consciousness 152, 154
Israel 164

J

Jacob 165
Jews 165, 169
Joker 150
Jordan 164
Jungian 159
Jupiter 72

K

KA 239
Karnak 50, 67
Kheop 177

Khesau herbs 223
Khoiak 56, 61
Khonsu 12, 99
Kingship 149
Knife 220, 230, 252

L

La Vey, Zeena 118
Laboratory 63
Language
   Code 78
Left 140
   Path 155, 159
Leo 211
Liber Al vel Legis 12, 137
Libra 212
Lion 107
Liturgy 70, 201
Loudness 55
Lunar 68
   cycle 69
Luxor 50
Lyra 153
Lyre 70, 74

M

Macedon 115
Magic
   Invocation 79
   "sampling" 42
Maia 122
Manetho 84, 169
Mariners 219
Mars 72
Marsh 184, 189
Mass 33
Massacres 74
Massey, Gerald 13
Master 100, 101
Mastery (sekhem) 240
Matrifocal 149
Medamud 189
Medinet Habu 156, 178
Mediterranean 60, 165
Melilot 56

Memory 82
Men 26
Menes 27
Menstruation 178
Mercury 72
Meret 185
Mesopotamia 140
Microcosm 189
Min 74
Monad 154
Monsters 71
Moon 72, 201
   Dark 174
Moral 76
Moses 70, 127
Multiracial 164
Mummy 65
Murray, Margaret 145
Music & Musicians 185, 189, 190
Muslim 147
Mystery play 34

N

Nagada 29, 130, 149
   Hypothesis 133, 137
Nails 99
Narmer pallet 28
Nature 118
Navaamshas 215
Necropolis 93, 178
Nectanebo 90, 144
Nekhbet 83, 115
Nekhen 112, 141
Nephotes 203
Nephthys 18, 29, 55
Nero 75
Neteru 118
Nietzsche 198
   anti-hero 145
Nightmare 82, 148
Nile 141
Nirvana 154
Niticris 182
Nomads 165

Non-being 161
Nu 238
Nubia 165, 188
Nuit/Nwt 12, 17, 157, 173

O
Ochre 44
Oedipal complex. 156
Offspring 238
Ombos 141
Opener of the year 122
Opet 67
Oracle 71, 148
  of the Potter 169
Osiris 56, 62, 133, 159
Ovid 76
Oxyrhynchus 77

P
Palestine 164
Parts 63
Patriarchy 151, 155
People 73, 199
Per-Aa (Pharaoh) 227
Perfumery 61
Peribsen 131
Persian 113
Pessimistic 117
PGM - Papyri Graecai Magicae - Magical Papyri 11, 17, 42, 91
Phi-Neter: power of the Egyptian Gods (Book) 91
Philae 92, 189
Philosophy
  systems 71
Pillar 131
Pisces 214
Plague 61
Plato 26
Plough 201
Plutarch 23, 83, 116
  Isis & Osiris 22
Pole 152
  Star 153, 154
Political religion 196

Possession 188
Post mortem 141
Postmodernism 162
Predator 149
Priest 192
Priestess 178, 192
Primeval 150
Progeny 231
Prophetess 179
Prostitution 178, 186
  Sacred 177–237
Psammetichus/Psamtik 93, 203
Ptah 232
Pyramid 177
  Texts 135

Q
Qettu 251
Quseer 88

R
Ra 17, 53, 81
  Barque of 102
  Creations Of 238
Ram 84
Ramses II 32, 74
Ramses III 156, 168
Rape 151
Reactionary 162
Rebels 113, 229
Red 32, 210
  Bull 102
  Ochre 79
  Redden 99
  Redness 73, 101, 110
  Sea 88
Rekhyt 33, 73, 168
Revolutionary 151
Roars 107, 223
Robber 143
Rock 86
Rudra 44
Ruin 145

S

Sacrifice 83, 90
Sagittarius 213
Satan 9, 23, 145, 155, 200
Saturn 72
Savage 158
Scepter 207
Scorpio 212
Scorpion 44, 141
Sea 60
Sebau 253
Seed 243
Sekhmet 96, 240, 241
Semen 174
Seneqenra 166
Serpent 106, 109
   god 242
   Winged 110
Set (Sati?) Goddess 241
Seth 14, 79
   Bad character 167
   Constellation 154
   god of Power and Might 37
   Great of strength 156
   Raging of 58
   Tantrik 155
   Typhon 78
Sety I 127, 153
Seven 147
   seals 92
   Spells 83
Sex 155, 158, 175–195, 192
   violence 151
Shadows 231
Shu 17
Singers 184
Sinister 161
Sixth 237
   day 69
Sky 173, 218, 224
   religion 152
Slaughter 229
Smu 76
Snake 44, 54

Sokar 62
Solar 68
Solstice 122
Sothis 260
Soul 146, 198
Spartans 144
Spear 218, 225
Spectacle 82
Spell kit 183
Spitting 46, 216, 253
Stab 219
Stansfield Jones, Charles (Frater
   Achad) 198
Starmaps 152
Statue 70, 74
Stinking 223
Storm 69, 150
Strabo 177
Stubbornness 55
Sun 72
   Rise 78, 222
   Set 78
Superman 152
Surge 110
Sword 104

T

T3y 184, 185
Tanis 126
Tankhem 183
Tantra 155, 183, 195
Tar 64
Tattoos 185
Taurus 209
Te Velde, H 23
   Seth, God of Confusion: A study
   125
Tefnut 17
Temperament 32, 163
Temple
   Rules broken 80
   189
   of Set 10, 116, 149, 161, 196
Ten Commandments 127

Tent 98
Terror 107
Thebes 50, 166
Thelema
   Religion of the will 197
Theophoric 122
Theosophical society 116
Thera 60
Thunderstorm 43, 58, 223, 224
Tomb 185, 242
Trampled 217
Trance 188, 190
Transaction 78
Transition 41
Trickster 158
Trumpets 33
Tsunami 61
Turpentine 64
Tutmoses I 142
Tutu 146
Two
   Lands 232
   Ways 200
Typhon 18, 20, 23, 78, 80, 208
   Sign of 20
Typhonians 84, 169
   Typhonia 37

U

Unas 130
Unguent 63
Urgod 160
Ursa Major 72, 91, 153, 201

V

Venus 72
Vietnam War 120
Virgo 211
Vision 82
Votary/Votaresses 179, 180
Votive 90
Vulture 85, 86, 93

W

Wadi Hilal 88, 113

Wadjet 260
Warfare 32, 73
Wax 222
   dolls 41
West 140
Wheel of the year 121
White 112
Wind 110
Wine 223
Withershins 201
Womb 181
Words of power 221
Wound 100, 106
Wyatt, John 55

X

Xenophobia 165, 166

Y

Yam 60
Yoga 20, 154

Z

Zeitgeist 124
Zeus 178
Zodiac 173, 209

If you enjoyed this book
and want to know more
sign up for free Mandrake monthly book newsletter, here's how:
Visit the
mandrake.uk.net
website
A subscription page should pop-up

or type this link into a browser

http://eepurl.com/THE9P

www.ingramcontent.com/pod-product-compliance
Lightning Source LLC
Chambersburg PA
CBHW061249230426
43663CB00022B/2958